The Impact of Electricity

THE IMPACT OF ELECTRICITY

DEVELOPMENT, DESIRES AND DILEMMAS

Tanja Winther

Berghahn Books
NEW YORK • OXFORD

First published in 2008 by
Berghahn Books
www.berghahnbooks.com

© 2008, 2011 Tanja Winther
First paperback edition published in 2011

Library of Congress Cataloging-in-Publication Data

Winther, Tanja.
  The impact of electricity: development, desires, and dilemmas / Tanja Winther.
    p. cm.
  Includes bibliographical references and index.
  ISBN 978-1-84545-495-1 (hbk)—ISBN 978-1-84545-292-6 (pbk)
  1. Rural electrification—Social aspects—Tanzania. 2. Rural electrification—
Economic aspects—Tanzania. 3. Sustainable development—Tanzania. 4. Power
resources—Social aspects—Tanzania. 5. Power resources—Economic aspects—
Tanzania. 6. Power resources—Environmental aspects—Tanzania. 7. Social
structure—Tanzania. I. Title.

  HD9688.T34W56 2008
  333.793'209678—dc22

                                                               2008014707

British Library Cataloguing in Publication Data

A catalogue record for this book is available from
the British Library.

Printed in the United States on acid-free paper

ISBN 978-1-84545-495-1 (hardback)
ISBN 978-1-84545-292-6 (paperback)

For Anna and Joakim

CONTENTS

LIST OF ILLUSTRATIONS

Maps

Figures

Plates

ACKNOWLEDGEMENTS

This book is based upon fieldwork in Zanzibar, first and foremost in the village of Uroa. I am thoroughly indebted to the men and women who accepted my presence there and who helped me in my efforts to answer the question of what impact the arrival of electricity has had on people's lives in rural Zanzibar. My closest friends, helpers and acquaintances also appear in crucial parts of the book and for this reason I have changed their names in the text.

The staff at the Zanzibar Electricity Corporation (ZECO) provided information and assistance. In particular, I wish to thank Omar Khamis 'Baomar' and the current project manager of the electrification project, Juma Othman Hija, with whom I have also worked as a consultant, along with his team. At the Zanzibar National Archives I received valuable support from H.H. Omar. Mwandawa Chaude Ramadhan and Bishara Mohamed Rashid assisted in conducting census interviews and focus groups. Bente and Suleman Said also provided regular support.

Both Haakon With Andersen (Centre for Technology and Sociology) and Jarle Sletbak (Norwegian Institute of Technology) of the University of Trondheim and anthropologist Kjersti Larsen, of the University of Oslo, provided advice and inspiration at the project's early stage. Asbjørn Tenfjord and A.S. Linjebygg, the subcontractor during the early phases of the electrification project, helped me in 1991.

I also wish to express my gratitude to Desmond McNeill, Harold Wilhite and Dan Banik at the University of Oslo's Centre for Development and the Environment (SUM) who have read and commented on various parts of the book's earlier drafts. I also thank my other colleagues at the Centre for providing stimulating and encouraging discussions over the years.

I am particularly indebted to Aud Talle at the Department of Social Anthropology in Oslo who provided guidance during the most significant period of the research process. Marianne Lien, of the same department, provided critical comments on the material touching on economic life and consumption. Acknowledgements also go to many other fellow anthropologists in the department. An earlier version of the manuscript was read by Pat Caplan, Jo Helle-Valle and Unni Wikan whose comments and questions have been vital in the revision process.

I wish to thank Marion Berghahn for her trust in the idea that electricity matters, and also her colleagues at Berghahn Books for splendid cooperation during the editing phase. Joanna Deacon proofed the English language in an early phase and Fadhili Makame proofed the expressions in Swahili.

Despite the generous feedback I have received from many people in the process, all possible mistakes rest of course solely with me. The main body of research conducted for the purposes of this book has been financed by the Research Council of Norway.

Finally, family counts. My sister Silja, my brother Ivar and my wonderful parents continue to provide support and inspiration. So does Astri, my 98-year-old grandmother. Not least, my husband Henrik Bentzen has supported me immensely. During fieldwork in 2000–1 he also helped me to organise, type and produce statistical data. As for our daughter Anna, who was two years old at the time, she created situations where the limits of Uroan social aesthetics were tested by simply opening doors and following her instincts. To our surprise, when she kissed a dear male neighbour on the cheek he became quite embarrassed. Boundaries may tacitly exist but sometimes their relevance and significance are only revealed by moments such as this. In a wider perspective this also implies that one cannot anticipate how a given change, such as the arrival of electricity, will affect social life. The empirically based, ethnographic account to be presented here, then, will explore such changes as they are actually perceived and experienced. This is the point at which the story of electrification in rural Zanzibar begins.

LIST OF ABBREVIATIONS

ADEME	Agence de l'Environnement et de la Maîtrise de l'Energie (French Environment and Energy Management Agency)
AfDB	African Development Bank
ASP	African Shirazi Party
CCM	Chama Cha Mapinduzi (Party of the Revolution; current ruling political party of Tanzania and Zanzibar)
CUF	Civic United Front
FINNIDA	Department for International Development Cooperation, Finnish Ministry for Foreign Affairs
HDI	Human Development Index
IEA	International Energy Agency
IMF	International Monetary Fund
INA	Indian National Association
MKUKUTA	Mkakati wa Kukuza Uchumi na Kuondoa Umaskini Tanzania (Tanzanian National Strategy for Growth and Reduction of Poverty)
MWCELE	Zanzibar Ministry of Water, Construction, Energy, Land and Environment
NORAD	Norwegian Agency for Development Cooperation
NRECA	National Rural Electric Cooperative Association, USA
NVE	Norwegian Water Resources and Energy Administration
RUREL	Rural Electrification Project in Zanzibar
SADCC	Southern African Development Coordination Conference (in 1993 transformed into the SADC; Southern African Development Community)
SFPC	State Fuel and Power Corporation, Zanzibar
SUM	Centre for Development and the Environment, University of Oslo
TANESCO	Tanzania Electric Supply Company Ltd
TASAF	Tanzania Social Action Fund
Tsh.	Tanzanian shillings (in 2001 Tsh.850 = US$1)
TVT	Television Tanzania

TVZ	Television Zanzibar
UNDP	United Nations Development Programme
WEC	World Energy Council
ZECO	Zanzibar Electricity Corporation (formerly SFPC)

Chapter 1

INTRODUCTION

The gradual evolution of electricity has historically provided societies with a means for using energy in a multitude of ways. Electricity not only conditioned rapid industrialisation and economic growth in many parts of the world in the past century but also continues to play a crucial role in various aspects of everyday life throughout the world today. We do not have to adopt a neo-evolutionary theory of human development to acknowledge the significance of energy and electricity. However, it is important to question how, and in what sense, energy matters.

Today 1.6 billion people, mainly in South Asia and sub-Saharan Africa, remain without access to electricity. This group constitutes about one quarter of the world's population, of whom 80 per cent live in rural areas (IEA). On the Tanzanian mainland today less than 5 per cent of the rural population have access to electricity and only 1 per cent of these people have actually got themselves connected. Most of the countries in question, such as Tanzania, tend to have a low rating in terms of development according to international comparative studies (e.g., Human Development Index, UNDP). Thus poverty appears to be linked to people's limited access to electricity. Although the dynamics of such links are somewhat under-researched, there is a general consensus among governments and other development organisations that electricity has a positive impact on human development. More specifically, current development strategies tend to stress the following view: access to electricity at affordable prices is a vital condition for increasing poor people's well-being and producing national economic growth.[1] Nevertheless, the issue partly remains open as to how electricity affects social life and people's well-being. This question is certainly not only of academic interest. The answers to this question and its documentation may also have an effect on affluent countries' willingness to invest in electricity for development. This reinforces the claim that the issue of electricity in the development context merits academic research.

The Zanzibari case has a particular position here. Over a period of 20 years, the rural electrification project in Zanzibar has constructed a grid which, by 2006, covered 66 per cent of the areas in which the rural population live. This provides a level of access to electricity which is extremely high in the African context. This book offers documentation of, and explanations for, the long-term effects of this intervention, mainly based on material from the village of Uroa, which was electrified in 1990. A premise in the chosen approach is that mutual influence is at work in the relationship between technologies and the people who relate to them. Not only does electricity have an impact on social life, the local socio-cultural context also affects the ways in which electricity is received, perceived and used.

Towards an anthropology of energy

Rural Zanzibar provides methodological and analytical advantages for the task of understanding people's relationship to electricity because this technology arrived quite recently, in the 1980s and 1990s. The consequences of electricity's introduction, use and rapid normalisation are thus tangible. Although the ethnographic material is limited to the Zanzibari context, I will argue that cross-cultural comparisons and analyses are a key to understanding the dynamics inherent in the relationships between people, electricity and the services that electricity provides. In anthropology relatively little has been done to understand people's use of energy, with electricity being a particular case in point (Wilhite 2005).[2] This is striking from the point of view of the user because new forms of energy are spreading as a fundamental element in social life across the globe. Wilhite is an exception and argues the case for an 'anthropology of energy' (Wilhite 2005; Wilhite 2006; Wilhite in press). Apart from the importance of energy for everyday existence, a central argument for innovative, culture-sensitive energy research is the acknowledgement that energy-related activities constitute the most important threat to the global climate caused by human activity.

The present work takes as its focus for study the moment in which the switch from fossil fuels to relatively clean electricity (mainly hydroelectric power, imported to Zanzibar from the Tanzanian mainland) was made. The study's purpose in this respect is not to quantify the shift's environmental implications. Rather, it is to qualitatively explore the various ways in which electricity has environmental relevance. It is the book's ambition to address the question of electricity in Zanzibar within a framework of sustainable energy consumption. This forms part of the new agenda for an anthropology of energy, where sustainability is taken to mean both environmentally, economically and socially sustainable energy policies and practices.

Addressing development

The main case study, the electrification of the village of Uroa on the east coast of Unguja Island, Zanzibar, will reveal that people themselves had a high degree of control over this process. They participated in a broad sense by not only establishing the 'need' for energy, but also by overseeing its introduction, collaborating in its implementation and deciding the new technology's use in the village. This qualifies for the use of the term 'participation' and implies that Uroa provides us with a case of 'best-practice' (cf. Chambers 1995: 30; Nelson and Wright 1995; cf. also Cornwall and Jewkes (1995) for a definition of participatory research).

Linked to the critique of development in the late 1980s and 1990s and the evidence of failed projects, there have been massive attempts during the last twenty to twenty five years, informed by anthropological findings, to redirect development processes away from top-down structures towards 'participation' and 'local control' (Grillo 1997: 7–8; Green 2003a: 123, 140). One of the important premises for this shift was the turn to 'agency' and 'knowledge' in the late 1970s, a move initiated by Norman Long and pioneered by Fredrik Barth (Gardner and Lewis 1996: 59; Leach et al. 1999: 36). Furthermore, feminist studies in the 1980s had documented the many ways in which developmental efforts had negative effects on women and marginalised groups, this also being the case in Tanzania (Caplan 1984). They called for bottom-up approaches attuned to the local social context (Rogers 1981; Caplan 1984; cf. Leach et al. 1999; Gardner and Lewis 1996). In short, 'local participation' generally came to be the presumed standard in multilateral and bilateral development programmes and continues to be relevant.

More recently, however, a range of observers have noted that the emphasis on participation and bottom-up development, linked to the mainstreaming of empowerment as a developmental goal, has had modest and sometimes even unfortunate results (Hobart 1993: 1–3; Grillo 1997: 10; Crewe 1997; Nustad 2001; Green 2003a: 123, 140). In particular, and also relevant to the case of Uroa, there appears to be a general hierarchical element to intended change. This limits the degree to which local control can be realised. I discuss the consequences of this constraint and suggest how it can be approached. Furthermore, the mainstreaming of gender in development strategies that followed the Beijing Conference on Women in 1995 has apparently not been successful in terms of promoting gender equality. A range of evaluations have documented how development efforts directed at women and gender equality became weakened towards the end of the 1990s (see NORAD 2006 (Aasen) for a synthesis report). The material to be presented aims to contribute with knowledge that could better serve such equality policies and practices in the realm of energy planning.

The 'success story' of electrification in the village of Uroa did not depend on a planned, participatory process instigated at the behest of more or less distant developers. Rather, it was the realistic prospect of obtaining access to electricity that made certain men in the village act. Moreover, the degree of local control over the process was shifting. Nevertheless, as I intend to show, this unexpected initiative and result (as seen from the developers' side) could be helpful in understanding both the potential and the limitations of participatory development in practice. For now I reiterate that the case to be presented, largely through the lens of agency-oriented approaches (Long 1989; Hobart 1993; Grillo 1997; Arce and Long 2000), will reveal participation in practice.

In addition to this, the fact that the intervention in question centred on the construction of an electricity grid makes the case even more relevant to the development debate. Such infrastructure projects have sometimes been considered to be particularly difficult to realise within a participatory framework (Chambers 1995: 41; Lane 1995: 185). However, the case of electricity's arrival in Uroa contradicts the thesis that technology and participation are hard to combine. The experience resonates with Paul Sillitoe et al.'s contention (they primarily deal with natural resource development) that '[t]he notion of technology transfer remains, not as a top-down imposition but a search for jointly negotiated advances' (2005: 13). Therefore, with the increasing emphasis on infrastructures among development agencies and governments at present, the possibility of including participation in these schemes should not be disregarded.

Research questions

The examination of the impact of visual material illumination is indicative for qualifying the relevance of electricity's impact and interrelationship with people in rural Zanzibar. Some of the effects of electrification are obvious. Unprecedented artificial light at night-time in specific locations indicates and instigates shifts away from what once was. On closer examination changes can be found in the way men and women work, visit one another, pray, have sex and relax. Electricity also affects the stakes for entry into marriage and a man's number of wives. Furthermore, a portion of the village population now gathers once a month to pay their electricity bills to a state company. In this way individual finances become common knowledge. Zanzibari authorities also gain increasing control over their citizens.

This book sets out to explore the consequences of such practices, modified due to electricity's arrival, by focusing on a set of interrelated questions. First of all, how has the introduction of electricity restructured social boundaries at the village level and beyond? To what extent has electricity contributed to, or ameliorated, social differentiation? Who controls the new technology and why? Who benefits and who is excluded? By examining these questions I explore the ways in which electricity has impacted on and otherwise affected the relationship between the 'haves' and the 'have-nots', the sexes, different generations, people of distinct origins and other social categories. I also look at the extent to which electricity has affected human–spirit relations. Secondly, I ask how electricity has made an impact on the relation between the state and ordinary people. Thirdly, I consider whether electrification in rural Zanzibar may be considered a success in development terms. Fourthly, as electricity is rapidly becoming normalised at present I account for the driving forces behind the increase in consumption. Finally, the environmental aspects of the arrival of electricity are obvious on one level but subtler in other ways. I seek to show how. In sum, the underlying goal of this book is, in the light of one particular case, to provide prospects for environmentally and socially sustainable development in relation to energy-use in rural Zanzibar and beyond.

The choice of an untypical village

It is a fact that the outcome of the governmental electrification in Zanzibar project turned out differently in different villages. I have concentrated on Uroa for two interrelated reasons. First of all, upon arriving in Zanzibar in 1991 to study the rural electrification project as a student of power engineering, I became interested in the instances in which the initial project plans had been modified. The study of the causes behind such changes, I thought, and soon discovered, could potentially and effectively be the key to understanding how Zanzibaris perceived the new technology and how they behaved in relation to the project staff. The project was funded by NORAD and managed by a Norwegian engineer at that time. In short, Uroa fascinated me because of the untypical manner in which the village became connected to the grid: *it was the only village in rural Zanzibar (at that time) where electrification had been initiated by the people themselves*. Thus Uroa was partly selected because its history of electrification is unique. Secondly, upon returning to Zanzibar ten years later to conduct long-term fieldwork as an anthropologist, fieldwork that provides the main base on which the material to be presented is founded, I expected to find many users of electricity in the village. Already in 1991 23 per cent of households had become connected to the grid, which was an exceptionally high connection rate in the rural Zanzibari context. I had also met two women who used electric stoves, a topic of social and environmental interest, and I expected to find more users in 2000. Thus the choice of Uroa in 2000 also seemed to provide the ideal opportunity to observe many people's electricity-use and at the same time to allow for the comparison of such practices at two distinct points in time. I have subsequently revisited Zanzibar and the village of Uroa in 2004, 2005 and 2006, partly in my role as a consultant.[3] The opportunity to return to the same locality over a period of fifteen years has been crucial to the task of exploring social change and electricity's long-term impact.

The ambition to account for causal explanations needs some elaboration. The mentioned, observable changes can be traced back in time to electrification. However, when I seek to account for the shifts produced by the arrival of electricity, other explanatory factors for change may be relevant at the same time. For instance, significant socio-economic changes, such as the introduction of seaweed production and tourism, coincided with the arrival of electric current. The wish to establish causal links involves accounting for the various 'mechanisms' at work and not simply presenting cross-sections of life at two distinct points in time.

As a fishing village with a growing industrial sector related to seaweed and tourism, Uroa resembles many other places in Zanzibar. To help establish what would have been the case without electricity (i.e., the counter-factual) I have also gathered data in the (by 2001 still non-electrified) neighbouring villages of Ndudu, Pongwe and Marumbi. Furthermore, to help put the Uroan material into perspective in terms of how the village became connected to the grid, I shall briefly draw on the experiences of other villages, such as Chwaka, included in the electrification project. These 'conventional' villages provide a contrast in the narrative. In the final chapter I touch on the untypical village of Binguni, where electrification failed. However, Uroa and its residents remain the primary focus for study throughout the book. The material will confirm that the manners in which new technologies are introduced matter to how people appropriate or reject them.

The significance of social change must be validated by means of people's experiences of the consequences of such shifts. Below I account for the main approaches that will be used for exploring change and continuity after electricity's arrival in rural Zanzibar. At the same time I discuss how one may come to understand electricity's position and significance for the people we are concerned with here.

Electricity matters[4]

Lesley A. White postulated that a population's utilisation of energy is directly proportional to their progress as a human culture (White 1943).[5] Today the notion of culture has changed and linear models of development have, at least on the surface, been abandoned. Instead, the present task is to focus on the ways electricity matters to a particular group of people.

Electricity was not selected as a topic for investigation based on knowledge of what people in rural Zanzibar consider important in their lives.

Admittedly I sometimes wondered during fieldwork if I overemphasised electricity's importance. Perhaps I was ignoring other more significant traits of social life and catalysts for change? If so, I would now be treating electricity as a fetish, constructing an account taking a relatively marginal technology as the basis of a superstructure within which everything else is considered (cf. Miller 1998: 3).

When the Swahili-speaking people of Uroa were asked to evaluate electricity's significance, they would often state that electricity is 'important' (*muhimu*, but not *lazima*, which has stronger connotations of 'necessity'). Some would bring up electricity when articulating what it means to live a 'good life' (*maisha mazuri*). On the other hand, it was also maintained that 'to the Swahilis, electricity is a little problematic' (*kwa Waswahili, umeme ni tatizo dogo*). This ambivalence inherent in the discourse of electricity will be explored later.

There is another way to approach the same question. We can investigate electricity's degree of importance by focusing on what people do and how they interact. Often electricity is completely irrelevant or trivial. However, sometimes, a man would risk his own well-being to acquire an electrical appliance. Electricity-related issues also appear as prime foci in many situations of conflict. Furthermore, a glance at people's financial priorities suffices to show electricity's importance in their lives. Although most families in Uroa have very modest resources, by 2006 more than half of the households in the village had obtained an electrical connection. In 2001 such an investment represented three to four months work for an ordinary fisherman. In 2006 the amount of work needed to obtain a connection had increased to four to six months. This speaks of electricity's significance as perceived by the people themselves. Electricity matters.

I dwell on this issue for two reasons. One reason relates to the task of selecting an object of study. Positioned within the sub-field of material culture, Daniel Miller has argued that the selection of physical objects should be validated according to the sort of things that 'matter' to the people under study. The term 'mattering' implies staying close to the values of those under observation. In contrast, 'concerns' and 'what is important' are said to be more abstracted notions used by the analyst (1998: 10–14). Miller's perspective raises questions of representation and validity. Do our choices of selected, physical objects and corresponding accounts reflect processes of significance for the people under study? I think the question also touches on ethical aspects in the sense of what purpose research should have. In addition, and of practical importance, how do we know what matters to people before undertaking fieldwork?

Apparently, due to the multitude of material fields open for study and the ghost of fetishism, the selection of a topic for study requires particular justification when we are dealing with people and their objects. Due to the questions raised above, I would suggest that this fundamental step in the research process should receive more attention in general. On the other hand, if we take seriously the idea that dwelling on objects' materiality provides a way to understand social processes, we should not fear fetishism. Empirically-grounded research implies a ceaseless attunement to the concerns and values of the people under study. Naturally, we should be willing to adjust the focus of investigation (as many ethnographers have done) if the selected one turns out to be a 'dead end'. This has not been required in the present research. The structuring of the book is my way of highlighting electricity's significance. In doing so, the findings are contextualised vis-à-vis other material fields and social and cultural life in general.

The second reason why this section was introduced by touching on electricity's degree of importance concerns the approaches I used for doing so. The reader might agree that the glimpses of people's relationship to electricity in practice provided the most substantial material for concluding its importance. I hasten to add, though, that verbal expressions and interpretations are by no way insignificant in, or excluded from, the present work. However, the object for study calls for a practice-oriented approach (Bourdieu 1977). I explore the routines of everyday life and how these articulate values and ideologies. By doing this I search for signs of change involving the way people use objects to mirror and reproduce who they are (Miller 1994).[6] The concept of 'habitus' is useful as it highlights the incorporated and partly unconscious elements that guide people's living. To some extent electricity's arrival can be considered as a moment when practices were temporarily removed from their mundane state, that is to say the one in which things are taken for granted (cf. Bourdieu's term 'doxa'). New technologies require new solutions for organising social life. These result in increased consciousness that in turn informs new discourses and can provide valuable moments giving insight to the observer. Here, the analysis of Uroan development discourses and the close investigation of electricity's arrival have the potential to reveal issues of general importance in this socio-cultural context. Likewise, the scrutinisation of everyday life is likely to enhance our understanding of the nature of the change in question and of its implications.

What sort of good is electricity?

The object we are dealing with at present is of a multifaceted kind. Electricity physically enters the village and finds its way to various households. In people's conceptualisations *umeme* (electricity) is powerfully present. Invisible yet dangerous, and with a remarkable capacity to produce various effects, the current is both feared and desired. As a commodity electricity is consumed immediately and paid for in bulk after consumption. However, once the wires are laid, the meters installed and the bills paid, electricity ceases to be the central focus of concern. Instead, people focus their attention on other issues apart from the current itself. In the analysis a corresponding shift occurs from chapter 7 onwards where the use of electricity becomes the central topic. Electricity is always consumed in combination with electricity demanding equipment.[7] Bulbs, freezers and TV sets are purchased and made to function in people's homes. These devices constitute what I shall label 'primary objects'. Chapter 8 deals with these and with people's strategies and careful considerations for obtaining them. In everyday life, however, people relate more closely to the services such primary objects produce with the help of electricity than to the appliances themselves. Apart from the instances when a device is obtained or becomes broken, people tend rather to think of lighting, cooling capacity and television programmes (that is, entertainment, information and so on) when they use or talk about such devices. These services, or electricity's 'secondary objects' as I shall also denote them, will also be treated as objects in analytical terms.

I stress that I regard the whole chain as related to consumption. Consumption is intrinsically social and meaningful as 'people need goods to commit other people in their projects' (Douglas 1982: 23; see also Douglas and Isherwood 1996 [1979]; Miller 1994). In any given context people strive for 'ritually match[ing] goods to occasions' (Douglas 1982: 29). My task is to demonstrate how people become associated with objects related to electricity and how they engage other people in this process. Purchasing an appliance is one way to create such associations and daily use is another. Both practices may carry social significance. We should also recall that 'food is not only for thought'. In Zanzibar, quite a few people also struggle to achieve subsistence.

Electricity and people's particular ways of using the services it provides are rapidly becoming normal parts of everyday life in rural Zanzibar. A central theme in the present work is to demonstrate the conditions, dynamics and qualities of such normalisation processes. The process whereby novelties become normal is actualised in this time of significant, material change.

Fieldwork and ethical considerations

A mixture of qualitative and quantitative methods has been used. Participation in everyday life and in-depth interviews were central means for obtaining insights into social life and how people perceive the recent changes. Furthermore, I conducted an extensive census which covered 23 per cent of Uroan households.[8] In addition the material is also founded on technical data. This reflects the topic for research and my background and interest in technology. Making active use of electricity data may not be so common in anthropology, but this broadening of sources does not alter the task of investigating social life. The anthropological method has always drawn on a range of data. I include volts and kilowatt-hours in mine. Finally, in addition to the general literature, I draw on written material that has been obtained from the Zanzibar National Archives and from project reports.

The supplier of electricity in Zanzibar, ZECO, is an important actor in the present context. I regularly visited their office in Zanzibar Town. Staff provided me with technical data and answered my questions. We also had informal conversations. The relationship between the utility and its rural customers is a central issue in this book. One of the important 'interfaces' (Long 1989) where these groups meet face to face is during ZECO's monthly rounds to measure electricity consumption. By accompanying one of the employees on these visits to various villages, I could observe this interface from a close distance. In all, we entered around 500 households together to register consumption. I also obtained insights into which appliances people keep.[9]

Given that I was introduced as an 'engineer' during my first visit to Uroa and during my regular contact with staff in the electricity company also in subsequent periods, my identity as an engineer has partly followed me ever since. In relation to the utility company this was a clear advantage in order to obtain trust and information. My enduring association with the rural electricity project also probably simplified the task of obtaining a research permit in the village. Electricity appears to be a politically innocent and neutral topic of study.[10] However, vis-à-vis the people whose lives I wished to understand, my engineering identity, or rather my association with the utility, needs further reflective comment. With the topic of study apparently being the same as in 1991 when I visited Uroa as a student of engineering, it is little wonder that many people regarded me as a Norwegian engineer involved in electrification. Correspondingly, I sometimes acted as my co-villagers' advocate on matters related to electricity. I was also approached by groups in several villages who asked me to mediate their requests for a supply. Taking 'their side' in the utility–customer relationship posed few problems in everyday life. However, I felt the situation quite awkward for interfaces where utility and customer were confronted with each other in antagonistic ways. In chapter 6 I describe one such incident in which it is likely that my position was perceived to be ambiguous.

The more I got to know people personally and in a variety of contexts, the less relevant became my affiliation with the electrification project and the utility company as such. Nevertheless, I should also acknowledge that my position in the field did have effects. Kirsten Hastrup has argued that 'we should realize, and creatively exploit, our intricate implications on the world' (1995: 51). Such reflexivity has general relevance, but here I wish to bring up two episodes in which my focus on electricity triggered responses I had not anticipated. They call for ethical reflections.

When I asked an officer at ZECO about the number of electricity customers in Zanzibari villages he said that, unfortunately, such information was not available. However, he helpfully suggested that ZECO could organise a mapping of every electrified house in Zanzibar. In this way all illegal consumers would also be detected, he was pleased to note. Terrified of being the cause of such a hunt, I rapidly withdrew my request. This episode revealed to me the way in which an apparently neutral question may produce large, and for the people in question; unfortunate effects. I hope to have lived up to the trust I was given, also in terms of how I represent my findings, but I cannot be certain of the effects I will produce. Pointing to the difficulties in the utility–customer relationship is meant to improve the situation, particularly for the rural customers. On an aggregate level the consequences might also be experienced as unfortunate. This is so because increased knowledge of how customers think and act has the potential of increasing the utility's control of its customers (cf. Ellen 1984: 137).

Secondly, upon observing that people in Uroa do not cook with electricity I occasionally raised the question of why this is so. One man, who is centrally positioned in village administrative life, told me he had noticed my interest in electric cookers. Now, he said, they were planning a general meeting at which I could tell the whole village about the benefits of using such appliances. While carefully turning the offer down, I realised that he saw me as a promoter of such appliances. Apparently I had stirred up a normative discourse on electric cookers. I do not know this man's motives for suggesting such a meeting. However, what I learned here, and in many other, yet different, situations, is that fieldwork is a process in which the potential for mutual influence is always present. I further account for the intersubjectivity involved in the ethnographic experience by way of a discussion on its textual representation.

In this diachronic account of life in rural Zanzibar the text is also often presented in the 'ethnographic present'. This is a choice of writing style that I use as a literary device to underline my arguments. However, this choice also has a specific motivation and a wider significance. Hastrup argues that the ethnographic present is a 'necessary construction of time, because only the present tense preserves the reality of *anthropological* knowledge'. (1995: 14, original emphasis). Earlier writers' use of the present tense reflected their ahistoric mode of anthropology. Today, Hastrup maintains, this writing strategy is important for providing transparency as to how anthropological knowledge is actually produced. Fieldwork is the main locus for such production. Therefore the experience of fieldwork should be reflected in the text.[11]

Hastrup sees the ethnographic encounter as a dialogue where the various parties speak on equal terms (ibid.: 150). Here, no one can claim privileged access to knowledge. 'Participant observation' involves engaging in daily interaction with those under study. In this dialogue there are speakers and listeners, selves and others, who are all mutually implicated (ibid.). In turn, identities are constructed reciprocally. These are the reasons why 'subjectivity' should be part of the final text when the anthropologist must transcend the ethnographic dialogue, and at this point the relationship in question is no longer symmetric. Hastrup emphasises that such subjectivity, together with reflexivity, involves making explicit the discursive field that is the locus of knowledge production and the various actors' shifting positions within it (ibid.). The ethnographic present is one device for this purpose. Another means is to strive for clarity as to how various participants in the field mutually influence each other. Consequently, in this introductory chapter I attempt to clarify my position(s) in the field as they might have been perceived by the people I knew. I shall also do so in later chapters when I find my interrelationships with Uroans particularly relevant to what was said and done.

Learning 'the art of conversation'

Fieldwork can be a strange experience. Despite the concrete object of study and my links with the village past, I felt a bit uneasy in the beginning. In October 2000 my husband, daughter and I had settled into a guest house on the beach in Dikoni ward, Uroa. Our daughter certainly helped us make initial contact with our neighbours. However, left on my own, I remember how awkward I felt trying to 'make friends' with my neighbours. The first time I met Meja, who was to become my closest acquaintance, she was sitting on a bench outdoors (*baraza*) with her female friends. When I came over and started to greet them and talk to them, they repeated my phrases and giggled. I tried to laugh with them but felt quite uncertain about what they thought of me. I said I wished to learn about electricity and life in the village in general but this did not help much. It was not until I later asked to watch them cook food that the ice seemed to break. By engaging practically in everyday tasks, I started to feel like a real person in their eyes.

The change of arena towards a more private space was probably one of the reasons why interaction began to take on meaning. I got the opportunity to be with one woman at a time. Differences in styles always appeared more significant in public space, especially in the initial phase. However, another important point is that Uroan women perceive cooking as a meaningful activity. Sharon Hutchinson describes fieldwork as 'the art of conversation' (1996: 45). For conversations to be meaningful, both parties must have a genuine interest in the topic. In Uroa, due to women's interest in cooking, they would elaborate at length on such tasks, in particular detail while engaging in them. Highly skilled, they also seemed to take great pride in explaining this practice to a relatively ignorant, but presumably interested, foreign woman. We also see the relevance of Hastrup's point that, in the ethnographic encounter, no one can claim superior access to knowledge. In this way cooking turned out to be a good point of entry into women's homes and lives. I ended up spending many hours in smoky kitchens where I would watch, smell, taste and talk about food. Subsequently women included me in other everyday activities as well as in healing rituals and ceremonial life.

A shared language is of course an important prerequisite for meaningful interaction. My level in Swahili was quite moderate during the first months.[12] However, I gradually came to be able to converse meaningfully with most people on any topic. From time to time I used a tape recorder during in-depth interviews, particularly with elderly people, whom I sometimes found difficult to understand (and vice versa). Afterwards I either transcribed the interviews myself or received assistance. I also engaged women and men (young and old) to write diaries and elaborate on given topics. On a few occasions I used assistants for conducting interviews, without too much success (see below).

Space and work are, to a great extent, divided into female and male realms. Being a woman, wife and mother – I was known as 'Mama Ana' by everyone I knew in Uroa – both opened up and limited the kinds of spaces I could frequent and participate in with ease. Access to private homes posed no problem because this space is principally female during the daytime. In contrast the fish market and mosques are male spaces. Although I might have gained entry into such places too, I preferred not to. When on occasion I visited the market I felt my presence broke with the social aesthetics. Conversations amongst men stopped when I approached. Even men I knew well would appear shy and uncertain of how to relate to me in their male friends' presence.

On my own, however, I frequently and easily conducted conversations with ordinary men. In the realm of electricity men are primarily the ones in charge. In addition men relate more with Uroa as a place than the women, who often settle in the village at the time of marriage. Perhaps for these reasons the men tended to be more eager to explain and evaluate village life than women. In this way the many stories I gathered about the village past nearly all stem from men's accounts. I was also invited on fishing trips, farming expeditions and went to the utility office in town with men. I observed them paying their electricity bills.

As a rough simplification I can say that I spoke with men and did things together with women. I took notes when it seemed appropriate, such as during conversations with individuals in their homes or outdoors on a bench. Here the subjects were often initiated by me but I also followed a nondirective approach (cf. Hutchinson 1996: 44). By 'being around' in certain households, participating in everyday life and following people in social space (cf. Wikan 1990: 47), I gained insight into important issues and, not least, the manner in which things are done in Uroa. My closest acquaintances also helped me explain words and topics and commented on my interpretations.

Being a non-Muslim had few implications regarding my access to social arenas (though the sexual division is influenced by Islamic teachings). Well-meaning acquaintances often recommended that I try to fast for some days during Ramadan so that I would become pure and feel better. Nobody condemned me, though, for not fasting, not praying and not wearing a head veil (although I did wear one during ceremonies). Rural Zanzibar is not a place where religious orthodoxy reigns. Nevertheless, when one day during Ramadan an imam who I had known for some time refused to greet me with a handshake as usual, I was suddenly able to feel the differences at work. His rejection of me was probably more linked with my being a woman than my being a non-Muslim, though. This, as least, is how one observer of the incident explained it to me. Whatever the truth of the matter, I experienced seeing myself through his eyes for a moment, and this evoked a rather unpleasant feeling in me.

Richard Shweder describes the 'surprise' of fieldwork (1997). By this he refers to the way we, in the task of trying to understand other people, also may find something within ourselves. The incident just mentioned was a moment when I set aside my own categories and felt the differences at work in Islamic, rural Zanzibar. Yet in this 'other' position something in my constitution also conditioned such resonance. Shweder says that participation in other people's lives may activate 'dormant or unknown emotional and cognitive structures within oneself' (ibid.). In this way fieldwork is not only full of surprises with regard to discovering cultural differences or the unforeseen consequences the ethnographic dialogue may produce (cf. Hastrup 1992, 1995). Inherent also is how one may come to surprise oneself. Shweder came to feel a sense of dread about eating leftovers of temple food in Orissa, India. People had warned him that a god would be upset if he did, but practical circumstances made it both possible and tempting to act contrary to such advice. He realised that he could not eat this food due to his own emotions and Shweder interprets this as a case where a certain, inherent emotional scheme in him was activated. In a similar way I had difficulties using my left hand for eating long after fieldwork had ended. Furthermore, people in Zanzibar humbly approach the prospect of waking up in the morning with good health. Even now, I 'must' add the sentence 'If God wishes' when telling my children that we shall meet in the morning. It seems dangerous not to. I shall not go into the question of whether such cognitive structures are really dormant within a person or if long-term fieldwork makes one adapt to new schemas. What matters is that in the field 'we' become mutually implicated, this process doing more than simply conditioning the knowledge that is produced. It may be particularly valuable for obtaining insight into the lives we seek to understand (Hastrup 1995). I consider this linked to Unni Wikan's evocative suggestion that we let 'their concerns resonate with ourselves' (Wikan 1992). In consequence such insight may serve, firstly, to bridge understandings and dissolve difference. Secondly, one may come to experience the meaning of difference in a similar way to those one wishes to understand.

Towards the end of my stay I received assistance from two young women from Zanzibar Town who were also fluent in English. They were to help me conduct group interviews with women in Uroa on topics such as light, spirits and people's fear of walking in darkness. I did not feel like a master of Swahili and wanted to ensure that these important issues were covered properly. However, such assistance did not bring me new information. On the contrary, I realised that my neighbours actively kept certain aspects hidden from view. The fact that the interviews were conducted in groups could have contributed to making Uroan women keep their opinions and fears to themselves, but other factors seemed more important.

First of all, the lack of personal bonds probably presented a barrier. In addition, there seemed to be a social distance between the educated town women and the Uroan women I knew. When my assistants turned up in the village they were covered in black veiling (*bui-bui*) which was typical for town. From their clothes wafted the aroma of incense. Uroan women are always dressed in colourful *kangas* (two-piece wraps) and they only use incense on special occasions. Notably, in encounters between the two groups, village women changed their way of greeting. Instead of the usual *Habari za kutwa* ('News of the day') they would say *Salaam aleikum* ('Peace be with you'), an Arabic expression. There was thus a difference of aesthetics in this meeting in which town aesthetics appeared superior to village ways. It is probable that my neighbours hesitated to reveal their true opinions on these occasions because they felt unsure of what the educated strangers from town would think of them. Again, the notion of fieldwork as an 'art of conversation' is revealed (Hutchinson 1996). Barriers for understanding other people exist in a range of ways. Long-term fieldwork provides particular advantages for overcoming some of them.

A final reflection in this section concerns how the census interviews were conducted. Here the 'art of conversation' was turned into asking and responding to standardised questions which also had ethical implications. The census brought valuable data that I make use of in the forthcoming chapters. Most people seemed to appreciate these interviews, which lasted for about an hour and which also included open-ended questions. However, the interview schedule was not tailored for the most materially-deprived households. Elderly people tended to have few material resources and I tried to be particularly sensitive in my approach to them. I asked them the general question of what they would need to live 'the good life'. This triggered answers as distinct as a good health, money and a nice house. If there was no electricity, I generally did not ask what kind of appliances people would want if they had the money. I had noticed that some elderly people with few resources showed little enthusiasm for this topic, so I avoided it. However, questions I considered relevant, such as 'How much do you spend on kerosene per month?', sometimes asked too much of this group of elderly, poor people. Consequently, I was yelled at and simply boycotted by two elderly women, respectively. These interviews were interrupted and I subsequently avoided asking people who were elderly, single and poor to join in the census because it seemed improper to ask them questions about consumption. I thus learned a lesson about the ethical difficulties of studying consumption in a context where some people feel they lack material resources.[13]

Mary Douglas conceives 'poverty' in social terms in contrast to 'destitution' which she relates to subsistence problems (1982: 16). Poverty is related to personal dignity, the author says with conviction. She discusses poverty in relation to consumption at large, consumption which is linked to people's need for goods in order to involve other people in their projects. When a person feels a lack of resources for committing others to his/her projects, s/he experiences the pain of that indignity. Therefore, when I appeared with my standardised questionnaire, it might have reminded some individuals of their deprived state vis-à-vis other people in the village. In other words I might have obliged them to focus on their own indignity. Although I tried to be considerate I sometimes remained unsure of the consequences of what I was asking for. On the other hand, most people eagerly gave me their answers. Some people even criticised me for not showing up sooner to ask them 'the questions' (*maswala*). The difficulty of not knowing when generally unproblematic inquiries did become too much followed me throughout these sessions, though.

In contrast, similar episodes did not occur in informal conversations because words would be floating freer. I often initially suggested a topic but this would not be imposed on people. Douglas speaks of the 'enjoyment of sharing names' as just as important as the 'enjoyment of sharing goods' when she treats people's objectives for consumption (1982: 28–31). By 'names' she refers to people's possession of knowledge that is linked to physical consumption.[14] Among the poor of Uroa, also, who are left with few material choices, the exchange of 'names' seemed to provide some sort of pleasure. This was notably so when they could be in control of what was said and the manner in which such knowledge was shared. For the fieldwork encounter I find Douglas' notion of 'dignity' to be related to Hastrup's perspective on protagonists' equal positions in the field. What appears more difficult within studies of consumption than in other fields is to avoid obliging marginalised groups to focus on their own poverty. If they are, which in my experience is more likely to happen during standardised interviews than in contexts where the art of conversation can be maintained, the ethnographic dialogue is no longer constituted by symmetric relationships.

An outline of the book

In this book the mundane electric current will act as our guide through a multifaceted, social landscape. We follow electricity's first illumination of Zanzibar Town in the late nineteenth century and its gradual diffusion into rural areas towards the end of the millennium. We also visualise how electric current is brought into some people's homes and made relevant to everyday life. To give an indication of the spread of the topics to be explored, suffice to say we will move from the construction of high voltage lines and end up in people's kitchens to explore food as a symbol of fertility. In what follows, each chapter dwells on a particular part of this tour.

Chapter 2, 'Powers of the past', introduces the location and the people in question and treats historical Zanzibar. We follow electricity's trajectories since its introduction in Zanzibar in the 1880s up to the post-revolution era. In this way electricity is used as a means of grasping important elements in Zanzibari history which also had effects on people living in the countryside. At the same time we are introduced to the technology in question as seen from the viewpoint of a utility company. Despite the distinct policies that have been employed over the years, electric distribution systems also have certain inherent characteristics.

Chapter 3 describes the overall goals and immediate achievements of the rural electrification project, RUREL, which brought electricity to the countryside in Zanzibar from the 1980s onwards up to the present day.

From chapter 4 onwards Uroa will be the central focus of analysis. Firstly, we hear the story of how the electric grid reached the village. Following David Nye (1990),[15] the chapter is titled 'Electrifying Uroa' to emphasise people's own participation in the process. In this place, participation became a reality to an exceptionally high degree. People in Uroa mobilised their forces to obtain the new technology. Conflicts also formed a central part of the picture and we shall come to see the political nature of any project of a certain scale.

Chapter 5, 'Discourses of development', documents recent socio-economic changes in Uroa and discuss these in the light of Zanzibari and village discourses of development. Communication technologies play an important role therein. I also show that there has been a boom in money-making activities over the last fifteen years. Kinship relations appear to be in decline. An important objective here is to demonstrate development's increasing impetus as an idea and as a way of living. The shift provides people with increasing legitimacy for referring to change as a value in itself. This contradicts other important Zanzibari values. Consequently, economic stratification increases and a battle over values is articulated, particularly between genders and between generations. Uroans' ambivalent relationship with tourism captures some of the general tensions people experience at present. Hopes for, and signs of, a better life continue to manifest themselves along with new types of challenges.

In chapter 6, 'The electricity company in the village', I focus on people's experiences as electricity customers. I show that a serious discrepancy exists between the type of knowledge customers are expected to possess and what they know in reality. This knowledge gap has important and unfortunate consequences. The investigation involves a scrutinising of various elements within the electricity system. I focus on moralities inherent in distinct types of connections to the grid which, through people's acknowledgment of them, become established ethics. These are not always in accordance with utility regulations. Mutual distrust characterises the utility-customer relationship and I account for why this is so. What is more, the government is gaining increasing control of its rural population due to electrification. The reinforcement of the ties between the state and rural households puts the latter group in a vulnerable position.

In chapter 7, 'Uroa by night', we explore outdoor space. Electric light at night-time has restructured the place, both time-wise and spatially. Electricity causes a faster pace of life. The meaning attributed to place also shifts with artificial light. This involves a modification of the arena where spirits and people meet. Furthermore, inherent in the materiality of electric light is its strikingly visible means of expressing who has power. I suggest that electric light produces new kinds of differences. This shift is relevant not just within the village but also to Uroa's position vis-à-vis other villages and Zanzibar Town. I also show how men's expectations of electricity appear to influence marriage patterns.

Chapter 8, 'Introducing objects of desire', treats people's strategies when introducing electrical appliances into their homes. Women do not purchase or own such devices and one of my objectives is to account for the 'maleness' of these items. Brotherly cooperation is an important part of men's strategies for acquiring such possessions in a morally tenable manner, this meaning without breaking the code of modesty. Nevertheless, in some instances which concern what I label as 'dangerous acquisitions' the balance is threatened. The phenomenon is closely linked to processes where objects become normalised (Shove 2003). The study of how Uroans acquire electrical appliances will carry insights to the question of understanding the general dynamics embedded in consumption.

In chapter 9, 'Reorganising interior space', we move indoors to study the spatial reorganisation following electricity's arrival. Both electric light and television sets, or rather people's new habits concerning their use, have had considerable effects. The man 'has come home' with these new consumption practices. Spouses now enjoy more time with their extended families, and the importance of kinship networks is reinforced. The chapter investigates these shifts by focusing on the living room as a meaningful place and pays particular attention to power relations between men and women.

Chapter 10, 'Negotiating tastes in food', can be seen as a response to the question of why electric cookers are not in use in Uroa. Both freezers and electric cookers are kept at a distance from Zanzibari food. I wish to account for this by drawing on selected parts of Pierre Bourdieu's work in *Distinction* (1984). The question of tastes in food is a fruitful way of exploring how people create boundaries between themselves and others. In Uroa it is equally important to note, however, that people minimise distinctions in many contexts. Furthermore, men and women express different opinions when asked about their taste in food with relation to various cooking technologies. These gender differences are important and we shall explore a cook's concerns and preferences and compare these with men's accounts of food, taste and the human body.

Chapter 11, 'Electricity makes a difference', summarises the effects of electricity's arrival in rural Zanzibar. The consequences of electrification are discussed with regard to how people in Uroa perceive them, in the light of the government's objectives, according to the relational and structural consequences, and in relation to current debates on development and poverty. Electricity's materiality and organisation is noted with particular regard to the constraints and tensions the technology produces in rural Zanzibar. I end by way of summing up the central elements in Uroans' present experiences of continuity and change.

Notes

1. See, for example, IEA: 'World energy outlook 2002' and 'World energy outlook 2006'; UNDP: 'Human Development Report 2001'; Tanzanian Ministry of Planning, Economy and Empowerment (2005: 104–10; 2006: 9).
2. Science and Technology Studies (STS) have primarily focused on the social aspect of how technologies come into being. Here, system theory and actor–network approaches analyse how various elements within technological systems are interlinked. Authors such as Bruno Latour (1994) and Madeleine Akrich (1994) have scrutinised the way technical objects, including electricity meters, continue to carry 'scripts' which determine the way users will act. Thomas P. Hughes's book, *Networks of power* (1983), on the history of electrification in the U.S. and other Western countries, is a classic. The body of literature on the historical significance of electrification and related technological innovations is considerable, for example, David E. Nye, *Electrifying America* (1990); Ruth Schwartz Cowan, *More work for mother* (1983); Wolfgang Schivelbusch, *Disenchanted night* (1988); Carolyn Marvin, *When old technologies were new* (1988). Sociologists have also contributed considerably to understanding the consumption of electricity in a sustainable perspective. A central book here is Elisabeth Shove's *Comfort, cleanliness and convenience: The social organization of normality* (2003).
3. In 1991 I stayed for three months in Zanzibar. I conducted more interviews in Uroa than in other places, and I also stayed two weeks with a family in the village in order to observe everyday life. Given the data gathered, the personal contacts I had made and the relatively high proportion of electrified households, Uroa became an easy choice for the period 2000–1. The fieldwork lasted for ten months this time. Brief return visits to Zanzibar were made in 2004 (two weeks), 2005 (five weeks) and 2006 (two weeks). On

the latter two occasions I was engaged as a consultant by the electrification project in Zanzibar. In 2005 the project in question involved designing information material and establishing teams that would organise public meetings and practical demonstrations of electric appliances in non-electrified villages (SUM 2005). The project was initiated by the Norwegian Embassy in Dar and the project management team in Zanzibar as a response to my earlier findings which bore witness to a high level of frustration and uncertainty among electricity customers in rural areas. The information teams' purpose was to improve potential customers' awareness of the electricity system, including the billing and accounting system, and also to seek to establish a good relationship between future customers and the electricity company (ZECO). The teams held meetings in thirty nine Zanzibari villages (Unguja and Pemba). 3,601 adults attended the meetings (two thirds men and one third women) which means that the project reached 8–9 per cent of the relevant population face to face (i.e., people living in villages that would be electrified during Phase IV). In addition to project and utility staff (male and female), men and women from rural areas who were already familiar with electricity played an active role during the meetings. An analysis of the questions people asked during these meetings revealed that they had become considerably more aware of utility regulations than had been the case in Uroa in 2000. In 2006 I conducted a social impact evaluation study of Phase IV of the rural electrification project (SUM 2006).

4.	The term is inspired by the title of a book edited by Daniel Miller (1998) called: *Material cultures. Why some things matter.*

5.	This and other linear and Western biased models of development, termed 'modernisation theory', have been widely criticised. In effect such models have not only proven to be empirically wrong, but have also been shown to tend to value some (developed) groups as more valuable than other (underdeveloped) groups. Throughout this book I try to avoid the premises embedded in such models.

6.	While building extensively on Bourdieu's work, Miller refers to the French author's tendency to 'structure' (Miller 1994: 298). He criticises Bourdieu for not accounting for how individuals translate 'habitus' into action (ibid.: 297). To allow more methodological room for tracing aspects of change Miller makes a slight shift towards material objects themselves. This resonates with anthropological work on technology. However, he follows Bourdieu when he argues that normative schemes tend to be repeated in a range of domains (material or otherwise). This is why apparently trivial practices are the ideal locations for the objectification of fundamental moral principles (Bourdieu 1977: 87–90, Miller 1994: 217, 315). Therefore, in contrast to the explicit self-representation of people in speech, material culture often appears to entail a more inconspicuous and non-provocative position (Miller 1994: 315; 1998: 9). In reality Miller maintains, echoing Bourdieu, that objects are often loaded with meaning and norms. This position of material objects (otherwise often perceived as 'context' for social life) is exactly what makes them valuable for investigation. The 'subtle connections' between objects on the one hand and human lives and their values on the other is what we look for (Miller 1998: 9; 1994: 315). However, in contrast to Bourdieu, Miller uses this perspective explicitly to investigate signs of change. To him objectification is not a one-way process where the material domains and discourses (that is, symbols) incorporate overall structures and rationales (that is, prior values) in individuals. Instead, he regards objectification as a dialectic process (1994: 54 n.). In this way people's relations to artefacts both reflect and create cultural ideas. This dynamic perspective is important when I examine how things and spatial organisation objectify or represent values and identities.

7.	This is why energy economists speak of the demand for electricity as a 'derived demand'.

8.	114 of the 480 households in Uroa were covered. I interviewed both wives and husbands. In most cases I spoke with each of the spouses on distinct occasions. Fifteen of these households were visited and interviewed by two field assistants.

9. I joined meter readings in the villages of Marumbi, Chwaka, Jendele, Dunga and Bambi, as well as Uroa. I also had access to ZECO's data basis and lists of customers, their consumption, arrears and payments.

10. Due to the difficult political climate in Zanzibar, I remained excluded from all formal meetings in 2000–1 and in 2004. A secret investigation committee was established by the district authorities to survey my actions. According to people who sympathised with the political opposition in Zanzibar, this is standard procedure at present. To the government all Westerners are seen as spies working for the opposition. As the 2000 general elections approached and tension increased in the village my husband and I found it best to take a break and visit the mainland.

11. Hastrup emphasises that anthropological practice is linked to both experience and writing in which a 'new world of betweenness is created' (1995: 25). Such insights are not outlived when the ethnographer leaves the field. In sum, Hastrup maintains that '[t]he ethnographic present is what potentiates anthropology' (ibid.).

12. Before taking on the major fieldwork I attended Swahili classes at the Peace Corps Institute in Oslo.

13. As a result, the census sample is not quite representative for the whole population. This is reflected by the fact that 43 per cent of census-households had obtained electricity whereas the real figure was 33 per cent at that time. I have not attempted to compensate for this slightly biased data which affects the figures to be presented. The sample was also selected strategically to cover various wards in Uroa.

14. Consumption in a narrower ('real') sense is the 'consumption that physically destroys goods' (Douglas 1982: 29).

15. To provide the most appropriate language I shall sometimes use the passive forms 'electrification' and 'electrified'. Throughout the work I nevertheless maintain the position that people are not passive receivers of electricity.

Chapter 2

POWERS OF THE PAST

The people and the place

Zanzibar is a semi-autonomous state within the United Republic of Tanzania. Situated in the Indian Ocean off the coast of mainland Tanzania, Zanzibar consists of the two islands Unguja and Pemba and some smaller islets. Approximately one million people inhabit the islands. The polity's administrative and commercial centre is Zanzibar Town, located on the west coast of Unguja. The village of Uroa lies on the opposite side of the island.

Zanzibar forms part of what tends to be known as the 'Swahili community' that stretches along the East African coast from Somalia to Mozambique. The first Swahili settlements are said to have emerged between the eighth and tenth centuries (Nurse and Spear 1985: 68–9; Spear 2000). Their settlements consisted of dense villages located either on the beach or in close proximity to the ocean. They fished and traded various products (iron, pottery, etc.) with neighbouring communities on the mainland. They also farmed and kept livestock (Nurse and Spear 1985: 68–9). Trade gradually grew in importance, with large vessels beginning to arrive from Asia. From the twelfth century onwards, Indian Ocean trade expanded and many Swahilis became engaged in the trading business (Middleton 1992: 11; Spear 2000). This was also when Islam began to make inroads (Spear 2000: 258). The interaction between the early Swahili settlements and Asian traders contributed to forming what is today perceived as the nature of the Swahili community. The question of Swahili identity has, nevertheless, been subject to fierce debate, a matter I will return to shortly.

Due to the population's common history, their particular social structure, their shared religion (Islam) and the shared use of the Swahili language (which is of Bantu origin (Spear 2000)), many scholars have

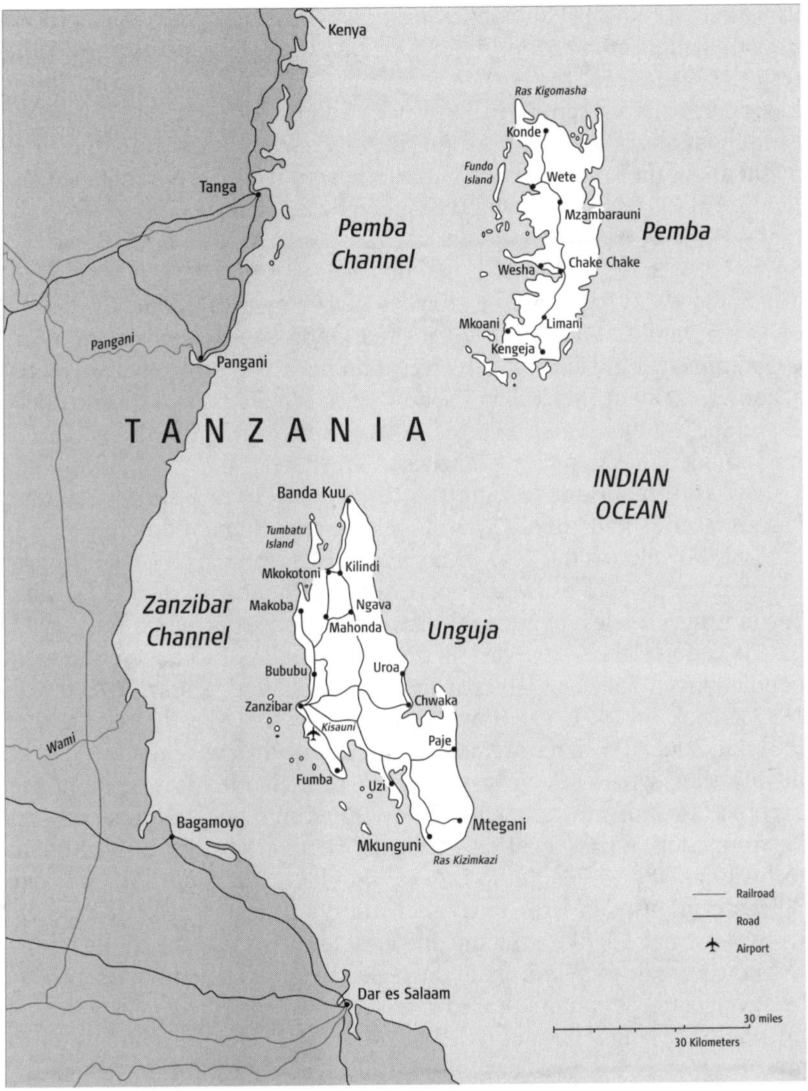

Map 2.1 Zanzibar: Unguja and Pemba Islands.
Source: University of Texas Libraries, USA.

argued that Swahili civilisation should be regarded as an integral whole (Nurse and Spear 1985; Mazrui and Shariff 1994; Middleton and Horton 2000: 2–4). Mazrui and Shariff have, however, pointed out the unfortunate effects of the way Swahili identity has been constructed over the years. The authors perceive this to be linked to the underlying ideologies at play. The Kenyan and Tanzanian states are said to have been using the Swahili label for political purposes. This has served to marginalise the population in question in quite distinct ways, though with the same result (1994: 44–5). The authors also criticise much Western research for having been ethnocentric in its way of adding to 'the confusion about Swahili identity' (ibid.: 43). As a result this research 'was to raise further doubt about the substance and indeed the very reality of Swahili identity' (ibid.). They claim, in line with recent linguistic and archeological research, that the importance of Asian influence has been overestimated (Nurse and Spear 1985; Spear 2000). The previous emphasis on overseas trade (e.g., Middleton 1992) has therefore probably slightly misrepresented the history of the Swahilis. Today the African or indigenous element in what constitutes 'the Swahili' has, correspondingly, come to receive greater acknowledgement (Mazrui and Shariff 1994; Middleton and Horton 2000: 27–8; Spear 2000; see also Larsen 2004 for a treatment of the politics of modern identities in present Zanzibar).

It is also important to note that there may have been less contact between rural and urban Swahili settlements than Middleton (1992) implied (Mbwiliza 2000: 7–13). Middleton's rich material on rural historical 'country towns' such as Uroa, as opposed to 'stone towns' such as Zanzibar Town, is nevertheless of great relevance in the present context (e.g., 1992: 83–9). Various labels have historically been employed to denote the early populations in Zanzibar, labels such as 'Hadimu' and 'Shirazi' (Middleton 1992; Depelchin 1991: 13). However, I note historian Mbwiliza's critique of the emic value of such terms. Mbwiliza holds that they were not used by the people themselves but vis-à-vis others in a hierarchical fashion. For example, Hadimu was gradually incorporated into people's mode of self-determination during the 1920s with the creation of colonial institutions (Mbwiliza 2000: 10–11). If this is so we should treat the terms Hadimu and Shirazi cautiously. In Uroa today they are not in use in everyday speech. Only older men I spoke with and one local historian recognised the terms.

These introductory lines about the region in question point to the need to be aware of not adopting so-called gate-keeping theories too quickly, at least not without a critical perspective. What Mazrui and Shariff remind us is that group identities, such as 'Swahili', are always politically constructed and shifting. African and Western scholars of the Swahili region now emphasise the openness, permeability and also the ideological aspects of coastal identity (Fair 1994: 192–7; Askew 1999; Mazrui and Shariff 1994; Parkin 1994; Middleton and Horton 2000; Caplan 2004: 11–12). This is in keeping with the general anthropological trend concerning the question of the boundedness of 'culture'. That said, ethnographic studies reveal that the Swahilis have maintained a sense of common identity, even today (e.g., Fair 1994; Fuglesang 1994; Larsen 1995; Caplan 1997, 2004; Nisula 1999; Middleton and Horton 2000). The articulation of a shared, Swahili identity is also to be found in the rural areas we are concerned with in this book.

References of identity: Swahili and Zanzibari

In rural Zanzibar people use the term 'Swahili' to describe who they are, for instance, in the sense of what they do, like or fear. 'Swahili' is also associated with traditional practices (*mila*) such as wedding ceremonies. Islamic elements are integral to such practices. Furthermore, the issue of Swahiliness is held to account for people's general disposition for, for example, jealousy (*wivu*) and secrecy (*siri*). In relation to serious health problems, spirits and magic remedies, 'Swahili' takes on a particular meaning. Suffering difficulties as a result of occult powers is, by definition, a 'Swahili problem' (*tatizo la Kiswahili*). In this way the notion is used to refer to a particular knowledge system (cf. Barth's notion 'traditions of knowledge' 1993; see also Hobart 1993). Linked to the sources of human malaise, but also to remedies, healing and prosperity, the forces related to such phenomena have a tremendous impact on a person's well-being. This will be my primary reason for using 'Swahili' as a label for practices and moralities related to the occult.[1]

'Zanzibari' is another important reference for identity. People in rural Zanzibar call themselves *Watu wa Zanzibar* (lit. 'People from Zanzibar'). This label is linked slightly more to place than to people's inner qualities. Zanzibar is primarily used as reference to denote distinction in relation to other places and, thus, other people. To be Zanzibari has, of course, a constitutional significance, because citizenship is defined according to this criterion. Registration for elections and reports of the actions of the Zanzibari government continuously remind people of which polity they form part. Radio and TV programmes are the most important means for such propaganda. Furthermore, a Zanzibari is also by definition a Tanzanian. Those with the closest affiliations to the governing party would occasionally use 'Tanzanian' as a label for self-identification. The same people would also refer to their 'African' identity. Nobody in the village would contest these labels but few would use them. In everyday village discourse Zanzibari and Tanzanian are rather opposing identities. Here, the latter uniquely refers to the mainland (former Tanganyika).

A large majority of the population in Uroa support the present government. Many would distinguish between Zanzibaris and Pembans, particularly when tension rises in the village. For example, on the day after the clashes in Pemba on 28 January 2001, the body of a police officer who had been killed was brought back in a coffin to Uroa. In this time of anger and sorrow some people described Pembans as particularly evil and quite different from 'Zanzibaris'. In contrast, the few in Uroa who sympathise with the opposition emphasise the unity of the population: 'We are all Zanzibaris' (*Sisi sote watu wa Zanzibar*). They reproach the government for failing to provide Pemba with development in terms of infrastructure. They also want fair elections and changes in the Union constitution. Individuals with origins in Pemba are stigmatised and partly excluded from Uroan social life.

In brief, what it means to be Zanzibari is a contentious matter in rural Zanzibar. Subsequent chapters will explore the ways various types of differences are constructed at present, in particular that between town and village. In the present discussion we are concerned with such relationships as they were formed in the past.

Uroa: remote but connected

Here, on the east coast, the land is characterised by coral ragstone. Due to the poorer quality of the soil, in comparison with other parts of Unguja and Pemba in particular, Uroa and neighbouring villages were not suited for clove plantations. This industry was introduced at the beginning of the nineteenth century during the heyday of the Sultanate period and had a fundamental socio-economic impact in Zanzibar (Depelchin 1991; Middleton 1992; Nisula 1999). The arrival of cloves provided the polity with immense wealth for the ruling classes and brought about transformations that are still felt on the islands. In fact, several writers hold that the present political impasse in Zanzibar – with its focus on ethnicity – is rooted in the introduction of cloves and the particular colonial context in which the industry was organised (Sheriff 1991c; Nisula 1999; Tambila 2000).

Arab rulers were in need of labour and exploited people from the mainland who became slaves on the plantations. The rulers also appropriated land which had previously been utilised for indigenous settlements. In consequence a proportion of the Swahili population in these western areas appears to have moved towards the coral ragstone zone on the east coast (Andersson and Ngazi 1998). It is, therefore, likely that Uroa received new groups at that time. Life in Uroa appears otherwise to have been relatively unmarked by the changes elsewhere in Zanzibar. They were not slave owners and people today do not perceive their ancestors as having been involved in slavery in any sense.

The population and its neighbouring villages were close to self-sufficiency apart from imports of iron and textiles (Sheriff 1991b). The fish market in Uroa is said to 'always' have been there. Farming was (and still is) managed by shifting cultivation, and the exchange of products with inland villages provided agricultural products that were hard to grow in Uroa. As women tended (and tend) to move at the time of their marriage, it is probable that a substantial part of these exchanges took place between members of the same family networks. Today 43 per cent of the women residing in Uroa come from such inland villages, according to my 2001 census.

If the 45 km distance to town seems short today with buses running every hour, this was not so in the past. Rashid remembers his father who would sometimes walk to town to sell dried fish. He would spend two days on such a trip. 'It was very hard to travel from here to Zanzibar Town.' As for contact with non-Swahili rulers, this seems to have been modest. In more recent times a few families are said to have come from Oman to sell shark in Uroa. Some remained in the village for certain periods. An Arab family ran a shop in the early 1960s. They sold rice, flour, sugar, 'mostly like today's [shops]'. However, they did not otherwise intermingle with the village population. Rashid recalls: 'We were just boys and afraid of those Arab children. They had the *falme* (king/sultan)'. The Arab family left Uroa right before the revolution in 1964 and life is said to have been relatively peaceful here at the peak of the conflict. This contrasts with what happened in Bambi, a village in which many Uroans were born and where they had (and have) relatives. Many Arabs had resided in Bambi and these Arabs were, according to my informants, all killed during the revolution.

I also met men in Uroa and other villages who spoke with enthusiasm of their relationships with Arabs in the past. Such collaboration seems to have provided people with business opportunities otherwise hard to find. These connections made investments possible and meant that enterprises could be established.

However, in general, the Arabs appear to have evoked fear in Uroa. Accounts from pre-revolution days tell us how distanced from, and fearful of, them Uroans felt, and such feelings are reproduced at present. The Arabs working for the British administration had constructed a small dispensary in Dikoni, Uroa. Destroyed by the passing of time, this building had been left untouched until the time of fieldwork. When asked why the former hospital had not been abolished or rebuilt, people replied: 'Because it belongs to the Arabs and they might come back to reclaim it'. This argument is replicated for Zanzibar at large when people express their fear that the opposing party will win the next elections.

Many Uroans refused to send their children to the primary school in Uroa due to its association with Arabs. For secondary education in town 'African boys were very few. ... Two to three were picked out. If you were the son of a Sheha [village leader] you got a place'. Village life was, thus, to a certain extent influenced by segregation. However, apart from education (and possibly other privileges granted to particular people), the village community appears to have maintained an internal egalitarian structure. This corresponds to Middleton's observation that rural settlements, such as Uroa, had a relatively egalitarian organisation. Their cognatic decent system (cross-cousin marriages are still relatively common) and local, economic interdependency formed ideals of equality (Middleton 1992: 83–9). Even today the value of equality and the subsequent emphasis on modesty heavily influence the ways in which people interact. As I will show in chapter 8, there is a considerable risk involved if a person obtains more than is considered appropriate by their peers. This is highly relevant to the way people obtain electrical appliances today.

Despite the relatively little contact Uroans had with Arabs – with the British they had even less since they never settled in the village – these are both nevertheless important groups of actors in people's imaginations of the past and present. Laura Fair has emphasised that all underprivileged groups in Zanzibar had a feeling of unity in colonial days (Fair 1994: 361–76). Events and ideologies in the centre affected life in the countryside. Partly because of this interconnectedness between rural areas and town, the remaining part of this chapter provides a condensed, but far from complete, account of electricity's colonial history in Zanzibar Town. By adopting a similar approach to that used in other parts of this work, electricity leads us to issues that mattered in Zanzibar in the past too.

There is another benefit to using electricity as a means for catching glimpses of Zanzibari history. We gain insights into how the electricity company operated; how overall policies and various constraints merged with initiatives and pressure from customer groups they sought to attract but also to discipline. By studying such interfaces we approach the technology under study from a perspective that will also apply to the following pages. I shall highlight aspects that have relevance for the topics to be explored further in the contemporary setting. Questions of morality are central.

The colonial period

The House of Wonders

Electricity appeared strikingly early on in Zanzibar Town, if only for a very limited part of the population. During the second half of the 1880s one of the Sultan's palaces, *Beit al-Ajaib* (House of Wonders), was equipped with electricity. Apparently this building, which served as a ceremonial palace, was the first in sub-Saharan Africa to have electricity. The House of Wonders is said to have derived its name from the building's spectacular architecture – and its electric light. The illuminated building was an emblem of power and influence.[2]

The Sultanate lost political and economic autonomy in Zanzibar during the nineteenth century (Depelchin 1991: 17–20). In 1890 Britain declared Zanzibar its protectorate and in 1891 the British took control of the Sultan's finances. European officers were appointed to run the administration (Depelchin 1991: 14–7; Sheriff 1991c: 249–51). The British kept the Sultanate as part of their colonial governance through indirect rule.[3] However, to ensure that a Sultan of their liking was put into office in 1896 they bombed the Sultan's Residence *Beit al-Sahil* ('Sultans Palace', today the Palace Museum) on the Stone Town shoreline (ibid.).

During the course of this event the House of Wonders, lying close to the residence, was also damaged. Plate 2.2 shows a picture of the inside of the

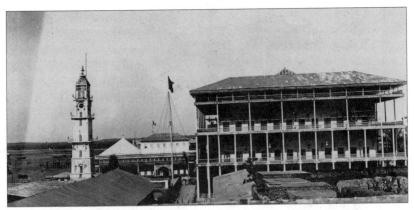

Plate 2.1 The original House of Wonders (*Beit al-Ajaib*), c.1895.
Source: Courtesy of Torrence Royer.

Plate 2.2 Inside the House of Wonders after the British bombardment of 1896.
Source: Courtesy of the Zanzibar National Archives.

building after the bombardment. The electric chandeliers appear to be relatively intact but I do not know the extent to which other parts of the electric supply might have been destroyed in the attack.

The building was reconstructed in 1899 due to the general damage. A former, separate tower and lighthouse on the coast had also been demolished and was now incorporated into the new building. This served as a seat for the British administration until its withdrawal in 1963. The history of the House of Wonders thus speaks first and foremost of the supremacy of the Sultanate. Electric light both conditioned and emphasised the Sultan's power. Secondly, the intended destruction marked the regime's decreasing influence in Zanzibar and, correspondingly, the means and ambitions of the British to take control in the region. Thirdly, the British takeover of the reconstructed House of Wonders signals how they remained in power afterwards.

Gradually the British administration in Zanzibar extended the electricity supply. In 1906 a concession was granted to a New York firm 'to supply electric light and power within a radius of five miles from the Sultan's palace'.[4] Stone Town was the area in question and had long been home to the wealthy part of the population, which mainly coincided with ethnic belonging.[5] The Zanzibar Electricity Company was launched. The company bought the Sultan's plant and used its 'surplus' to supply certain houses. Reading this in the aftermath we see how the Sultan's power was further reduced, and doubly so. Hypothetically there might have been conflicts over which supplies (the Sultan versus the other houses now connected) to prioritise as the capacity became more critical, but I have not found documentation that could support this. In 1908 the company installed 'a modern plant' fuelled with wood and more customers could become connected.[6] Supply in this early phase was meant for street lighting and the domestic and commercial use of electric light.

The company introduced two types of tariffs, one in which customers paid for each unit consumed, thus requiring an electricity meter.[7] As an alternative they also offered a 'contract rate'. This latter system was to cause problems for the utility company in disciplining and controlling their customers.

Attempting to control customer behaviour

The 'contract rate' defined the price each customer should pay according to the chosen lamp-size.[8] A daily period of six hours burning was presumed. The tariff was probably intended to make connection attractive since customers would be paying a fixed price per month. It also saved the company from having to invest in meters. In 1909 around 6000 lamps of medium size had been installed according to a government report, 'the Indians being particularly keen on electric light'.

Problems occurred, however. First of all, the growing supply attracted commercial actors to Zanzibar and merchants saw an opportunity to sell new electrical products. In turn some customers appear to have changed their lamps. In a note to the public written in 1910 the Manager of Zanzibar Electric Light Company warns:

> It has recently come to our knowledge that large quantities of Electric lamps have been for some time past imported to Zanzibar for sale by certain merchants ... [and that] several of our customers who are on the contract system supplied by us with Electric lights, have been fitting up for their use in their premises *lamps of higher powers* than are contracted and paid for. ... It is hardly necessary for us to point out to such customers that such practices are fraudulent and amount to a criminal offence. ... [The] company will in future be reluctantly compelled to take such legal action as may be necessary (ZA-AB6-14/1, original emphasis).

The light company had also discovered customers' failure to meet a second condition. The note continues: 'We also take this opportunity of informing our customers ... that *all lights* must be *put out* after twelve o'clock. ... Any use by them after this is illegal' (original emphasis).

However, the company's threat to proceed with legal action was ineffective. In an internal memo circulated in May 1912 the Director stated that company tests had shown 'that nearly 75 per cent of all contract lamps are left burning for the whole night, no attempt is being made to save the current'.[9] To solve the problem the Director suggested that the current be charged on a twenty-four-hour basis. Tariffs were increased correspondingly.

Thus we see how the utility company had certain expectations of customer behaviour. When consumers failed to turn the lights off at midnight, as the contract prescribed, the company modified the premises for accounting. Initially the customers had also had the opportunity to choose a twelve-hour (all night) contract for a higher price. However, the company by this point had little trust in its customers turning off the lights at all, so they made supply (legally) available twenty-four-hours a day. In this way the company no longer had to check when the lamps were lit or extinguished. Instead, the tariffs themselves redefined (and controlled) proper behaviour. Since these involved higher rates, one could say that the customers were punished as a group for some individuals' disloyal behaviour. The relationship between a customer and a utility thus does not only concern these two parties. Because tariffs are made general, trust and distrust are also relevant to how customers regard each other.

It was also in 1912 when the government bought the electricity company. By means of this the British administration gained full control of the electricity supply in Zanzibar (cf. Myers 1993: 191). With the change of ownership and increasing tariffs 25 per cent of all contract customers made a common complaint. The request produced considerable internal activity but did not make the utility company change its tariffs. To calm down the group of complaining customers the Director informed them that 'during the coming month of Ramazan [sic], all Jamats and Mosques will be allowed the privilege of using electric current from sunset to sunrise without extra charge'.[10] This gesture to Muslim communities seemed directed at buttressing the government's decision to keep rates as they were. The Ismaili community also enjoyed privileges for a longer period of time.[11]

I do not wish to overestimate the significance of this protest, but it is clear that the initiative concerned the shift in utility ownership. More specifically the customers were concerned with the new management's intentions, suspecting it of profit-mongering. This suspicion on the customers' side, namely of being a target for the utility company's commercial ambitions, has quite striking parallels in a variety of contexts.[12] On their side, the utility company appears to have balanced various concerns. The Consul General's unusual (to my knowledge) involvement in this case, and the free current provided during Ramadan, show that some degree of effort was made to meet the request. In this case the high number of people complaining, represented through an apparently Muslim-led commercial enterprise, seems to have given them a certain influence, albeit not enough to make the utility company actually change its tariffs.

We now turn to a group of people who played a central role in Zanzibari economic life, at least until the 1930s (Bader 1991): the Indian National Association (INA). They also used their influence in relationship to the government as electricity customers, and with considerable success.[13]

The Indian National Association (INA): pushing for lower charges

During the First World War coal prices rose considerably. Electricity was produced by coal at the time, and in 1916 the company was running at a considerable loss. This triggered the ordering of diesel generators. However, immediate measures were also taken. On 1 May it was announced that of the 485 street lights in Zanzibar, 300 were to be put out. In addition a range of measures were taken to reduce consumption and, at the same time, ensure the company's income.[14] The note refers to high coal prices and expresses the company's hopes that prices might later 'resume a normal supply at reasonable prices'. It mentions the plans to acquire new power plants but not the particular technology to be used.

Only one week later the INA sent a complaint to the company. The group was quite sympathetic with the government's need for action but showed concern for public safety:

[The] reduction of street lamps has been carried out to such an extent that many public streets have been absolutely kept dark at nights and there is every danger to the public safety and of thefts being committed in such darkness (ZA-AB6-14/36).

Electric street lighting provides people with a sense of security. This is also the case in today's Uroa. It is striking how fast, following the arrival of street lamps, the idea or experience of not having such light increases the feeling of risk.[15] The shift in Zanzibar Town in 1916 from electric light to darkness felt uncomfortable and dangerous. It might also be significant that the group which made the protest probably had a large proportion of shopkeepers among its members (cf. Bader 1991: 163–83).

The INA objected primarily to the time of year when these measures were taken: '[This] Monsoon season [is] when public streets remain so damaged'. The month of May corresponds to the rainy season in Zanzibar. However, this was also the time when Zanzibar hosted seamen and traders waiting for the southwest wind to take them back to the East. Therefore, by 'damaged' the Indians'/merchants' association might have been referring not only to the rains but also to the effects of the larger crowd of people occupying the isle. It is uncertain whether INA's efforts had immediate effect, but seven years later they reappeared on the scene. They had not forgotten about what had been promised.

In 1923 the INA wrote a letter to the Chief Secretary to remind the government about its promises to reduce charges whenever conditions returned to normal (referring to coal price decline).[16] This initiative led the government to reply to the association that, unless unforeseen circumstances occurred, the rates for electric light would be reduced from 10 to 8 annas per unit. Eleven days later the INA thanked the government for its decision. However, they kept up the pressure, stating their hopes for a further reduction in charges after one year or so.[17]

I find the association's language and arguments quite significant in comparison with other groups of customers at that time, and also with rural customers today. The INA obviously closely followed the change in coal prices. They showed some degree of insight into the utility company's technical and operational situation, though on a general level ('latest machinery'). Significantly, they referred to utility policies in other countries where 'a limit of 5 per cent return on invested capital is common'. In short, the INA possessed a high degree of relevant knowledge which provided them with resources they could use to influence the government. Their communication of this along with their network in India and elsewhere, their representing of a large number of customers, and their central role in Zanzibari economic life, forced the government to take their arguments into account. One and a half years later, the rates were reduced yet further.[18] The government knew they were being closely watched by the INA.

A utility company's commitment to stable consumption

Of concern to any electricity supplier is the attainment of a demand that is as regular as possible. Production must adjust to a real-time demand, which continuously varies. Relatively high peaks in consumption/load imply inefficient use of capacity in production gear and distribution lines. Technical losses also increase with increasing load. Therefore for higher peaks, with low consumption at other times and customers paying by the unit, the return on investments is inevitably less. The load-factor expresses the extent to which an electric system is exploited, and utility companies seek to keep this as high as possible.[19] Because various types of customers contribute to the load-factor in different ways (and for a range of reasons, as we shall see) energy policies and tariffs differ for various groups.

From colonial times up until now, the peak load in Zanzibar occurs in the evening. The isles lie six degrees south of the equator, thus the shift from day to night does not vary throughout the year. Every day is twelve hours long and the evening top-load coincides with the arrival of darkness. Furthermore, due to the sub-tropical climate, there is no need for heating buildings, unlike in many other parts of the world. The variations in natural seasons have a limited impact on domestic customers' electricity use. Figure 2.1 illustrates how consumption (the load) has varied in Zanzibar during ordinary weekdays in recent years.

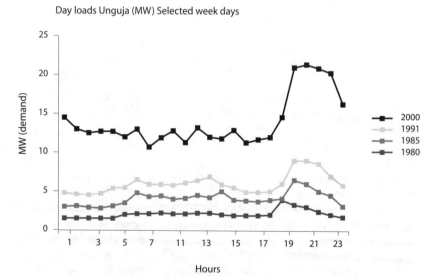

Figure 2.1 Daily variations in electricity consumption in Zanzibar up to the year 2000.

People's use of electricity is a topic to be explored in chapters 8–10, but some aspects are relevant to the present discussion. One family in Uroa possesses a water kettle. Only in the 'cold season' (*wakati wa baridi*), that is the rainy season, would they heat their bath water by means of electricity (or any other means). Similarly, another family that keeps an electric cooker primarily uses this when the firewood is wet. On the other hand, residents with leaking palm roofs would not use electricity at all when the rains were pouring down. Freezers and fans are systematically turned off during the rainy season. When time-use and the power of various appliances are considered, I would estimate that electricity consumption decreases slightly in Uroa during the rainy season. However, for Unguja at large, comparisons of the utility's day-load curves from selected months in 2000–1 show no significant variation that can be traced to changes in the natural seasons.

There is good reason to believe that the evening peak throughout the year is – and has been – related to the consumption of electric light. Electricity suppliers are generally oriented to reducing such peaks in demand. We shall now take a closer look at the company's concern with reaching a regular supply demand and how this concern affected their relationship to various types of customers. I concentrate on how they regarded and contrasted two distinct customer groups: factories (using the 'power' tariff) and domestic-light consumers, respectively.

In Zanzibar factories operating during daytime were (and are) attractive customers from a technical and economic point of view. When a producer of soap and oil approached the British Resident in February 1918 to ask for lower rates, this triggered a process of internal discussions.[20] The factory emphasised its potential capacity to triple electricity consumption if prices went down. After one year power rates were generally reduced whereas light charges remained the same.

Internal correspondence on this matter reveals that the settlement of tariffs is subject to negotiations. The dialogue between the British Resident's office (BR), the Chief Secretary (CS) and the Director of the Railway and Electricity Department also tells us how various customer groups were regarded. First of all, the CS notes that the customer uses 'an exceptional amount of current'. The Director agrees but thinks the question of lower tariffs should wait until he has been able 'to run the Diesel engine for seventeen hours instead of ten as at present'. The CS agrees and asks: 'Shall I reply this [to the customer]?' However, on the following day, someone higher up (presumably at the BR's office) intervenes:

> I consider all rates should now be reduced. We are making large profits at present … and this is not right, as we increased the rates owing to exceptional circumstances last year which no longer obtain (ZA-AB6-14/54).

The superior wants action for the reduction of prices and asks for details on rates, costs and returns. This shows the officer's removed position from daily operations. Moreover, his initial justification for recommending reduction in charges was ultimately turned completely around in the process. Consider the dynamics between these officers of distinct rank. In January 1919 the Director shows in detail that they are making a profit. He suggests that the price of 'power' is reduced because: 'It will be greatly to the benefit of the undertaking to obtain a larger consumption of current during the hours of daylight'.[21] Both superiors agree. The CS emphasises that no reduction should be made in the charges for light. The senior officer who finally authorises the cut in power rates (the same person as the one quoted above, who stated that all tariffs should be reduced) concludes with regard to ordinary light-customers:

> I think any reduction in lighting rates should be approached with caution. Govt. is justified in taking a profit just as much as it makes a profit from shipping. My view is that the profit thus accruing is used for the general development of the Protectorate, & this is far better than distributing the profit to a host of Indians and others in small sums (ZA-AB6-14/82).

We thus note that subordinate officers had a considerable say in the forming of electricity policy. The reference to technical aspects was accepted as a reason for lowering power tariffs. Factories had a favourable consumption pattern and were also often owned by British or other European companies.[22] This all probably contributed to their being treated sympathetically. Furthermore, by showing and claiming their potential to increase the use of electricity, factory management gained additional influence over the government's tariff policies.

Light-customers, in contrast, were now regarded as milking-cows for the Protectorate. For light-demand, the government either had trust in its weak correlation with price (low price elasticity) or, alternatively, did not regard a potential decrease in light-demand as a problem due to its contribution to the peak load. Also, the (presumably) British officer might not have been too concerned about this group's situation. His rather disgraceful way of speaking about a large proportion of the company's customers reflects the racist discourse openly articulated at the time (Nisula 1999: 210–18). That the 'host of Indians' had, in fact, been overcharged and had thus contributed to the profit was completely disregarded by the officer. Instead he was worried about distributing 'small sums' to those who had initially been providing them.

In sum, large consumers of electricity received benefits compared to small light-customers for a range of reasons. However, as we can see, when claims were made in unison, light-consumers also had negotiating power. What influential actors succeeded in doing was to manipulate the utility company's justifications for selecting their policies. We are now to make a leap in time to consider the situation of another light-customer. Matters of morality and knowledge continue to be my concern.

Customers on 'the Other Side'

By 1951, the electricity system was established in Ng'ambo ('the Other Side'). This part of Zanzibar Town was mainly inhabited by indigenous Zanzibaris and mainland Africans (Myers 1993: 43).[23] The 1950s was a transformative period, also with regard to electricity. Towards the late 1940s the company had been running at a loss and it publicly announced a 66 per cent increase in domestic charges. Interestingly, given the apparently modest political role contributed to the Sultanate, there is evidence that Sultan Seif bin Hamood had a say when the utility was about to introduce the new rates in 1949.[24] Following the Sultan's objections, protests from the INA, and the Town Council's similar reaction, a public note asked customers to disregard the previous note about increased rates. Without reference to the Sultan it said that 'His Highness' (that is, the British Resident) was 'considering' the issue. As a result, only power charges were increased in 1951. Domestic charges remained as before.

The electric power-supply was reconstructed. In 1954 Saateni Power Station was opened.[25] The direct current system (d.c.) was changed into alternating current (a.c.) which was a milestone because a.c. can be transformed into higher voltages. In consequence, the current may be transported much farther without nearly as much energy-loss as would be the case with d.c. These costly changes, together with the economic losses accumulated over the years, led the government to nearly double the tariff for ordinary kWh-customers in 1955. A fierce dispute followed with the Town Council amongst those who complained, but the British Resident had the final say.[26]

In this context we will now hear the case of a customer who was living in Ng'ambo in 1957. She had been disconnected from the supply and claimed to have been unfairly treated. Her general situation resembles that of many rural customers today. However, unlike the people I met, this customer made a formal complaint. We also gain insight into how the utility company considered her case and how they communicated their conclusions.[27]

Letter from customer to the Chief Secretary in Zanzibar, 1 July 1957 (ZA-AB6-30/1):

Mtumwa bt. Juma
c/o Mr. Ali Yusuf
Post Office
Zanzibar

Hon. Chief Secretary, Zanzibar.

Sir, I forward herewith my petition in regard to the disconnection of electric current to my house recently. ... I am an old woman, aged 60 years, living far off from town, i.e. Kisimamajongoo, and that I cannot write or read, and at the same time not well-to-do so as to afford luxuries, like radio. ... I have to state that I did not receive a bill from P.W.D. which I always do. ... Moreover, on 28th June, [19]57, my agent had been at the Head Office of P.W.D. where he consulted the clerk concerned, who said that I am supposed to refer to the gazettes or listen to the radio ... – and that unless I pay the connection fees of Shs.22/50 then I will not be able to get the current. ... I assure you that had I received the bill in time the above disconnection would not have occurred. Winding up, I am certain that I have been unfairly treated and that I supplicate for your consideration to exempt me from paying the connection fees of Shs.22/50; for which kindness I shall be much obliged.

Yours faithfully,
(L.T.P. of Mtumwa bt. Juma)

Copy to Hon. Director of P.W.D.

Internal note from Chief Secretary's office to the Director of Public Works, 11 July 1957 (ZA-AB6-30/2):

The Director of Public Works,

I have received a letter from Mtumwa binti Juma ... in which she claims that her electricity supply was disconnected and that she has been required to pay a reconnection fee although she did not receive the account for the electricity she consumed in the previous period.

A copy of this letter has been sent to you, and I shall be grateful if you will let me have your views.

A.H.Hawker, for Chief Secretary

Internal reply from Director to Chief Secretary, 19 July 1957 (ZA-AB6-30/3, original emphasis):

Hon. Chief Secretary,

With reference to your letter ... I have to advise you that the usual practice in this office is to disconnect on or about the 27th of the quarter month all electricity supplies for which the account has remained unpaid for the *previous quarter*. The actual disconnection date is published in three consecutive issues of the Official Gazette,[28] in the local papers and is broadcast over the Sauti ya Unguja. ... What usually happens is that after disconnection at least twelve to twenty consumers report to me asking for exemption of the reconnection charge ... giving a variety of reasons. ... A common reason for non-payment is that they have never received the bill. Owing to the non-existance [sic.] of a postal service in the Protectorate, it is not possible for me to refute their statement but likewise I never accept such a statement as a justifiable reason for non-payment. All electricity bills are dispatched to premises by a billman who frequently, because of the absence of the occupant, or because the occupant is in purdah,[29] has to slip the bill under the door.

In this particular case, I can see no difference from the usual number of complaints ... and suggest that no exemption be given in case a precedent is created. It is true that this consumer has not been disconnected before, but that is usual with most cases as we have no bad offenders in this respect. Once a consumer has had to pay a reconnection fee for disconnection for non-payment, they take good care that it does not occur again.

AG. Director of Public Works

Letter from Chief Secretary to the customer, 24 July 1957 (ZA-AB6-30/4):

Madam,

I have the honour to refer to your letter dated 1st July, in which you submit a petition that the reconnection charge raised by the Director of Public Works in respect of your house be waived.

I am informed that the bill for the first quarter of 1957 was delivered to your house and this constitutes notice of the debt under section 25(2)(b) of the Electricity Decree (No.29 of 1954). The actual disconnection date was published in three consecutive issues of the Gazette, was published in the local press and was broadcast by Sauti ya Unguja.

Under these circumstances therefore it is regretted that the reconnection charge cannot be waived.

I have the honour to be, Sir, Your obedient servant,
R. P. Read

For Chief Secretary to the Government

First of all, we note the paradox that a customer who is unable to read and who possesses no radio is supposed to acquire information by such means. In the circumstances she is also forced to describe herself in this degrading way. It appears that the utility company made no attempt to reach her personally to claim the debt. A quarterly payment system implies that meters are only checked every third month. Hence it is unlikely that a meter-reader warned her that the disconnection was due. The strictness of such a regime is significant and puts people unable to read (or listen to the radio) at a disadvantage. Today meters are read monthly. This creates more opportunities for personal contact and gives customers more chance to settle their bills before they are disconnected. However, personal contacts also pose particular dilemmas as we shall see in chapter 6.

My second observation concerns how the officers concealed their own uncertainty of whether she had actually received the bill. The internal reasoning infers, first of all, that they generally did not know if customers received their bills. Secondly, many disconnected customers gave this explanation after having been disconnected. Thirdly, since many said they never received the bill, this argument was not accepted. However, to the customer the CS maintains that the bill was indeed delivered. Not only is this conclusion morally dubious but it also speaks of an asymmetric relationship. The customer is in no position to detect or relate this deviation from the utility company's general experiences and policy to the statement of her particular case. In addition the reference to Zanzibari legislation serves to alienate the customer further and to increase the authority of the decision. She is forced to pay the reconnection fee if she wants the current back.

The Director nevertheless seems to have a certain degree of sympathy with the customer, possibly due to the fact that she, unlike most customers (past and present), is a woman. She is also old and poor. His note to the CS is rather lengthy compared to other similar cases. He also refers to the danger of creating a precedent if she were treated differently from other customers. Therefore, seemingly, he at least considers accepting her request. His last comment about her former fulfilment of paying her arrears also signals a certain degree of understanding of her situation. However, as he concludes, few customers repeat their mistakes once they have been punished.

With his aim to discipline customers and the word 'punish', we touch on one of electricity's features that is radically different to those of other commodities. Unlike sugar, rice or oil, the difficult thing about electricity in many places is that it is first consumed and then paid for.[30] In addition, the costly and solid physical connection between customer and utility company binds the two parties to one another like spouses in a marriage: tied to each other through the good times and the bad times and with a high cost in the case of separation.

In general the utility company wants to attract consumers. At the same time, it also penalises consumers for disobedient behaviour. The officers' choices of artefacts and tariffs are means for serving both goals. Such choices are conditioned by political, economic and technical restraints. Furthermore, the utility company relates differently to various types of customers. They all possess unequal resources and unequal types of knowledge. Accordingly, they are treated differently. I do not mean to say that similar complaints to that made in the last case would have had a more positive outcome for other kinds of customers. In the event of disconnection everybody seems to have got the same treatment, though a poor person is, of course, more likely to end up in such a situation.

Rather, a crucial moment occurs when contracts are negotiated. The type of products manufactured mattered to the British management. We see signs of this in the fact that the cinema in Zanzibar got a special price.[31] Furthermore, a request for lower charges from the ice factory was considered by the British Director since '[they] make a product almost essential to life in the Tropics'. The involvement of the British in commercial enterprises has also been noted. Finally, we saw that some actors had particular influence on tariffs in general. This was the case either because they represented a strong organisation or because they were a technically and financially attractive type of customer. Throughout, political considerations played a role in utility company decisions. In sum, we start seeing the contours of the variety of 'heterogeneous' elements that make up our socio-technical system of concern. We also see the ways in which such systems are reshaped.

With the colonial government's focus on already privileged groups, the spread of electricity in colonial Zanzibar Town did not create, but rather emphasised, a system of social classification. Through their use of tariffs, technologies, bureaucratic language and propaganda, the utility company clearly reproduced the social order as they perceived it.[32] The provision of street lighting shows the regime's consideration for security in certain areas and less so in other districts. Along with Edward Said in his book *Representing the colonized*, we may say that the contrast between darkness and illuminated space reflected the 'geographical imagination' of colonialism and imperialism (Said 1989: 212, found in Myers 1993: 176, who uses Said's image to capture the general division of Zanzibar Town). However, the utility company/government also met resistance. It is very likely that the government's major concern was – particularly as the political antagonism increased – to keep the Protectorate running smoothly and peacefully. This was a condition for achieving the administrasion's goals in the late 1940s which were to provide development of the British economy, justify the British presence in Zanzibar and prepare for an end to that presence (Myers 1993: 178–9, building on Berman 1984). For all these concerns the avoidance of conflict seems important. Nevertheless, it is clear that it was the British administration that mainly decided the premises for electricity policy and supply in colonial Zanzibar.

Zanzibar was soon to be turned upside down, however. In December 1963 Zanzibar gained independence. The British left political power in the hands of a non-representative, Arab-dominated group (Nisula 1999: 15, referring to Lofchie 1965: 257). In January 1964 the revolution was a fact.

Many Arabs and Indians were killed or fled the islands in the months and years that followed. Surprisingly, the electric power supply remained stable during the revolution according to the utility Board who summed up events in April and May 1964.[33] The accounting department had suffered heavily 'due to depletion of staff'. As to the utility management, there had been relative continuity in personnel. Manager E. Clark, now about to leave, concluded that it had been 'so necessary' that the supply services were maintained without disruption at 'the height of the disturbances'. He seems to have presumed that with power cuts the violence during the revolution would have been even more severe. In European history, correspondingly, light has been considered so synonymous with order and symbolic power that in the Paris of 1830 destroying lanterns was defined as an adjunct to general revolt (Schivelbusch 1988: 105; see also Garnert 1993: 123–6 and Nye 1990). The darkness that prevailed stood for 'disorder and freedom' (Schivelbusch 1988: 98). Such acts both had symbolic and pragmatic relevance as the darkness created an area in which government forces could not operate (ibid.: 105–6). If electric light can be said to reduce uncertainty in everyday life and to underscore perceptions of order and human control, as we shall also encounter in chapter 7, it is easy to see why the prospect of darkness during the days of revolution evoked fear and nowhere more so than in the minds of the administration.

The post-revolution era

A new, socialist era arose in Zanzibar and the electricity scheme changed accordingly. In colonial days the driving force for change in the electricity supply rested primarily with customer initiative, available technologies, and the authorities' concern for income, security and prestige. Related to this primarily commercial philosophy, it was important to be running a modern plant and to be offering modern solutions to customers. Developments in Europe and North America were important references in this respect, but the utility company also compared its achievements to other parts of the British Protectorate. Neither should one underestimate the influences customers with connections in Asia received within their respective global networks. There were also signs that the poorer parts of the population were gradually taken into consideration. However, such steps seem to have been more a result of external pressure on the administration, such as those from the Town Council, than a product of intended policy.

In contrast, the revolutionary government emphasised its egalitarian commitment.[34] The first president of Zanzibar, Abeid Karume, declared his ambition to improve the living conditions of the poor. Land and property were nationalised and a range of other radical measures taken (see Myers 1993: 339–45; Larsen 1995: 56–7). Plans for development were centralised.

For help reconstructing society and running the electricity supply th government immediately turned to the Soviet Union.[35] A pillar in Karume's vision was that the entire population should live in 'modern' flats (Myers 1993: 350). Myers quotes from one of the President's speeches: '[A] mud hut, however well constructed, cannot compare with a modern flat. ... A person who lives in a miserable ramshackle hut cannot truly be said to be free' (ibid.: 366–8). Notably, for our purposes, such modern flats require electricity.

In 1968 East German experts helped formulate an overall plan for reconstructing Zanzibari homes. Ng'ambo was selected as a starting point for constructing tall, modern blocks. Here 229 buildings with a capacity to house 30,000 residents were to be put up, though only eight buildings were actually constructed (Myers 1993: 362–8). Similar buildings were built in some of the villages I visited during fieldwork, villages such as Bambi and Chaani.[36] Each block was 300 metres long and of between six to eight floors. Electricity supply and running water were integrated. The idea that the Zanzibari population would become happier, healthier and more developed by living on top of one another is surprising to anyone who knows a little about social life in this region (see also Myers 1993: 373–6). However, Karume did know and yet he still launched this massive project to relocate the population. He also promoted electric cookers as a feature of modern life. Karume is said to have patrolled the streets at night to check how women cooked their food. If failing to use electricity, according to several of Myers' sources in 1992, Karume would threaten to evict the offenders (ibid.: 356). This insistence, militancy, or blind faith speaks of a strong ideological commitment.

James Scott refers to the Tanzanian state as having been 'relatively benign' in the period in question compared with the Soviet collectivisation programme (Scott 1998: 223). The *Ujamaa* campaign was a development and welfare project rather than a plan of punitive appropriation, ethnic cleansing or military security.[37] Nyerere insisted that there should be no violence. Although this was not always the case and though the project proved to be a failure (ibid.: 224), the intentions for bettering people's lives through modernisation appear to have been key. This description could also fit for Karume's nationalisation programme. However, Myers both questions Karume's intentions with the housing projects and the socialist regime's objectives as such, partly by pointing to the new elite's range of privileges (Myers 1993: 359). What is clear is that a large proportion of the housing projects failed, and with a considerable cost (Myers 1993: 341, 377). If development was the overall goal, the wisdom of focusing on the reconstruction of houses was doubtful at best. Abeid Karume was assassinated in 1972. Before he died, however, he initiated plans for constructing a TV station in Zanzibar. TVZ, the first station in sub-Saharan Africa to provide pictures in colour, was formally opened on 12 January 1974.[38]

Karume's heritage is important when we consider electricity's position in present-day Zanzibar. Putting the rural population on the development agenda was the most important change after colonial days. People in the countryside today also constitute a central group within governmental energy policies. In addition, Karume's trust in TV as an important medium for education is still pointed to on various levels in Zanzibar society. Later governments installed TV sets in various villages for educational and political purposes. For example, Uroa's neighbouring village, Ndudu, which by 2004 had not yet been included in the rural electrification project, had a generator and TV set installed at the CCM party branch office. In Uroa there was a privately owned TV set before the arrival of the grid in 1990. This background is relevant when we consider today's patterns for watching TV. This medium has been used for educational and political purposes for a relatively long time.

The State Fuel and Power Corporation (SFPC), today known as the Zanzibar Electricity Corporation (ZECO), had been established as a parastatal after the revolution and is also today in charge of the electricity supply in Zanzibar. A range of international development actors have been involved in the Zanzibari electricity supply. A notable change in the provision of electricity occurred in 1979–80, when a submarine cable was constructed between Zanzibar and the Tanzanian mainland. Since then electric power, mainly hydroelectric, has been imported to Unguja.[39]

The cable raises and reflects political issues regarding the relationship between Zanzibar and the Union. The settlement of rates, payments and arrears are central questions.[40] The cable can be seen as a symbol of Zanzibar's dependency on the Union (Maliyamkono 2000: 213–30). I heard a range of speculations as to what would happen to the electricity supply if Zanzibar got a different government from the present one. The interconnection is a political issue.

The submarine cable also forms an important backdrop for the object of study. With a capacity of 45 MW, the government of Zanzibar saw an opportunity to promote development by increasing electricity consumption. Development in rural areas continued to be of central concern. Scattered diesel generators existed in many villages, but these were regarded as unreliable and demanded expensive and unavailable fuel. In the early 1980s the government of Tanzania asked Norway for support in order to extend the electricity grid. This 'Rural Electrification Project' (RUREL) was at its peak when I first went to Zanzibar in 1991.

Notes

1. I emphasise that the term Swahili has a much wider application. Some people might become disturbed by my limited and specific use of the notion in this way. However, I

hope that the ethnography as a whole will justify this choice of distinguishing a signifying practice from other practices (cf. Ferguson 1999: 93–102).

2. In comparison, only a few years before (1879), Thomas Edison had made the first public demonstration of the incandescent light in Menlo Park, New Jersey, USA (Nye 1990: 3). Edison's team's invention was a so-called 'brush arc light' (carbonised cotton filament) enclosed in a bulb (ibid.: 2). Other kinds of electric lighting had existed for several decades. However, these former types produced smoke and were not enclosed in a bulb (ibid.: 29–30). The first central electricity stations in the world became operational in 1882 in London and New York (Schivelbusch 1988: 65). In Zanzibar the first steam driven electric plant was installed in 1885 according to Khamis Khamis at the Zanzibar National Archives (personal communication by Torrence Roye). At today's Palace Museum in Zanzibar Town I was informed by staff that the House of Wonders was electrified in 1886. A description from 1909 of activities in the British Protectorate identifies the year to have been around 1890 (ZA-SB1-8: 428). Lifts were installed around 1930 according to the Palace Museum. It thus seems that the building received its name without regard to the lifts. On the other hand, I have not actually come across documentation of when the name 'House of Wonders' was attributed to this palace.

3. '[Frederick Lugard] developed the doctrine of indirect rule, which Great Britain employed in many of its African colonies. According to his views, the colonial administration should exercise its control of the subject population through traditional native institutions. Lugard expounded his theory in *The Dual Mandate in British Tropical Africa* (1922).' (Columbia Encyclopedia, Sixth Edition, Copyright (c) 2005, Internet: http://www.encyclopedia.com/html/L/Lugard-F1.asp).

4. ZA-SB1-8: 428.

5. Stone Town had been constructed on an islet separated from the rest of Unguja by a creek. The area was inhabited by the upper classes, initially Arabs and Indians and other prosperous Zanzibaris. Later, its southern section developed into a 'European garden suburb' (Myers 1993: 43). Stone Town was the seat of colonial rule. Africans resided on 'the Other Side' of the creek, Ng'ambo. Sheriff has warned against seeing race and ethnicity as the basis on which difference was constructed in the colonial period. He points instead to politico-economic factors and the fact that race and class were far from constituted in a one-to-one relationship (1991a: 7). However, as Nisula argues, it should be possible to regard ethnic and economic factors at the same time (1999: 16–7). Quite in keeping with Nisula's work on the health sector in Zanzibar, my material on colonial electricity policies shows that the British had quite specific ideas about divisions based on race. Hence ethnicity is important too, because it affected practices that had effects.

6. ZA-SB1-8. The term 'modern plant' was used by the colonial officer who described the system in 1909. Three generators were situated in Malindi, where the Zanzibar Harbour is located today. Three Belliss & Morcom engines, each of 220 b.h.p, were coupled with three Electric Construction Company's dynamos. The supply was 220 V direct current (d.c.). The distribution system was overhead and steel poles were used to carry the cables.

7. The notions of 'unit', 'electricity unit' and 'kWh' (kilowatt-hour) are synonymous and will be used throughout this book. One unit corresponds to the work done when 1 000 watts (W) are maintained for one hour.

8. Lamp-size is my own term and is connected to the lamps' power and brightness. It was dimensioned in candle powers (c.p.) at the time and ranged from 32 to 16 to 8 c.p., respectively (ZA-SB1-8).

9. ZA-AB6-14/3.

10. ZA-AB6-14/15, 20. The protest in 1912 was led by Ali Mohamed of Jan Mohamed Hansrag & Co. and Moloo Bros. of the Main Street. The letter was signed by 183 of the around 700 contract customers at the time. The protest initiated meetings in which the Consul General also participated. In the Director's final reply to the group, he assured

them that the government had not bought the undertaking to make large profits out of it. However, a fair return on capital invested must be made and charges could not be reduced.

11. In 1913 the Consul General, Waldron Clarke, is said to have agreed with the Ismaila Council to provide a reduced charge for the Jamat Khana. However, upon the Council's request in 1918 to maintain reduced tariffs this was declined by the Chief Minister who said they had to pay the same amount as any other mosque (ZA-AB6-14/44–8).

12. I see clear signs of this in areas where the electricity system is organised as monopolies in colonial Zanzibar and present-day rural Zanzibar, but also in present-day Norway where free competition in energy sales were introduced in 1991. In the latter case, customers acknowledged that energy companies make a profit. However, popular discourse still held that the introduction of a market for electricity would bring lower prices to the customers. Morally, electricity is different to other goods. It is seen as infrastructure that should be available to everyone for a reasonable price.

13. I use 'utility', 'company' and 'government' interchangeably in the following. Since 1912 the utility was owned and run by the government. In addition, because decisions were often made by the Chief Secretary, the government's influence is apparent.

14. Three types of rates were adjusted. For the 'contract rate', no lamps were to be used in upper stories in domestic buildings. Secondly, the price of electricity purchased by meter was increased by 50 per cent (from 8 to 12 annas per unit). Thirdly, the 'power' rate, relevant for customers using more power-consuming appliances than electric light, was charged double (changing from 4 to 8 annas per unit) (ZA-AB6-14/21–8). The rupee was used as currency in Zanzibar up to 1936. 16 annas are equal to one rupee.

15. Many European towns had been 'enlightened' by other kinds of technologies (oil, gas) before electricity gradually took over (Nye 1990: 29–30). Frequently electrification did not represent a discrete change from darkness to light as in current Uroa. In Zanzibar Town oil lamps had been on the agenda too. A maintenance agreement dated 8 December 1904 shows that oil lamps existed in Zanzibar in 1904/05 (ZA). The Markets and the Sultan's Palace are mentioned in particular, as these had special 'red lamps' (Palace) and 'central draught lamps' (Markets). However, also 'ordinary lamps' were used. I do not know which year oil lamps were introduced in the streets of Zanzibar and have not found traces of how long after 1905 they were in use.

16. ZA-AB6-14/117.

17. ZA-AB6-14/124.

18. ZA-AB6-14/128–31. The company was making a considerable profit at the time.

19. The load-factor is defined as the ratio between average demand and the maximum demand. In theory if the load is constant there is a load-factor of one. In Zanzibar (2000) it was 0.55 which is similar to Norwegian utilities.

20. ZA-AB6-14/53–7, 74–86. The request came from Esmailjee Jivanjee & Co. The firm used 200 units per day at the time.

21. ZA-AB6-14/78.

22. ZA-SB1-8.

23. Influential Indian merchants, such as M.H. Tharia Topan, had considered themselves as landlords in parts of Ng'ambo since the pre-British period (Fair 1994: 105). From 1890 they started to collect rent from house owners to the protest of residents in both Ng'ambo and Stone Town (including many Indians) (ibid.: 108–9). In 1927/28 Topan also initiated court cases to claim compensation from the British administration. Among other things he demanded ground rent for electric poles in Ng'ambo 'erected on "his" land' (ibid.: 113). This indicates that electricity was introduced in Ng'ambo in the 1920s, at least in certain parts. However, it is likely that a more extensive grid was constructed towards the end of the 1940s. In 1951 the Zanzibar Town Council addressed the Chief Minister concerning an extension of street lighting in Ng'ambo (ZA-AB6-56/118). In 1952 there were an average of four street lights per street in the area (ZA-AB6-56/128).

Today the name Ng'ambo is seldom used. The name now relates instead to a specific and particularly deprived part of town with 'an almost total lack of electricity' called Jang'ombe (Myers 1994: 452, 455).

24. The effects of the general strike in 1948 could also have been relevant. Here, the British administration and other privileged groups who made up the largest proportion of electricity customers were on the same side in the conflict initiated by workers and peasants (Fair 1994: 63–76). This might have given rise to a particular concern within the British administration with avoiding confrontations with groups they needed loyalty from.

25. ZA-AB6-5/3A. Saateni is located on the other side of the creek. The 'small village of Saateni' applied for light in 1938 (ZA-AB6-56/97). Myers refers to the post-revolution confiscation of 35 houses in the Asian middle-income housing estate at Saateni (1993: 347).

26. An interesting debate on the shift from d.c. to a.c. arose in 1957. A group of customers represented by Sheikh Muhammad Said Riami and others complained about a jump in the all-in scheme. ('We are shocked …') Customers on this contract would now have to pay for 150 units per month regardless of their use. The group appears to have asked for special reductions. Being mainly users of light, they claimed: 'Those who use cookers, fans, refrigerators and other appliances are very few indeed, mostly perhaps Europeans and how many are they?' They continue: 'We did not demand from the Government that they should change from DC to AC.' The Chief Secretary replies that 'DC is outmoded' and says that AC was introduced 'solely in the interest of the general public'. The CS also dryly recommends: '[You] are not compelled to use any particular tariff, or indeed to use electricity at all if you find it too expensive'. Towards the end of the letter, he proclaims: 'Your reference to arbitrary, undemocratic and unfair methods suggests that His Highness's Government have some mysterious purpose in the fixing of electricity charges' (ZA-AB6-20/1, 10–1). The change of technology caused speculations about its character and consequences. We see the central role of artefacts in producing and redefining relationships.

27. ZA-AB6-30/1–4.

28. In 1954 the Zanzibar Official Gazette was issued weekly (AB6-43/33).

29. *Purdah* refers to a veil women (Muslim or/and Indian) use for covering their bodies. Fair describes how in Zanzibar Town poorer women sought to copy Arab styles by changing their clothing (1994: 219). During the 1920s women of 'quality' began wearing the black *bui-bui* which covers a woman from head to foot. Today women living in town or travelling to town use *bui-bui* outdoors if they can afford one. The notion can also mean 'a screen' or generally be taken as a system that keeps women secluded. In his note, the CS seems to refer to the way women were (temporarily?) kept separate from men/strangers.

30. In recent years the utility has introduced pre-payment meters. By 2006, 13,000 customers in Zanzibar Town were on this TUKUZA system. The system involves a different customer–utility relationship. Due to technological limitations, according to utility staff, it is unavailable in rural areas. The question of cost involved in changing meters is also probably relevant.

31. This was in the 1920s (ZA-AB6-14/143–4).

32. Consider this quote (ZA-AB6-15/36): 'I do not anticipate that cooking by electricity will be adopted in many European households because unless strict attention is paid to the use of the various heat controls, the cost would exceed that of firewood or coal, and I know from experience that a disinterested person, I mean a Goan or African cook, will never take sufficient care to be really economical. It will be in households where the housewives themselves superintend the cooking that the benefit will be felt.' In this internal document from 1928 the director promotes the idea that electric cookers be introduced to customers on a hire system. The quote relates to his evaluation of the types

of households that would be appropriate for using such technology. At first glance the quote appears strikingly racist. However, it also reflects a class society and a pragmatic view that people who pay for their own consumption will take care to reduce consumption. European households apparently had cooks who worked for them. He probably had Arab and Asian households in mind when estimating the potential users of cookers.

33. ZA-AY1-30/6C, 7.

34. Zanzibar and Tanganyika merged in April 1964 to form the Union of Tanganyika and Zanzibar, a name which was later changed to Tanzania. Zanzibar kept its own government and remained in control of internal matters such as infrastructure.

35. ZA-BA88-23. Soviet electricity experts had already been sent to Zanzibar in June 1964. A Soviet consultant participated in initial meetings with the Zanzibari top administration and the Soviet Consul in Zanzibar. Here the parties exchanged opinions on the 'desirable lines of [the country's] developments'. The Minister of Communication and Works, Mr Moyo, and Vice-President of the Republic, Mr Hanga, participated in these meetings.

36. The electricity supply in Chaani and Bambi was upgraded with the rural electrification project in the 1980s. In 1991 residents in Chaani told me they were satisfied with the return of the current since water pumps could be used again. Secondly, they mentioned the importance of electric light. People residing in such blocks in Bambi were visited in 2000 and did not use electricity for cooking. Kitchens were located on the ground level. Women brought food downstairs to the semi-open kitchen and cooked with firewood.

37. Tanzania's first president, Julius Nyerere, used this term as a label for Tanzania's socialist policies. *Ujamaa* involved the forced relocation of at least 5 million people into peasant cooperatives (Scott 1998: 223) and was officially instituted with the Arusha Declaration in 1967. Myers refers to Karume who frequently said: 'the Arusha Declaration stops at Chumbe', that is, by the port in Zanzibar Town (Myers 1993: 339–40). However, though *Ujamaa* never reached the island state, the two, respective programmes had many similarities.

38. Communicated by staff at Television Zanzibar (TVZ), March 2001.

39. Diesel generators are only used as back-up in Unguja. In Pemba the first generator was installed in 1959. Pemba so far continues to rely on diesel production for electricity. However, in 2007 there were plans for a direct submarine cable from the mainland to Pemba, but at the time of writing (2008) the issue had not yet been decided upon.

40. In a letter from the Zanzibari Minister of Water, Power and Minerals to TANESCO in 1980 the tone reflects dissatisfaction and some degree of hostility. The Minister is quite dissatisfied with a suggestion for tariffs (ZA-DB1-33). Over the years the ZECO and thus its owner, the Zanzibari government, has failed to pay its debt to TANESCO on the mainland. There were signs in 2001 and 2004 that Zanzibar had started to pay back its debt.

Chapter 3

THE RURAL ELECTRIFICATION
PROJECT (RUREL)

> The Rural Electrification Project is one of the projects initiated by
> the Zanzibar Revolutionary Government. It was included in
> the Government's Development Programme because the
> Government firmly believes that electricity is an essential input
> for economic and social development in both urban and rural areas.
> General Manager SFPC, Mtoni, Zanzibar, 7 September 1991

This extract is taken from the General Manager's speech during the
handing-over ceremony for Phase II of the Rural Electrification Project in
Zanzibar (RUREL). The President of Zanzibar, several Ministers, Members
of the House of Representatives, the Norwegian Ambassador and other
prominent guests were present. Tents were put up for the large crowd that
had been invited. We all sat on chairs while listening to the various
representatives making their speeches. A brass band had started the
ceremony, and there was an atmosphere of accomplishment and joy. The
event marked the completion of Phase II and the handing-over of the
results. Having up until then been the property of the Norwegian
government, it now formally became property of the government of
Zanzibar. According to the General Manager high power lines (33 kV) now
covered 85 per cent of Unguja. Clearly, we were to envisage that the arrival
of the network implied that development could begin in rural areas.
Transformers and 30 km of low-tension lines had also been installed in
various places. This encouraged and speeded up the use of electricity. The
project subsequently continued into a third and fourth phase, both also
involving Pemba Island.

The project had been formally initiated in 1983 when NORAD was
requested by the Ministry of Finance in Tanzania to assist in the

development of rural electrification in Zanzibar (Norconsult 1994). Zanzibar was facing severe economic problems at the time. Earnings from the important clove export deteriorated due to declining clove prices in the world market and the reduced quality and quantity of harvests. Furthermore, the heavy control on exports and imports of goods, money and people contributed to Zanzibar's poor economic situation at the time. The initiative to extend the electricity network probably came from Zanzibar but the Union government also had interests in strengthening economic and political ties with the island polity. In addition, bilateral cooperation takes place between states. Therefore, requests for support are addressed through the Tanzanian administration.

On behalf of NORAD and after a field visit in October 1984, senior engineer Steinar Grongstad at the Norwegian Water Resources and Energy Administration (NVE) prepared a proposal for an implementation programme. In May 1986 an agreement was signed between Tanzania and Norway for the latter's financing and implementation of what was to become RUREL's first phase. The total budget for Phases I–III (1986–95) came to around $US10 million.[1]

A project committee was established. It played an important role in planning and running the project. Decisions to deviate from original plans also had to be authorised by the committee. The group consisted of representatives from the Zanzibar Ministry of Water, Construction, Energy, Land and Environment (MWCELE), the electric utility company in Zanzibar (ZECO), the Norwegian Agency for Development Cooperation (NORAD), Noremco (main contractor) and staff from within the project. Asbjørn Tenfjord, from the Norwegian subcontractor Linjebygg AS, was appointed Project Engineer and resided in Zanzibar. The Project Engineer was formally situated under the General Manager of ZECO, but RUREL was run quite separately from the daily tasks and leadership of the utility company. The Project Engineer remained in charge of project management on behalf of Noremco. During Phase III Muhammed Mjaa took over as Project Engineer. Throughout the project employees 'borrowed' from ZECO participated in RUREL to a great extent and were paid by the project. The number of people engaged in RUREL was around sixty in Phase I, rising to about one hundred in the third phase.

Objectives: improve health facilities, create modern villagers and ensure Zanzibar's future income

Rural electrification in Zanzibar had the following priorities (Centre for Development and Technology 1990): first of all, the project would improve and extend the islands' water services (domestic water supply and irrigation schemes, particularly for rice irrigation); secondly, electricity was to be provided for clinics and health centres in the districts; thirdly, the change to mainly hydroelectric (imported) power, would reduce Zanzibar's economic dependency on diesel fuel and engine spare parts. Many villages had been supplied with water pumps run by diesel generators in the 1980s. Also, various smaller power stations in rural areas were running on diesel, as they continue to be on Pemba up to the present day. Presumably the transmission of electricity through a rural grid was considered cheaper for providing the same services. In the light of Zanzibar's accumulation of debt to TANESCO over the years, one might say that the substitution of one technology for the other resulted in the transfer of problems from the local to the Union level. The premise for such a conclusion is that the Zanzibari government until recently has been unable to fulfil its economic commitments (either in terms of welfare promises to its own population or its obligations vis-à-vis the mainland). Unfortunately, this has proven to be the case.

The practical problems related to diesel engines also appear important (though they are not explicitly stated in the policies we are concerned with). People involved in RUREL stressed that the maintenance of diesel engines had often failed. This not only resulted from a lack of money. The people in charge would also often fail to check (and thus change) various parts, such as packing and filters, regularly. With the lack of such maintenance engines might break down completely. In contrast, once an electricity grid is installed 'it is there'.[2] The contrasting 'scripts' of these two distinct technologies (Akritch 1994) account for some of the reasons why 'electricity' is regarded as 'easy' and 'clean' in comparison with diesel. This impression is strengthened by the fact that the electricity grid is centralised in its structure and organisation. Responsibility and control, as we shall see, rests with the utility company in Zanzibar Town.

A fourth goal, to be realised in a long-term perspective, was to connect domestic and industrial customers to the distribution system. There was also an environmental aspect linked to this, as I discuss below. Fifthly, rural electrification was introduced to prevent migration from the countryside to town. According to the rural development policy of the Zanzibar government:

> Rural electrification will extend electric power facilities to areas where it is most needed for social and industrial development. It is the Government and the Party policy to spread town amenities to the rural areas so that the rural population may remain in their Districts to develop the land. This can best be achieved with the help of electricity (Zanzibar Government, cited in Norconsult 1994: 2–4).

The notion of 'town amenities' is important as it connects electricity use with 'town-ness', a perception I discuss in chapter 7. Linked to this, one may ask what was meant by 'social' development. The 'social' could include more than the concrete priorities referred to above. It could also have had a more value-laden meaning. In any case, it is clear that the government had some overall intentions of its own. The question of making rural people stay in the villages was related to Zanzibar's economic challenges. Alternative sources of income, such as tourism, diversified agriculture and fisheries, were sought. Zanzibar had started to attract investors in tourism after economic and political liberalisation in the second half of the 1980s. A Norwegian evaluation report concluded: 'the RUREL project ... is part of the foundation for the future development of Zanzibar' (Norconsult 1994: 2–4). Rural electrification was thus seen as a key to the polity's economic growth. In more recent years there has been a shift of focus from development to poverty reduction in Zanzibari and Tanzanian development policies. The objectives of rural electrification have nevertheless remained similar over the twenty year period.[3]

The impact of international environmental discourses

Zanzibar's energy policies were also linked up to a discourse on the environment (Norconsult 1994). By the 1990s signs of deforestation in Zanzibar had been reported. Systematic replanting of trees and proper forest administration were seen as central means to prevent this. Relevant to our purposes here are the environmental concerns that also made the government aim for the reduction of fuelwood consumption. They regarded a change in cooking technologies (moving towards coal, improved stoves, and electricity) as a means of reducing women's work load and avoiding environmental degradation.[4] The perceived link between deforestation and cooking technology should be considered in the international developmental framework. Emma Crewe has shown that international development agencies (and Western researchers) regarded rural households' use of fuelwood as a major cause of deforestation. Despite early documentation provided by non-Western researchers that forests were often cut down for quite different purposes (that is, land use and commercial use), this idea persisted (Crewe 1997).[5]

A Zanzibar/FINNIDA report in 1993 acknowledged that urban consumption was a larger threat to deforestration than rural populations' use of fuelwood.[6] It appears, however, that the Zanzibari government's expectations for changed cooking technologies were founded more on international environment discourses than on Zanzibari realities. This impression is strengthened by the fact that few people among the officers I met in town (mostly at the ZECO but also in ministries and other offices) use electricity for cooking within their own households, even though they often own electric stoves. We here see the tendency for a discrepancy between people's articulation of the potential of electric cookers and what is practised, an issue to be elaborated on in chapter 10.

Another environmental argument for the change towards electricity seems particularly premised on external discourses. The government emphasised that substitution of diesel and kerosene would also benefit the environment. Air pollution is not a particularly striking phenomenon in Zanzibar. In addition, global warming is quite irrelevant in contemporary discussions about the challenges Zanzibar is faced with. When people speak about environmental problems (*matatizo ya mazingira*) in Uroa, they refer to the importance of not cutting down living trees. The government reminds them of this from time to time. Indeed, this is in accord with women's cooking concerns as found in Uroa; they only collect dry wood (that is, dead vegetation) for such purposes. However, for poles to be used in the water (for farming seaweed), they prefer living trees. This recently introduced activity might thus have a negative effect on the local environment. Private cooking has not.

To conclude, the government's expressed goal, also reflected in RURELs objectives, was to promote development in rural areas by ensuring electricity supply for public services. The government's incentives for doing so rested also explicitly with a concern for demographic spread and the polity's future income. Compared to the colonial administration, the one under discussion was obviously more attuned to supplying non-privileged groups with electricity. Putting the rural population on the agenda had started in the Karume era. The governments of the 1980s and 1990s continued this part of the modernisation project in which electricity played a central role. An environmental flavour was added to the argument in political rhetoric, but appears to have been somewhat detached from Zanzibari discourses and realities.

However, at this 'time of confusion', as Myers captures the recent era, a mixture of ideologies seems to reign simultaneously (1993: 401). The Structural Adjustment agreement signed between Tanzania and the IMF in the mid 1980s was an important turning point (ibid.: 403). Neo-liberalism now became the answer to how Tanzania's problems should be solved (as has also been the case in many other countries in the South). In the 1990s privatisation programmes were launched and Tanzania and Zanzibar began a transition to multiparty politics (Nisula 1999: 260; Myers 1993: 403). All these processes were pushed forward by the international donor and money-lending community.

Still, as Myers points out, the heritage from former modernisation programmes and economic liberalisation are blended at present. The confusion is, perhaps, well captured in the utility company's own dilemma. On the one hand, it is supposed to run on a commercial basis, that is, to be economically sustainable. On the other, it continuously runs at a loss primarily due to 'bad-paying' customers. The government, a large consumer of electricity, is the biggest sinner of all. Furthermore, as a modern infrastructure, it could be held against the government that all

Zanzibaris have the right to be connected. For the poor already connected a rise in rates would be particularly painful (and morally dubious, see chapter 11).

Political difficulties: the project interrupted

In the mid 1990s RUREL was interrupted for political reasons and the project was put on hold.[7] In a letter to NORAD in February 1996 the Norwegian Embassy in Dar es Salaam recommended that Norwegian aid to Zanzibar should be held back in view of the political situation. The general elections in Zanzibar in 1995 had been criticised for not being free and fair by the opposition party (CUF), international observers and the Western aid community in Tanzania. The Ambassador's letter also referred to suspicions that staff within the Zanzibar administration were being prosecuted and fired for having political sympathies that diverged from those of the ruling party (CCM).

My experiences from 2000 support the claim that political opponents were, and continue to be, oppressed by the Zanzibari government. However, I am not convinced that putting a ban on development aid was the best suited tool for improving this situation. First of all, one of the most important critiques I heard against the government was that Pemba severely lacks development in terms of infrastructures. This is a region where a large majority of the political opponents reside. The neglect is perceived to be the result of the government's intended policy to undermine one part of the population. In this way poor electricity supply in Pemba contributes to political antagonism. That is partly why I believe that strengthening the electricity network in Pemba, one of the goals in the planned Phase IV of the project, would have reduced the political tension (but this is, of course, not the only source of the conflict and reducing the tension around the energy issue would by no means be equivalent to finding an overall solution). On the other hand, it may be argued that improved infrastructure in Pemba would calm things down and therefore only serve to strengthen a political system with democratic shortcomings. With the ban the Zanzibari government received pressure both from external agencies and from Pembans experiencing delays in receiving infrastructural services (and other types of neglect). Maybe this has contributed to what seemed in 2004 to be a slightly improved political situation. However, based on my first-hand experience of how painful the (re-)invention of democracy in Zanzibar has been for ordinary people of all political affiliations, I think the boycott was, for donors, a far too easy solution. Considering the social costs, I find it morally doubtful to first have been putting pressure on Tanzania and Zanzibar to introduce elections and then, as soon as problems appeared (and old wounds were reopened), to leave the country. To me, institution-building and spreading infrastructure improvements appear to be interconnected prerequisites for improving conditions for human rights. The international community decided to abandon all such activities and joined the general boycott of Zanzibar in 1996, which lasted up to 2002–3. This appears particularly strange in light of the fact that bilateral cooperation takes place between nations. The government of Tanzania was not (and still is not) held sufficiently responsible for the developments in Zanzibar.

Leaving the issue of how political considerations form development policies aside, there are also political forces inherent in the electric power system itself. The submarine cable has a strong symbolic power, as mentioned. One particular episode in 1996 further demonstrates electricity's central strategic role. On this occasion one of the two main transformers at the Mtoni power station outside Zanzibar Town blew up. As the other transformer was out of order, Unguja apparently remained without electricity for several days. Zanzibari authorities interpreted this as a result of political sabotage.[8] Whatever reason caused the blackout, it demonstrates electricity's strategic importance and how vulnerable electrified societies become to a breakdown of the system. This is also a much discussed topic on the mainland. Due to low reserves of water at the hydroelectric power stations, reduction schemes result in power cuts from time to time. As a Norwegian engineer told me: 'If you can't get the kWh through to the people, the government will find itself in a weak position' (*Får du ikke frem kilowatten, sitter regjeringen løst i stolene*). Power cuts quickly cause dissatisfaction among commercial and domestic consumers and have high political costs. As also shown in chapter 2, electricity is a political issue with high stakes. It is time to turn to electricity's uses and to see how villages and potential customers responded to electricity's arrival. At this point I focus on the immediate results, or the project's outcomes.

Public services dramatically improved

> Before, we sometimes found the water dirty. There were stones, remains of copra and palm leaves and so on. Thus we had to empty the well [from time to time] and let the water go. We could only use the water for washing clothes. Then we had to wait until we could use the water for drinking again. Due to the poor quality, many people got diarrhoea, which also meant high costs for the family. In the dry season people used to sleep by the well, there was so little water. They wanted to be there first. After the pump, it is clean (*safi*) and safe (*salama*).
>
> Male meeting participant, Makombeni village,
> Pemba, Zanzibar, 2006 (SUM 2006)

Before RUREL the electricity grid on Unguja was only found in, and around, Zanzibar Town. A few villages (e.g., Gamba) had diesel generators which provided electricity for public services such as water pumps and a very limited number of households. In comparison, Map 3.1 shows the extent of the Ungujan electricity network after RUREL's three phase plan had been accomplished. The high voltage grid had grown to the extreme north, east and south of Unguja. Nineteen new villages in Unguja had been electrified and four had received extensions. According to the map's representation, 'development' had reached rural areas.

The sign of development's relevance in this picture becomes clearer when one considers electricity's use for public services. By 1995, twenty-two clinics, twenty-one water pump stations, fourty-three mosques and twenty schools had been electrified in these villages in Unguja (SFPC 1995: 15). In accordance with the General Manager's evaluation of 1991, various Norwegian assessment reports have been overwhelmingly positive about the project's accomplishments. It maximised 'the benefits of the masses' by giving priority to public services which made 'women the main beneficiaries of rural electricity in Zanzibar' (Centre for Development and Technology 1990: 32–3; see also Norconsult 1994). In this way success was primarily measured with reference to improvements in the public services.

The plain numbers mentioned above speak for themselves as to the high priority given to the public services in Zanzibar and the RUREL project. From the perspective of people who use these services, the quality is seen to have dramatically improved after electricity's arrival. My material from 1991, 2000 and 2004–6 supports the conclusion that electricity has had a significant and positive effect on the public sector and the services offered. I stress, however, that access to electricity alone is not enough to provide such effects. The supply of water pumps, pipes, equipment, spare parts and medicines is also required, and in 2000 this was not the case in Uroa with respect to provision of medicines. (In 2004 the situation had improved.) Electricity is thus one among several conditions for enhanced public services in rural Zanzibar. Without electricity much would have remained as it was. To illustrate electricity's immediate social impact I will here focus on water supply and health (education will be treated in chapter 5).

In coastal villages, such as Uroa, the previously used shallow well-water used to contain so much salt that for a person unfamiliar with it a cup of tea with sugar bore the distinct taste of salt. When the village water system was connected to a source located farther inland the quality became good (*baridi*, lit. 'cold'). Furthermore, according to health workers I spoke with in Makombeni in Pemba, diarrhoea (mainly caused by the consumption of dirty water) used to be among the three most common illnesses in the village. After electrification the number of cases went down and the illness has now become the seventh most-reported health problem in the village (SUM 2006). Electricity thus positively affects the quality of drinking water which in turn has a positive effect on people's health.

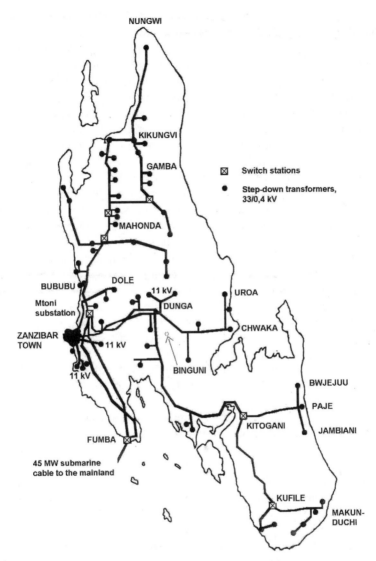

Map 3.1 The electricity grid in Unguja after RUREL's first three phases (1986–96).
Source: ZECO/Project Management, RUREL.

With a piping system and taps, electricity also conditions the simplified transport of water to the areas where people live. Thus, compared to the former situation when village wells situated on the outskirts of the villages supplied people with water, the change both implies improved water quality and more effective time-use. Based on data from Uroa in 2005 when the water pump had failed for some months, and also from interviews in many non-electrified villages, I have reason to conclude that each household has freed-up at least 20–25 hours per week since the arrival of electric water pumps. This primarily means that women and young girls spend their time differently. As a result girls are said to perform better in school than they used to. Women tend to spend more time generating an income or otherwise increasing their productivity. Even when there is no significant potential for earning an income, the advantage of saving time in this way should not be underestimated. In 1991 I observed with empathy women's sixteen-hour work days with nearly no time to sit down and relax. A decade later, with taps in the village and three hours saved per day, it is little wonder that the same women appreciated their reduced burden. The coming of piping systems and village water taps also encouraged people to obtain water inside their houses. The majority of households in Uroa now have access to water at home. This trend eases women's and girls' burdens further.

In addition to electricity's positive effect on water supply (better quality and easy access) there are also other, significant changes related to electricity and health. Health centres that have electricity and piped water now have working conditions that enhance the potential for proper treatment (cleanliness, light for examination and nocturnal treatment, access to medicines that need storage at a low temperature, sterilised equipment, fans and electric microscopes). Again, electricity, in combination with other public infrastructures, has a positive effect on people's health, which is one of the central means for poverty reduction as stated in the Millennium Development Goals (UN). Health is also a central parameter in the UNDP's Human Development Index.

On an overall level RUREL has provided 141 villages on Unguja and Pemba with electricity over the years. Of these sixty-four were electrified during the Phases I–III and seventy-seven during Phase IV. This implies that, in 2006, 66 per cent of the rural population in Zanzibar (Unguja and Pemba) had obtained access to electricity through the project (SUM 2006). With the extension of Phase IV from 2006–8, it is expected that more than 80 per cent of the rural population will be living in electrified villages. As mentioned in chapter 1, this represents an extraordinarily high degree of electrification in an African context. The corresponding effect on the quality of public services is significant. It also seems that the prospect of electrification produces village initiatives to plan for improved water services. During visits to villages which were to be electrified in 2006 and 2007, the Tanzania Social Action Fund (TASAF) was mentioned by the leadership in every village visited. Through this community-driven development programme each village may reportedly select and give priority to two development projects which the government in turn supports. The leadership's capacity to take action in such situations appeared varying, but with electricity in the neighbourhood improved water supply always came up as a subject during the visits.

I would like to add a word on water and its significance for human well-being. In the Human Development Report of 2006 (UN), *Beyond scarcity*, water and poverty are the main issues in question. Electricity is rarely mentioned. When it is, it tends to be negatively associated with some groups' conspicuous consumption of water (depletion of ground water) at the cost of other groups' access to water (e.g., ibid.: 144–7). Notably, the way electricity may play a role to improve the lives of marginalised groups and their access to water is not discussed. This is surprising given electricity's importance in providing sustainable water systems for ordinary people. The links between water and electricity deserve attention whether there is water scarcity or not.

Household connections, tourism and productivity

Various factors condition the rate of household connections to the electricity grid. Below, I provide an account of the common way villages in rural Zanzibar were electrified. I discuss this in relation to the number of households that gradually became connected. The role and geographic distribution of tourism and other income-generating potentials are also important when accounting for electricity's adoption and use by ordinary people.

Chwaka village serves as a good point of reference. As in most villages visited in 1991, people in Chwaka first learned about the plans for electrification through announcements made on the Zanzibar radio station. The news inspired some young men to get together and start planning for the arrival of electricity, but little was done on a village level. There were also meetings between village leadership and staff from ZECO at an early stage, but village leaders remained relatively passive. This may partly be explained by the fact that the village did not need to mobilise resources to attract the electricity grid. Like most villages, Chwaka was already included in the plans. Furthermore, it was standard procedure for RUREL to provide high-tension transmission lines and transformers. ZECO was to supply the low-tension distribution network and to be in charge of consumer connections, but sometimes had difficulties fulfilling its role. Although water pumps became connected in Chwaka there were many problems related to the supply to public and private customers. For example, in 1991, one year after electrification, the health centre in Chwaka remained unconnected to the line passing at a modest distance of 30 m. Some Chwakans blamed their village leaders for not doing their job. However, the lack of connections can also be attributed to a ZECO which did not immediately have the capacity to provide them.[9]

People in Chwaka, as elsewhere in Unguja, also considered electricity's potential for domestic consumption. By 1995, 10 per cent of private households in electrified Unguja villages (11 per cent in Chwaka) had become customers.[10] In comparison, as mentioned, Uroa had a connection rate as high as 23 per cent by 1991, one year after electricity's arrival in the village. In line with most villages Chwakans awaited, rather than promoted, the arrival of electricity. The effects of this generally quite passive role attributed to, if not assumed by, villages themselves were probably most significant in the early stages of electrification in rural areas. As time goes by and people become accustomed to the notion of becoming connected, factors other than the degree of participation during implementation also become relevant. However, as I will argue in the next chapter, I do not consider it to be a coincidence that Uroa, excluded from RUREL's initial plans, was the only village to have street lighting in rural Zanzibar. There is a link between the quality of the initial processes and some long-term effects as I shall argue presently.

Uroa's position as the most electrified village in Unguja was surpassed in 1995 by Paje, where 48 per cent of households were connected (SFPC 1995). Private consumption is increasing in both areas, however. In 2006 more than half of the Uroan households were connected.[11] It is not a coincidence that villages with the highest rate of connections are those most favourably situated in economic terms. As the SFPC report mentions, electrification is related to people's access to income-generating activities such as fishing, seaweed farming and tourism. The coastal, northern and eastern parts of Unguja have relatively good conditions in this respect and there are some important dynamics at play in the interrelationship between electricity and tourism. The planning of the grid's extension was partly informed by considerations for developing tourist areas. In 1998 the utility company's Electrical Masterplan report contained a chapter on 'Development Areas' which was uniquely devoted to plans for constructing new hotels in Zanzibar (SFPC 1998: 10–13). Electricity may be regarded as a condition for the arrival of hotels. Tourism also triggers expansion of the grid. An important question here is who should finance, and who should benefit from, such expansion.

There was a discussion going on in 2001 between hotel constructors and owners, on the one side, and ZECO, on the other. The question related to whether transformers (and thus the costs covered by hotels) should be dimensioned so as to cover potential consumption from neighbouring villages too. The moral obligation to stimulate village development (and bring them more customers) as seen by the utility company was not always acknowledged by private investors.[12] As we saw in chapter 2, there are always political considerations to take into account when a utility company exercises its mandate. Furthermore, given the current energy and power shortage in Tanzania and Zanzibar, the battle for supply has probably only just begun.[13] The question is what kind of customer groups will be given priority – and at what prices.

Another tremendeously important problem in relation to tourism is what kind of conditions investors are subject to in terms of taking local stakeholders on-board in their projects. As will become clear in chapter 5, rural Zanzibaris have close to no access to the general growth produced by the tourist industry, which has come to constitute a substantial part of Zanzibar's economy as a whole. The sector represented, in 2001, one third of the total consumption of electricity in Unguja. This is the sole industrial development of any significance that is due to electricity's arrival, and is one from which the local population is excluded. Here lies one of the most fundamental reasons explaining why electricity in rural Zanzibar has not yet produced economic prosperity for the general public.

There are other activities, though, in which electricity plays a role in production. I list them here. *(1) Shops.* Lights are used in the evening, making longer opening hours possible. Also TV sets are sometimes put on to attract men and children in the evening. Freezers and fridges are used for storing cold sodas for sale. The customers are mostly local but in tourist areas one may also receive foreign customers. *(2) Frozen ice.* Women produce and sell frozen, sweet ice to neighbouring children from their homes. *(3) Frozen fish.* A few individuals make agreements with hotels and supply the tourist sector with a supply of kingfish and tuna. *(4) Mobile phones.* Access to electricity conditions the use of mobiles and some people provide charging services for other people. *(5) Tourism.* As mentioned, hotels, when owned by foreigners to Zanzibar, seldom employ local people. One exception, to be treated in chapter 5, is an untypical joint-venture hotel in Uroa. Here jobs offered locally include management (a man), cooks (men and women), bar keepers (men), housekeepers (women) and diving instructors (men). There are also secondary effects during periods when new buildings are under construction, either in terms of labour offered locally or, for local shops and restaurants, immigrant workers who come to buy food and soft drinks. *(6) Inland farming.* For a couple of farms visited, electricity has had a significant impact on their level of production. Electricity is used for providing light during milking hours (for cows) in the morning and is said to make it possible to keep the premises and machines clean and proper. Farmers keep the milk in refrigerators until it is transported and sold. Water, obtained by the use of electric pumps, is used for irrigation (for vegetables and fruit). *(7) Chicken breeding.* In Uroa alone fifty people (out of a total adult population of about two thousand) had plans to start breeding chickens in 2006. Lights are used to keep young chickens and ducklings warm during their first three months. The alternative, kerosene, is considered much more expensive and would make it impossible to get a return on the investment. *(8) The governmental institutions* become more efficient in terms of administration and their services improve. In terms of labour available, the number and significance of positions depend on factors other than electricity alone. *(9) Stone crushing.* In Kibele village (inland Unguja) two electric crushing machines were said to be in use. The stones, derived from larger pieces of coral (lime)stone are used for road and house construction. (10) *Brick production.* Cement bricks are produced in many places in rural areas. The mixing process could potentially be done by means of an electric device, but no such device has been observed. (11) *Production of coconut oil.* Some attempts were made in Uroa to process coconut oil by means of an electric device, but with limited success. (12) *Grinding mills.* There are some mills which run on diesel in rural areas. In some villages, and amongst women's corporations in particular, people expressed the hope of obtaining electricity-driven mills in the future. And finally, (13) *People's general production capacity* is affected by the many little shifts in their use of time and space.

A summary of the immediate effects of electricity's arrival

From a health perspective and also in terms of Zanzibari macroeconomics, the overall results produced by rural electrification fulfil the project's stated objectives. The islands' water services have been considerably improved, both in terms of people's access to water and in terms of its quality. This has positive health effects and is also time-saving for women and girls in particular. Never did I see signs of, or hear complaints about, women losing valuable time spent with other women waiting for their turn by the well. Rural Zanzibaris have many chores and interests. Fetching water is not their favourite task.

Furthermore, health clinics have become electrified, with positive effects for the quality of the services offered. With the import of hydroelectric power Zanzibar, as a semi-autonomous state, has also become radically less dependent on imported oil. Because of this the economic challenge for the utility company and the Zanzibari government has become the paying of their electricity arrears vis-à-vis the mainland. The long-term goal of connecting industrial customers to the grid has also been successful, but mainly within the tourist sector.

Households continue to become connected to the network at a rate which is astonishing within an African context. In November 2006 around eleven thousand rural households in Unguja were connected to the grid. According to the Tanzania Census Survey of 2002 (adjusted according to the annual population growth) this means that about 20 per cent of all households in rural Unguja (whether located in electrified villages or not) have become electricity customers. In 2005 people from new villages to be electrified reported that they had sold some of their livestock and were ready for the current to enter (*ingia*) their homes. People's desire for electricity is striking. In the chapters to come, which will focus on the village of Uroa, we shall come to understand the driving forces for such increasing consumption. We start by hearing the tale of how electricity ended up there.

Notes

1. RUREL's first three phases were completed between 1986 and 1996. Phase IV (2003–6) continued the rural electrification project with a cost of about US$6 million. An extension of Phase IV will run from 2006–8.
2. This does not imply that electric networks do not need maintenance. However, the components and their configuration have a much longer durability than those engines used with fossil fuels. In the Zanzibari climatic setting regular bush clearing is important for maintaining the electricity grid.
3. Measured in terms of the UNDP's Human Development Index 2006, Tanzania was ranked 162 out of 177 countries worldwide, and was thus identified as a country with 'low human development'. The index combines the three main variables of economic performance (GDP per capita), life expectancy and educational attainment. Although policy rhetoric in Zanzibar has changed from a focus on 'development' in the 1980s and 1990s towards 'poverty reduction' more recently, the main goal of the electrification project has remained to improve the living conditions for the poor in rural areas. The eradication of absolute poverty is the overall objective of Zanzibari and Tanzanian long-term policies. See also Zanzibar Poverty Reduction Plan (2002) and the Zanzibar Vision 2020 (2002), where access to power, water and communication are specifically mentioned as necessary for promoting a more enabling environment for poor people living in Zanzibar (NVE/ECON/E-CO partner 2003). By 2003 the rural electrification project stated its intentions to achieve this goal through development of the economy through tourism, industrialisation, and children's education and by providing women with new opportunities. See also Tanzanian Ministry of Planning, Economy and Empowerment 2006.
4. A report prepared for the Zanzibar Forestry Development Project (1993a) stated that shifting cultivation and urban fuelwood constituted the main causes of deforestation in Zanzibar. The Finnish Development Agency (FINNIDA) also assisted in the same governmental project in assessments and recommendations of 'stove activities' in town (1993b). TANELEC, the electricity company located on the mainland, produced and supplied Zanzibar with 'simple and cheap' electric cookers at the time. Norwegians involved in the electrification project later regarded this access to cookers relevant for how the government envisaged such transformations.
5. With Foley and Moss' report of 1983 it was generally acknowledged that rural domestic consumption did not cause deforestation, according to Crewe (1997: 64–5). As a result, and also because many projects promoting stoves had failed, international donors stopped financing such projects at the end of the 1980s. Crewe regrets this and argues that cooking practices remain important for potential beneficiaries. She attributes the failure of stove projects to not taking the particular social, economic and climatic contexts into consideration. In this light, the Zanzibari/FINNIDA attempt to map the potential for a 'viable programme' for (charcoal and wood) stoves in Zanzibar Town seems to have approached the issue in a relatively context-sensitive manner. I do not know how implementation succeeded and to what degree such stoves were used. However, there always seems to be a danger of environmental arguments promoted by international agencies leading to initiatives that do not sufficiently take local

circumstances into account. We here touch on crossing concerns inherent in the notion 'sustainable development'. Various actors may perceive environmental and developmental issues distinctly.

6. Zanzibar Forestry Development Project (1993a).

7. Norconsult (1994) had recommended that the project continue into a final phase, Phase IV. The boycott lasted for 6–7 years and Phase IV was initiated in 2003. I do not treat the realisation of Phase IV in this book, apart from referring to the increased connection rates and changes observed at the user-end of the electricity chain.

8. Suspected of having neglected to guard properly on purpose, one person was put in jail. After two months he was released due to lack of evidence. He later left the islands temporarily. A new transformer was soon installed, financed by a loan from the African Development Bank (AfDB).

9. Because ZECO had difficulties providing funds and material for this task they asked NORAD to extend RUREL's focus to include construction of low-tension lines. For water pumps and other kinds of end-use, this step was considered necessary and therefore gradually introduced during Phase II and more so in Phases III and IV.

10. SFPC (1995: 15).

11. I should perhaps add that I do not intend to make this into 'a challenge' in which I regard the goal to be that all households should become connected. Electrification has clear drawbacks, as we shall see. The figures are given as a backdrop for understanding certain connections and electricity's position in current, rural Zanzibar. They also serve to position Uroa in the rural context.

12. Sources consist of newspaper articles and personal communication with hotel owners.

13. In 2006 the maximum demand in Unguja, Zanzibar, reached 45.6 MW, the capacity of the submarine cable. Since then, electricity supply has been unstable, culminating in May 2008 in a power outage in Unguja, apparently due to damage to the inter-connector to the mainland. As this book goes into production, Unguja has for one month remained without electricity. Due to the resulting water shortage and crisis in public services, the United Nations has called in experts in disaster response to assist the Zanzibar government in assessing the impact of the power outage on the island's population.

Chapter 4

ELECTRIFYING UROA

One night in 1989, two men secretly sit down in a kitchen in Uroa to perform a protection ritual. Local healers (*waganga*) in the village have provided them with water cooked with special herbs and advised them to drink this while uttering magic spells in Swahili. In turn, the two men say: 'I drink this water and remove the problem inside my body' (*Mimi nakunywa maji haya na ninaondosha maradhi ndani na mwili wangu*). Now their bodies are impenetrable and they may move on to the important task they, as the village Chairman and secretary, are obliged to perform. Tonight the whole village will be protected. An older man shows up as scheduled. They boil prescribed leaves from plants (*majani*) in a big metal pot on the fire. While their co-villagers are asleep the three men enter the darkness outside and slowly start to encircle the village. They murmur spells and distribute drops from the remedy little by little on the ground as they walk. When the circle along the village borders to the bush and the sea is completed, Uroa is closed (*fungwa*) and protected (*kingwa*) against evil.

Two men involved in the process provided me with this story eleven years later. In 1991 I had also heard about the incident but in less elaborate detail. The purpose and sequence of the protection ritual remained the same, however. Apparently the problem had started when two local healers were visited by certain 'bad people' (*watu wabaya*) in the village. By then village leaders were making plans for the arrival of electricity. The bad people had asked them to perform harmful rituals against electrification by calling down evil spirits (*mashetani wabaya*). However, refusing to do such a thing, the healers instead went to tell the Chairman. They agreed that some kind of precaution had to be taken. There were already signs that problems had started to occur. Not only was the fulfilment of the plans for electricity at stake, but village leaders and the population as a whole were in danger. After the protecting ritual had been carried out anyone who tried to commit harm would fail.

This story from the early days of electrification in Uroa indicates how the process was far from a trivial matter. It was a political battle with high stakes in play. This leads us to ask why some people seem to have been against electricity, whilst others defended and actively promoted its arrival. Whose project was it? Furthermore, the accusations of witchcraft and the precautions taken to deal with the evil powers point to the important role occult forces play in social life. When conflicts are high, knowledge about such powers becomes vital. In addition, it is not a coincidence that it was a project related to a spatial reconstruction of the village that caused these clashes. As I reiterate further on, physical steps in the direction of 'development' (*maendeleo*) often have their counterparts in resistance.

The people engaged in electrifying Uroa were situated in various geographical and social spaces. We shall meet several of them. My primary reason for telling this story (or rather, stories) is to provide a direct reference for understanding why and how Uroa ended up connected to the grid. This involves accounting for various people's strategies and dilemmas. It also means exploring the way technologies are negotiated, manipulated and conceived.

Uroa becomes connected

Uroa was connected to the electricity grid in Zanzibar on 10 October 1990. Originally, the village had not been included in the map for electrification. However, during a process of negotiations between the local administration, ordinary households, healers, and RUREL staff and management, electricity and its various uses became accessible.

The village water pump was soon run by electricity. Water supply, once a problem, became reliable.[1] Successively, several water taps were put up in the various wards. On 26 February 1991 the new health centre in Uroa was electrified. The current was, and continues to be, used for sterilising equipment, storing medicines in a refrigerator and providing light. At nighttime the health centre is normally not in use, but in emergency cases such as when women are in labour or during cholera outbreaks, the building is used and the fluorescent lights are switched on. The health workers regarded the steady supply of water, now available from a tap at the health centre itself, as the most important improvement after electrification.

Furthermore, the school, two mosques, and a range of households were connected (see below). In addition, on 2 June 1991, fourteen street lamps were turned on for the first time and lit-up the village main road. Electricity had entered Uroa. Or rather, as the stories told by people involved in the process will show, the village leadership had embraced the

Plate 4.1 Former main road in Uroa (photo taken in 2000).

idea of electricity's arrival and had taken action in order to make it come true. This implied convincing RUREL's management, meeting local resistance and seeking to mobilise the population to support their efforts. It also meant becoming directly involved in laying power lines and shaping a technology's configuration.

The significance of a meal

Men within the local leadership played a central role during the days of electrification. Juma Hassan Juma was the Chairman of the CCM party branch in the village at the time.[2] His management seems to have been crucial to the outcome. According to Juma and several people whom I interviewed in 1991 and 2000–1, he was the one who first suggested the idea of electrification. However, as indicated, the Chairman's efforts to provide electricity and his clearly effective leadership were not appreciated by all. His sudden death in 1993 was explained by his relatives as having been the result of evil people's work through spirits. In his family's and sympathisers' eyes, Juma's involvement with projects such as electrification ultimately cost him his life. In what follows, the narrative is mainly based on accounts provided by Juma himself and his supporters.

However, other people would supplement (though not knowing all the details) rather than contradict this narrative of how it all started.

Juma was working as a teacher in Chwaka in 1989. Every weekday he went by bicycle on the bumpy road leading to this village, which is located 5 km south of Uroa. In Chwaka he learned about RUREL's plans to connect Chwaka to the grid. Juma here obtained detailed knowledge of the plans for the project and how it was meant to be organised in Chwaka. It seems that his knowledge at this early stage highly influenced his successive initiatives and strategies.

The Chairman got in touch with the Project Engineer in RUREL and asked about the possibility of obtaining electricity in Uroa. More specifically Juma first brought up the idea among various groups of leaders in Uroa. Included here were Sheha and his committee and the Elders' Group (*Wazee Wanne*) in question.[3] One man, who had been a member of Sheha's committee at the time, described in 2001 how they had decided to approach the RUREL management at this early stage:

> Juma invited Tenfjord for a meeting to tell him about the problems of water supply (lack of diesel, great distance to fetch water). We explained that we needed electricity. They sat down on Sheha's *baraza* to talk. There were Tenfjord and a couple of other men from ZECO as well as Chairman Juma and Sheha Pandu Simai. Then we made nice food for him (*kwa ajili yake*). My wife prepared the food at the guesthouse we used to have on the beach. Octopus! Cooked rice! We asked Tenfjord if he did not want a house here in Uroa. He told us he wanted a place. We gave him a place, where Tamarind is now.[4]

A strikingly high number of Uroan men mentioned this meal when asked to tell the story of electricity's arrival. Octopus cooked in coconut milk is not everyday food but is quite common here on the coast. Cooked rice is served almost daily. The passion revealed by these accounts (they often added: 'and everything!' (*na kila kitu!*)) expresses people's own appreciation of the food. Linked to this, it marks their pride in a shared identity, as I return to in chapter 10. Furthermore, the way this meal was described twelve years later had strikingly seductive connotations. The underlying tone was that few people would be able to resist the taste of such food. To serve this to a Norwegian and his Zanzibari colleagues was thus considered a strategy for obtaining what they wanted. By accepting the invitation the Project Engineer already partly owed the villagers a supply of electricity, whether he perceived this or not.[5]

In the meal's aftermath, the Project Engineer advised Juma to write an application for electricity to ZECO. Subsequently the Project Committee received and accepted the change of plans to include Uroa in the electrification programme. Following this the RUREL staff examined the conditions for electricity in Uroa more thoroughly. In the village the issue of domestic electrification soon became a vividly discussed topic.

A passion for meetings

The Chairman summoned his co-villagers to a range of general meetings. As was common procedure, staff from the RUREL project participated in one meeting to inform the villagers about the project. However, in contrast to other villages, men in Uroa appear to have continuously discussed the plans for electrification, including the possibilities for household connection. There were 370 households in the village at the time. During one of the assemblies that took place before August 1990, sixty-two people (all men) put up their names on a list indicating their interest in electricity. By September the same year fifty-six people (i.e., fifteen per cent of the households) had bought an electricity meter and were ready to be connected.[6] Quite extraordinarily; this was nearly one month before the general supply was ready. This early, collective planning in Uroa also meant that the Chairman could inform the RUREL staff about where consumers would be located. It is difficult to establish whether lines and transformers would have been located differently had the RUREL staff not received this information. However, it is significant to the Chairman's feeling of participation that he told me he had advised the Project Engineer about where to put up such gear. He provided a map of the village and together they marked the location of points for public and private consumption (see Map 4.1).

Women's limited role in the process

Women do not attend general meetings in Uroa to the same extent as men and those who come usually stay for a shorter period of time than men. They have duties at home to take care of in the afternoon and up until late at night. In fishing villages such as Uroa men often return from the sea after midday and have the afternoon free to attend meetings.[7] In inland villages, like Gamba, I observed the opposite pattern in 1991. Men living in such villages often stayed away for several days to make a living on the sea. Probably as a consequence of this, women in Gamba attended meetings more often than men. In this way, they appeared to play a more central part in village formal life than what is the case in coastal areas.

Women in Uroa heard about electricity's arrival on the radio and through information from co-residents. Unlike their male counterparts they remained at a distance from the technology. This is also related to the fact that men are owners of domiciles. Fixed electric gear can be considered as extensions to houses and remain men's responsibility and concern. It is also relevant that it is primarily men who are involved in communal work of this sort. Finally, the under-representation of women in village leadership must also be taken into consideration. There were (and are) very few female

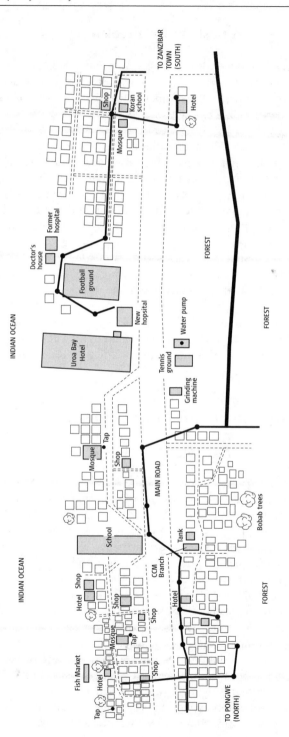

Map 4.1 Sketch of the village of Uroa in 1991 showing the distribution of the electricity grid. Produced by Mr Juma Hassan Juma of Uroa.

members of the various committees constituting the village leadership. A women's corporation called 'Patience brings happiness' (*Subira Yavuta Heri*) consisted of thirty-seven members at the time. The group had discussed the issue of electricity and its uses at an early stage, but concluded that electricity was out of their reach. They have a mill, but this has not, by 2008, been electrified.[8]

Creativity and capability – participation practised

Just as the plans for electrification in Uroa were about to be realised, I was told in 2001, a controversy had been exposed in the Tanzanian printed press (apparently both in *The Guardian* and *The Daily News*). It had become known that each private customer in Uroa was to pay an amount of Tsh.4,620 (US$20) to have electricity installed in his house. Now there were speculations about the purpose of this payment. Apparently the Norwegian government had disapproved of and interfered with the plans. Uroan leaders were told that electrification could not take place after all. Upon hearing this news the Chairman went to town. First he went to see the management at ZECO. During this meeting the management insisted that the project had to stop. However, Juma did not stop. He continued right on up to the Minister of Energy, Muhammad Hatibu Reja. The Minister listened to Juma's story, my acquaintances in 2001 continued. He understood that electricity would help village development. The amount was meant to cover the expense of the meter and fuse as well as the connection to the house. The Minister sympathised with the argument that the money was not bribery. It was a way to effectively collect what people had to pay anyway for connection. Apparently, Juma received support. The Minister informed ZECO that it must continue the project in Uroa. 'The Norwegian government' was also contacted by the Minister and accepted the decision. Finally, the 5 km long 33 kV tee-off from Chwaka to Uroa could be constructed.

After the area had been surveyed by RUREL staff, male volunteers from Uroa participated in clearing the bush and preparing for the erection of poles. In the aftermath (Phase IV) this became standard procedure according to the management. It was intended to increase villagers' 'ownership' of the project. In Uroa, however, the Chairman did not await instructions as to what their contribution should be, but came up with concrete suggestions as to how to proceed. In this coral ragstone area ditches for mounting the poles had to be blasted by using dynamite. Often during such operations the ground would be covered with fishing nets, according to the Project Engineer. Juma suggested instead that branches from palm trees be used for this purpose, and the project management followed up on the idea. Juma told me that he had been the one explaining to the workers how to do this.[9]

The RUREL staff were experienced and had devised routines for how to proceed with village electrification (though the practice of becoming involved in providing actual connections was quite recent at that time). However, what the above accounts show is that the Uroan leadership played quite a significant role throughout the process. This contrasts with the stories from other villages where leaders and residents met the new technology more passively. The Uroan Chairman's initiative, the meal and the cited incidents where protagonists perceived their own agency as vital for achieving electrification, are significant. In sum, these actions reflect a high rate of local participation.

The 'participatory paradigm' has had tremendeous influence on development theory and practice during the last twenty-five years. Evidence of failed projects in the 1970s and 1980s in combination with an analytical focus on agency and knowledge triggered a shift from top-down modernisation models of development towards local ownership and control of such processes. Despite the considerable challenges participatory methods have encountered in practice (Gardner and Lewis 1996: 111–3; Grillo 1997; Crewe 1997; Nyamwaya 1997; Pottier 1997; Nustad 2001; Green 2003a: 123, 140; Mosse 2004; Bornstein 2005: 119–24), the idea remains an ideal in development thinking. In its fullest sense participation implies, first of all, that people should identify their own goals for development instead of having such goals defined from a distance by others. This, we have seen, was the case in Uroa where the Chairman initiated the idea of electrification and, in doing so, defined access to electricity as a need in the village. The important condition, of course, was that electricity had become an option in the first place.

Secondly, full participation implies that the groups at the local level should be active and in control of the process leading to the fulfilment of such locally identified goals (Chambers 1995; Nelson and Wright 1995). Again, Uroa, at least at a first glance, appears to match the criteria. The village leaders were proactive in planning for electricity, writing letters, drawing maps, and organising meetings. In fact, many of these activities took place before the goal of electrification had been fully determined. Therefore one could rightly say that the goal of development and the means for getting there formed part of a single, multifaceted process. Most notably, Uroans influenced the shaping of the technology by untying and manipulating elements within the 'black box' (Latour 1987: 130–1) of transformers, wires, ditches and predetermined electricity policies. This strengthens the argument for regarding participation as just as relevant to projects focused on technological interventions as to other kinds of projects. Robert Chambers (1995) somewhat oddly distinguishes between two kinds of projects: those focused on 'people' and those focused on 'things' (i.e., technologies). Arguing why participatory methods are better suited for the approaches that focus on 'people', Chambers says (1995: 41):

[P]rojects concerned with people should become processes of learning, enabling and empowering, with open-ended time frames allowing for participation and change, while blueprint approaches with rigid time frames and set targets should be confined to things, limited to some physical aspect of infrastructure.

Based on the Uroan case, but also by reference to STS and other social approaches to technologies, I find this general distinction between people and things hard to justify. What this book seeks to demonstrate is the interrelationship between people and the physical objects they become associated with. From its arrival, to its organisation and use in the aftermath, the electricity system in rural Zanzibar, as elsewhere, is made up of things and people which never cease to influence each other.

The initiation, implementation, administration and use of street lighting probably represent the most striking and lasting evidence of Uroans' degree of influence in the process. Their experiences have attracted attention in other Zanzibari villages (SUM 2005).[10] One and a half decades after electrification, the Uroans' sense of authorship of the project is still expressed and experienced in the village.

The limits to local control

The aspect of control is central within the participatory framework, and ideally indicates that the power to determine 'needs' and exercise control over the 'process' should lie with the local groups themselves. In Uroa, the process of electrification involved shifts in power and control from the project management (and the politicians and donors above them) towards the local administration in Uroa. However, these shifts were more temporary than permanent and were triggered only in certain instances. Local control was never fully realised. Without acceptance and assistance from the project management, there would have been no project. The main control remained in the hands of the project management.

Here, the Uroan case supports a point that has been raised against participatory methods as such, a point which relates to the problem of realising bottom-up approaches. Knut Nustad has argued that one should acknowledge the intrinsically hierarchical nature of any process related to intended social change (Nustad 2001). He draws on Cowen and Shenton's use of the notion of 'trusteeship' on which the idea of development is inherently based (Cowen and Shenton 1995 and 1996 found in Nustad 2001: 483–4). Trusteeship, in turn, implies that somebody (other than those to be developed) must define the end before the process can begin. Participation in the full sense that I referred to above therefore constitutes a tautology and a contradiction in terms. This may partly explain the range of problems participatory methods have run into or produced in practice, but other factors also appear relevant.[11] In any case, the Uroan case reflects the unavoidable hierarchical ordering of intended change. This aspect is also relevant within the village. It is probably no coincidence that the street lighting, which otherwise followed the main road in Uroa in a straight line, made a detour off to the Chairman's house. Today this mercury bulb signals the elevated position and power of the house's former owner. Hierarchies exist between central and local actors as well as among the villagers.

At the same time, Uroa's case vividly illustrates the rich potential for participation, also when new technologies are in question. These observations, together with the fact that Uroans themselves initiated the idea of electrification, are partly why I advocate a model of development that highlights actors' (structurally constrained) choices. Donald Curtis, arguing in 1995 for a revitalisation of 'community development', asks: 'How has it come about that both development theory and constitutional theory have been so slow to recognize local initiative and responsibility as a basic reality?' (Curtis 1995: 115). In the same way as Curtis observed locally driven projects in Nigeria (he explains their motivation primarily by referring to the failing state), many Zanzibari communities have made, and continue to make, initiatives in various respects. Earlier I mentioned the activities now triggered in various villages motivated by the combination of access to electricity and TASAF money. Uroa's case is not unique in this respect. Furthermore, in terms of how the community reached an understanding with the project staff, the case has more general insights to offer.

Finding equivalence

A closer analysis of the relationship between the village leadership and RUREL staff helps us understand the process of electrification in Uroa further. I argue that this particular relationship was central (but not the only relevant factor) to how the process was experienced and how it ultimately turned out. Norman Long's notion of 'social interfaces' is a valuable starting point to explore the encounter (1989: 2). Interfaces can be regarded as particular intersections where groups or individuals situated in distinct social or cultural positions are confronted with one another. Taken that the two groups represented distinct types of knowledge at the time, I am interested in exploring the negotiating processes that resulted.

In the absence of a prescribed plan for electrification both parties had to improvise. Both had a genuine interest in seeing the grid reach Uroa but there were many questions to be answered, including how to convince the Project Committee and NORAD to incorporate Uroa in the project. As a result the two parties appear to have acted more on equal terms here than was the case in other villages in Zanzibar. Notably, the project management listened (and ate what they were offered). They did this partly because they were fascinated by the Uroan initiative and determination and partly because they had to obtain some kind of cooperation with the village in order for the plans to succeed. Accordingly, the RUREL staff adjusted their decisions and routines with reference to their encounters with the village leader.

In addition to this flexibility the staff supported activities on the local level to an extent unprecedented elsewhere. The lump sum of Tsh.4,620 that each customer was to pay for connection indicates how RUREL staff became directly engaged in organising provisions geared to individual households. This was quite unusual and shows the project staff's dedication to supporting village connection. The two groups of actors were not equally positioned. However, they had a common goal, and during the development encounter they provided space for each other to act. I suggest that the necessity for improvisation in Uroa is exactly what produced this important interrelationship and the positive end result.

Despite the turn towards 'folk theory' since the 1970s, and the more recent focus on 'agency' and 'participation', Hobart has argued that scientific knowledge tends to be regarded and treated as hegemonic compared to local types of knowledges (1993). Local knowledge, and the particular ways knowledge is linked to agency are correspondingly unacknowledged. This is how we (falsely) produce and attribute 'ignorance' to the local side. In Uroa the Project Engineer needed the Chairman as a partner to achieve the goal in question. From this position the central question became 'how' they could work together rather than 'who knows better'. Although he did not fully understand the man, he regarded the Chairman as capable and determined (which he demonstrated that he was). This, I hold, is one of the factors that explains the success of electrification in Uroa.

The communicative aspect in the relationship just described is important. It is likely to have relevance in other contexts too. Hobart continues to be pertinent. He refers to a standard (presumingly Western) model for communication that tends to be used in the development encounter and also in the analysis of it. Based on the Uroan case, I think Hobart is right in suggesting that the communication in question should not be regarded as a standard sender–message–receiver model, in which the actors share a world view and are capable of perceiving the 'meaning' of such messages. Elaborating on Wallace (1961: 29–44, quoted in Hobart 1993: 11), Hobart maintains that 'all that is required is that the parties concerned can find equivalences of some kind'. In the present case, finding equivalence is a central element as it presumes, first of all, that both parties share a goal and perceive the other to have something to offer. There was some degree of symmetry involved. Secondly, the model emphasises that actors do not fully comprehend each other, which is related to their references to distinct knowledge systems (Long 1989). Hobart even suggests that they ought not to understand each other completely and that, certainly, one cannot expect them to want to fully understand each other.

Thus the model allows for the very likely fact that actors in development projects interpret moments of interaction in quite distinct ways. The meal in Uroa where the two groups met, shared food, and discussed the plans for electrification is a case in point. The significance of the meal as perceived by the Uroans was probably not shared by the Project Engineer. When treating the Chairman's careful handling of conflicts and occult forces the discrepancy (between Project Engineer and Chairman) in their perceptions of causal effects will become even clearer. Nevertheless, there appear to have been moments when the parties spoke or otherwise interacted in a way that both parties found meaningful and appropriate to their common purpose. There was a sufficient feeling of mutual understanding and common interest. Moreover, there was room for differences of opinion, allowing things to move forward at a pace that was not detrimental to the process.

That said, it did take a bit of effort. The Chairman had to make several attempts to reach and convince the project management. The project management spent many days in Uroa before the construction of lines could begin. Thus I support Hobart's view that communication in such instances should be perceived as a matter of degree and 'the end result of much mutual work' (Hobart 1993: 11, quoting Reddy 1979). Hobart (and Reddy's) approach to 'understanding' thus serves the encounter in question. As the author stresses, though, such understanding is never perfect. The error on the part of the development practitioner or researcher would be to expect that the parties' mutual understanding was, or should be, complete.

Explaining conflict and resistance

Electricity was not introduced in Uroa without conflict, and the tension produced is also an important part of the story. Due to the protagonists' distinct positions in such processes, this aspect is of general relevance when new technologies are introduced (Long 1989; Bijker and Law 1994: 9). As observed, the leaders and their advisors regarded protection rituals as necessary. Signs of evil forces continued to be registered throughout the process. Below I describe some of the measures that were taken to meet the perceived threats which ultimately involved the whole population. The accounts mainly stem from a pro-electricity perspective at two points in time.[12] However, among people within the Chairman's 'faction', explanations became somewhat modified over time. I thus touch on how the causes for resistance and conflict were expressed on distinct occasions. Later on I focus on what such shifts may tell us about village dynamics and changes in general. In concluding the chapter I discuss the relationship between occult practices and local and national attempts to modernise the population.

In 1991 I was introduced to representatives of the elders' group of the Nyanje ward, where the Chairman was a resident himself. The group consisted of two men and a woman. Apparently, the battle over electricity had roots in people's different origins. Uroa consisted of two groups, in their eyes, the 'indigenous' (*wazalendo*), with affiliations to Nyanje, and the 'guests' (*wageni*), associated with Mji Mpya (lit. 'New Town'). The demographic borders between the two units were clearly described.[13] Each faction had a group of elders who gave advice and who assisted their respective members through the use of occult remedies. According to my informant the guests would always try to carry out harmful rituals directed against any changes proposed by the Chairman and his group. So when bush-clearing approached the village, the guests had continued their efforts to disrupt electrification. The elders in Nyanje saw their own role as having been central to the successful outcome (that is, electrification). One member described the vital remedies they provided labourers with:

> The workers discovered signs of blood in the forest next to where the poles were supposed to be located. Meanwhile, the oldest man among the elders (*wazee*) in Nyanje noticed something happening in his head. He was warned that something evil was going on and understood that the guests (*wageni*) were trying to stop the works. The old man asked his spirits for advice and passed the directions on to the Chairman. The workers were gathered and told to do the '*kombe*' (protection ritual). They were to read the Koran and wrote down some parts of the text on a paper. Then they should pour water on the paper and drink the coloured (black or red) water. After this, they could go on working.

In this way, a wide range of actors contributed to the obtaining of village electrification. Spirits, mediums, the Chairman, his helpers and workers all joined forces in this effort. 'Bad attitudes' were linked to a person's particular origin. However, seen from the other faction's perspective at the time, these links, causes for conflict, and strategies were not so clear-cut. When I had the opportunity to speak with one of the elders from Mji Mpya, he contested the labels 'indigenous people' and 'guests'. He also opposed the idea that people in Mji Mpya were behind the resistance. People's origins, he told me, had nothing to do with their like or dislike of the new technology.

In 2000 the question of 'origin' was generally perceived to have been of little relevance. People remembered the former resistance, though, and referred to it as a 'campaign' (*kampeni*) against the new technology. The question of who had been behind the campaign was no longer related to the question of origin. Instead, certain individuals' inadequate knowledge and their having been old were used as explanatory factors. The opposing elders had not 'understood the meaning of development' (*hawajafahamu maana ya maendeleo*). They had not figured out electricity's 'purpose/meaning' (*maana*) and they had thought it was 'dangerous' (*hatari*). More concretely, they had not realised that electricity would bring reliable water pumps and improved health services. Some of the opposing elders had apparently also complained that they would not be able to pay for the connection to their own houses. In brief, it was certain individuals' 'backwardness' and/or fear of being excluded from benefiting from electricity that had triggered their resistance (cf. Hobart 1993 and his treatment of the construction of 'ignorance').

Such accounts are perhaps not surprising in a retrospective light, due to men's and women's general appreciation of electricity's various uses today.[14] However, I also find it significant that the particular distinction between Nyanje and Mji Mpya was either not mentioned, or was referred to in contradictory ways. Ward boundaries in general seemed less fixed, at least compared to how Nyanje elders had described them in the past. When I repeatedly asked the young meter-reader (born in the village) in which ward we found ourselves during our rounds he would often hesitate as if the question was irrelevant. What is more various people gave quite different answers when asked to define village internal boundaries. I finally gave up the attempt to represent such boundaries on a map.

The reasons for the change of emphasis from geographic location/origin to a question of age and knowledge seem first of all to lie in the fact that elders interviewed in 1991 had all passed away by 2000. Old and long-term conflicts are likely to have informed the accounts during my first visit. Ten years later, those people interviewed had been less involved in the politics of the past. This might have reduced the relevance of former conflicts. On the other hand, there might have been a concern with reducing conflicts of the past if bringing them to light could cause new harm. Furthermore, as the population grows space is getting scarcer. Sons now frequently establish houses at some distance from their fathers', which contrasts with the common patrilocal *kiambo* system where sons stayed in their father's neighbourhood.

Also relevant to this picture are some recent shifts that have caused a reconstruction of categories. There are immigrant workers from the mainland and elsewhere arriving to work in the construction or tourist sector. This is the group defined today as 'guests'. They are (wrongly) thought to bring AIDS to the village. Tourists (*watalii*) have also become a new category of 'others'. What is striking today, compared to 1991, is the way Pembans (*Wapemba*) are identified and stigmatised in everyday life. This redrawing of boundaries caused by the introduction of a multiparty system in 1995 is also reflected in that many more evil spirits from Pemba are perceived to be around in Uroa today than was the case in 1991. Perceptions of boundaries depend on who the speaker is and in what context the question is asked.

Development as a political matter

What is clear is that the Chairman's group perceived the use of occult forces as central to making electrification a reality. Other projects, particularly those in relation to the construction of the Uroa Bay Hotel, also stirred up the situation in Uroa at the time (Winther 1991). The 'proof' that evil witchcraft had been activated frequently during this period of rapid change was explained by the high number of people who had died or become seriously ill, particularly in the ward of Mji Mpya (as stated in 1991 and in 2001). In addition children were apparently disappearing in the forest, a fact providing evidence that evil was going on. After my stay in 1991 there had been a general assembly to find out who was behind the trouble. Three men, who had been on the Chairman's side at the time, explained in 2001 the purpose of the meeting:

Uwesu: Afterwards there was this meeting at the branch office where the Shieh [Islamic leader] read the Halbadiri [from the Koran]. They went from one person to the next, touching their heads, saying: 'Every person who has done ill shall die' (*Kila mtu kufanya ubaya; kufa!*).

Ibrahim: Those who were afraid to go, we knew they were not good. Some did not go. Other people went and afterwards they died (*Wengine walikwenda, baadaye walikufa*).

Tanja: These must have been very strong forces?

Pandu: Superpower! [We laugh from what I perceive to be the shared joy of having found an expression in English that captures the power of such forces].

Tanja: Did anybody die as a consequence of the reading of Halbadiri?

Uwesu: Yes. After three months only, three people died. [Gives their names].

Ibrahim: Why did we know the Halbadiri had affected them? Because if it gets you, you become ill/destroyed (*unaugua*). Afterwards you suddenly feel like undressing [that is, cause yourself great shame]. You get wounds, the legs get swollen, and you pee in bed as small children do. If you try to move by foot, you can hardly walk, you have to rest many times. Because of this we knew! We did a lot to protect ourselves at the time. You could not sleep alone. You go to bed in the evening and close the door and the next morning you find yourself lying outside. Now there are no problems like this, now it is only development (*Sasa hakuna matatizo, ni maendeleo tu*).

This public anti-witchcraft ceremony (led by a Muslim teacher which imbued it with authority) shows the village leaders' moral condemnation of the 'evil' going on. By pointing out who was behind it the leaders intended to remove all sorts of problems, to purify the village and to clear the way for development to proceed. Maia Green claims that many anthropologists have tended to treat anti-witchcraft practices as 'modern' since their emergence often coincides with periods of change induced from outside (2003b: 139). On the surface of it a ritual intended to remove barriers to development could appear 'modern'. Some Uroans explained the resistance by referring to these people's backwardness and ignorance. However, what the previous discussion also showed was how electricity was not introduced in a social vacuum but rather in a quite specific political context. I follow Green who argues for looking at such anti-witchcraft practices in light of concrete political processes (2003b: 139). In historical descriptions of settlements such as Uroa John Middleton and Jane Campbell have noted their general dual structure (1965: 63–4). The power embedded in such antagonism has been used to account for some of the causes of the Zanzibari revolution (ibid.; see also Nisula 1999: 20 n.). The local political context today is no less important to take into account when we seek to understand the resistance against electrification and the accusations of witchcraft along with the successive protecting and cleansing rituals that followed.

To grasp how the arrival of electricity affected village life, simple dichotomies between traditional and modern traits do not take us much further. Rather, all Uroan practices, fifteen years ago or today, constitute a particular modern experience (cf. Moore and Sanders 2001). Continuities, and claims for their abandonment or maintenance, form part of the picture. It is by focusing on actors' strategies and their theories of cause and effect that we come closer to understanding the connections between the occult and material change.

I think Green is constructive when focusing on how categories are associated with status and how they are used for very temporal classifications (2003b: 124). In the above account Ibrahim's use of the notion 'development' illustrates just how contextually such notions are perceived. He here applied the word to describe the favourable current situation in which the level of conflict is regarded as low. However, in other contexts, he would often complain about current leaders' lack of initiative in making improvements in the village. He would say: 'today there is no development' (*leo hakuna maendeleo*) and contrast today's inefficiency with all the changes for the better in the past. In the two, rather contradictory, contexts development is used to describe a favourable situation of any sort. Notably, in neither case does he refer to development as the opposite of tradition (*mila*). What we see is how the various discourses of development, tradition and backwardness articulate people's pressing concerns.

In this chapter I have shown that governmental development policies may have a limited effect on how projects in fact turn out. Uroa's success was a result of local political processes. The Uroan leader had the ability to control important parts of the premises for implementation. From actually initiating the project to the ongoing money collection for street lighting, Uroans were not presented with central policy decisions camouflaged as technical solutions to their problems (cf. Green 2003a: 136). They defined their own needs. Through close association with the RUREL staff, the project became the result of the implementation of local energy policies combined with central ones. Together the parties found some sort of equivalence and this partial, but important, understanding and the open character of the process contributed to its success. The Chairman had the mediating role between village elders on the one hand and the project management on the other. Particularly with regard to the occult the two groups represented distinct knowledge systems. We may see this as a discontinuity in world views (Long 1989). However, the two groups never met in direct encounters in Uroa. The village leader took it upon himself to be the broker. He also had to handle the resistance from opposing internal groups in a way that would be alien to the Norwegian element of the project management. I find it vital that in Uroa it was local knowledge and local perceptions of agency that set the scene for various steps in the process towards electrification.

When focusing on political dynamics in a village we should not be surprised to find large scale projects, such as electrification, surrounded by local conflicts. Such resistance is not unique to this region.[15] At the same time we have seen influential actors' potential to reshape predetermined development policies and to form their own projects. The battle in Uroa was perhaps not a match between equals. The Chairman managed to bring the developers on to his side. However, the cost of the implementation was felt by both parties in the village. Today all Uroans express appreciation for their late leader's efforts.

Notes

1. There had been a diesel generator running the village water pump for quite some years, feeding water from the well to a tank in the village through pipelines. However, experience of lack of diesel had proven this technology to be vulnerable and unreliable. Also the generator had a small capacity and water consumption was increasing. These problems had forced women to walk to the well outside the village in order to provide their families with water.
2. There was – and, to my knowledge, still is – a CCM office in every village in Unguja.
3. Sheha is selected by the district authorities and holds the position of administrative head of the village. In 2001 I was told that district authorities seek advice from the various Elders' Councils in a village before an appointment is made. As CCM leader, the Chairman in theory deals only with party matters. However, in practice (1990 and 2001) the distinction between the roles of the Sheha and the Chairman seems quite blurred. In addition, both leaders need legitimacy from the Elders' Councils in important matters. Thus formal leadership appointed/selected by governmental authorities and traditional institutions are interconnected actors in village decision-making.
4. The Project Engineer later negotiated and bought the plot from the family who owned the land (or, strictly speaking, the trees) on the beach at the time. This family became

partners in the hotel project. Up until today they also form part of the hotel's management and staff.

5. I experienced a similar invitation to a meal in Marumbi in 2001, where I was asked to help provide electricity.

6. It has been easy to document this process since the Chairman and his staff kept all records.

7. During a general meeting in Uroa in September 1991, 136 men and 56 women attended the gathering. The issue that day was the CCM party and its organisation in the village. During my two-week stay in 1991 the Chairman participated in meetings nearly every evening.

8. The women's group has discussed the possibility of replacing diesel with electricity to run their electric mill. In 1990 they were thinking about the possibility of getting electricity for lamps in their homes. The leader of the group said, in 1991, that they knew about radios, cookers, fridges, fans and irons. However, the prices of these commodities were far beyond their means, so they did not discuss the possibility of getting any of them.

9. They were economically compensated by the project. The works were carried out within a period of one and a half months.

10. The main challenge in the process of obtaining street lamps was how to finance the investment and later organise the payment of the monthly electricity bill. This was solved in the following way: fourteen street lamps were put up along the road that ran through the village in its most densely populated area. Each lamp cost Tsh.5,400 (US$24). Money was collected from the people living near a lamp. According to the Chairman, each person paid what he or she could afford. In order to save on the cost of meters, the lamps were connected to private customers. In 1991 each of these meter owners were paid a stipulated sum of Tsh.100 a month to cover the cost of units. This money was collected as a local tax at the Uroa fish market. Upon my arrival in 2000 the bulbs were no longer working. Many people explained to me that the current village leadership had failed to maintain the payment system, so the public lighting had gradually disappeared. When new wires and two separate electricity meters were installed in 2001, the administration of street lighting was considered easier to handle. Tax was put on fish sold at the Uroa market to finance consumption. The lights were still in use (and bills were being paid) in 2004.

11. Many observers have treated the various difficulties related to participatory approaches to development. Participation has been used as a rhetorical device while central authorities and elites tend to want to keep things under control (Nustad 2001; Nyamwaya 1997). NGOs have been strategically created due to the participatory regime, also sometimes without allowing communities to play a major role in development (Nyamwaya 1997; Bornstein 2005). Beneficaries have not had real influence because 'workshops are structured encounters marked by hidden agendas and strategic manoueuvres' (Pottier 1997: 221). There is a lack of pre-existing groups to take command of their own development (Bornstein 2005: 120–4). The methods used, such as PRA, have tended to be rigid and difficult to use (ibid.).

12. In 1991 my informants were, to a large extent, picked out by the Chairman. He also had the task of translating most of the interviews. As a result most of the accounts of electrification matched his version of the circumstances. Towards the end of my stay I encountered some of the people from the opposing group by accident and got to talk to them with the help (for interpretation) of a friend from Zanzibar Town.

13. The first group were residents of the old wards Nyanje, Mtagoni and Kipandoni and had been living in Uroa for many years. Originally they had come from Bambi, a village where men in Nyanje (or their families) still often find their wives. The 'guests' residing in Mji Mpya had arrived fairly recently and originated from Bwejuu, Paje, Jambiani and Makunduchi. People living in the Dikoni ward, which is spatially separated from the

main village, are thought to have origins in Ndudu to a great extent. However, they also have close interrelations with many of the 'old' wards.

14. As anticipated, it became even more difficult to obtain 'the other side' of the story in 2000–1. Several of those blamed for working against electricity had died. Others had become very old. Some people I talked to (described by others as responsible for the campaign) said they appreciated electricity for its benefits but had no recollection of a conflict. Perhaps the lack of memory is a sign of former reservations. However, if and how this might have been articulated at the time remains an open and non-crucial matter.

15. I also know this from conversations with Norwegian engineers who were involved with such projects in rural Norway in the 1950s.

Chapter 5

DISCOURSES OF DEVELOPMENT

In October 2000 a group of Italian tourists approached some children on the beach in Uroa and asked to take a photo of them. A couple of women standing nearby got in between and refused to let the tourists do so. Then, instead of walking away, the tourists threw a heap of sweets (*peremende*) up in the air. When the children started eagerly collecting the candy in the sand, the foreigners took several pictures in defiance of the women's objections.

I did not observe this incident but the episode was afterwards vividly commented on and condemned by men and women in Uroa. The reactions seemed to capture a widespread feeling that 'tourists have no shame but there is nothing we can do about it'. In 1991 there were many critical remarks related to the arrival of tourism. An Italian hotel in Uroa was causing considerable frustration at the time. However, these days, people in general appear less preoccupied with the negative influence of tourism. The foreigners' presence seems to be accepted. As people in Uroa tend to say: 'we have become used to it' (*tumeshazoea*). Many also made the point – and showed, by including me in their community – that Zanzibaris like outsiders. Showing hospitality is a virtue.

However, in cases such as the one mentioned, or when bikini-dressed women wander around in the village, the reactions afterwards reveal people's hostility towards the foreigners. The anger appears to contain a sense of fragility and disempowerment. Tourists come and go and there is little to be done with their, on occasion, disrespectful behaviour. Spoken communication is difficult and the aesthetically informed ways of showing disapproval are not understood by the tourists. Olsen observed the way Nungwi women tried to communicate dissatisfaction with tourists' behaviour by turning their faces away during encounters (1999: 103). Western tourists did not get the message and continued their holiday unruffled. The Zanzibari aestheticised means for sanctions are not rendered effective for such interfaces. Nevertheless, tourism also produces aspirations for economic gain. Some people are involved in the business and young people in particular hope to be able to profit from this realm. There is, thus, already a certain dependency on the foreigners' money. This adds to the ambivalence of Uroans' relationship with tourism. The dilemma inherent in tourism also has its parallels in economic life more generally.

These introductory observations serve to set the scene for discussing discourses of development and recent socio-economic changes. Inferred here is the extent to which electricity is used as a means of generating income in Uroa. We should also bear in mind that 'development' is something intrinsically good to rural Zanzibaris. The term is most often used in connection with concrete, material or economic changes in a positive direction. This resonates with Christine J. Walley's findings on Mafia Island, in which people tend to refer to development (*maendeleo*) as 'the ability of individuals to "get ahead" economically' (Walley 2004: 63; see also Caplan 2004: 56–9). Other studies from the East African region (Talle 2002: 49; Fuglesang 1994: 227) have tended to emphasise development's more ambivalent associations. Mohamed Ali Saleh, in a study of modernity in Zanzibar, presumably Zanzibar Town, goes further (Saleh 2004). He refers to the negative associations people have with the term '*kwenda na wakati*' (lit. 'to go with the times'). The author perceives this expression 'to sum up the notion of modernity in Swahili society today' (Saleh 2004: 145). This conclusion appears a bit too general, though. In Uroa there is no abstract notion of modernity resembling that of Zanzibar Town. *Kisasa* (also translated as 'modernity') is seldom used and *kwenda na wakati* has a uniquely positive flavour to it. Again, this resonates with Walley (2004) and Caplan's (2004:5) findings on Mafia, where *maendeleo* at the same time means 'development' and is the closest one can get to any notion of 'modernity'. Thus it might seem that, in this respect, there are more similarities between rural Zanzibar and Mafia than between rural Zanzibar and Zanzibar Town.

Given that the rural Zanzibari notion of development is constantly in tandem with what people value, few speak of the tourist industry as 'development' in general terms. This is linked to tourism's ambiguous connotations in Uroa. Furthermore, when changes mainly perceived as development also turn out to have drawbacks, these effects are not spoken of as 'development's darker side'. The introduction of seaweed and electricity are cases in point. Here, the unfortunate effects are phenomena in themselves. This point is important when we scrutinise discourses of development. For some, the notion is seen as an attitude or even a morality. For others, development is also what they have missed. The notion is a central locus for the construction of difference in current Uroa.

Unreliable markets

On 22 April 2001 several hundred women were gathered on the beach in Uroa. Dressed in identical blue and white *kangas*, they had come to celebrate the birth of the Prophet in a *Maulidi* reading. Most women were sitting in the sun but some took shelter under a tent together with several men. Children and men performed the singing and reading. Their voices reached us by means of microphones, amplifiers and loudspeakers.

The seaweed company's local branch had initiated and organised the event. Its purpose was to thank God for the reopening of the 'market' (*soko*). Until recently, the Zania Seaweed Company had not bought seaweed from producers in Uroa. The local market had been closed for nine months, apparently due to low prices in the world market. Weeds already planted, harvested, dried, beaten free of sand, and collected were turning mouldy in their plastic bags and being thrown away. There had been little point in starting new fields for a long period. However, now, new hope was collectively expressed.

Towards the end of the nearly three-hour-long performance, everybody participated in the chanting. Some uttered individual prayers. The intensity of Meja's loud and repeated appeals for better times attracted the eyes of younger women. Having first adopted the skills of farming and having enjoyed earning her own money, she had come to know the capricious nature of the business. I also thought of her recent recovery and her fear of the spirit that continued to live inside her body. Upon the reopening of the market, she expressed her feeling of vulnerability but also her feeling of gratitude and genuine hope.

The arrival of seaweed in 1989 has had a tremendous impact on life in Uroa. As the quote from my fieldnotes indicates, it is an economically risky and physically demanding occupation. Not only does the market close from time to time, the price per kilo has also tended to go down over the years. From 2000 to 2004 (when the price per kilo was as low as 7c), a farmer would have had to double his/her efforts to keep a steady income (see Winther 2005 for further details). Still, 80 per cent of women in Uroa farm seaweed, which has come to be their main non-domestic occupation.

According to the Assistant Manager of Zania, men had their eyes on the business in its early phase. However, they became disappointed with the relatively little money and hard work involved, and most men withdrew. He referred, with a smile, to men's preference for 'relaxing' (*pumzika*) as a way of accounting for this. Fishing has been, and still is, the most important source of income for men (cash and subsistence).

Nevertheless, women's accumulated income from seaweed is quite substantial. Comparing the total sales of seaweed with sales at the fish market, seaweed accounts for at least 50 per cent of what men obtain in cash at the fish market (April 2004 is used as the date for reference). Fish is also sold directly either to hotels, in town (market), or in other kinds of direct exchange. From having had few opportunities to earn money in the

Plate 5.1 *Maulidi* reading to thank God for the reopening of the seaweed market, Uroa, April 2001.

Plate 5.2 Seaweed farm, Uroa, 2001.

This picture cannot go any larger at this resolution.
Can we get one with a better resolution?

past, women today thus have a considerable cash income. This produces more autonomy for women. As I have elaborated elsewhere, there is a strong articulation of any individual's right to decide on his or her financial matters (Winther 2005). However, this morality often contradicts other requirements for behaviour, such as sharing your surplus, the exchange of gifts and men's duty to provide for their families. Women's increased income, the multiple moral discourses at play and, most notably, the pragmatics of everyday life are highly relevant factors for the way electricity and appliances are financed (see chapter 8).

The arrival of seaweed can be considered as a direct step towards development from a female perspective. Everybody acknowledges this. However, I also heard voices questioning whether the new economic situation had in fact empowered women. A few complained, for instance, that despite the new opportunities for earning money it remained hard for women to get a divorce or obtain a house of their own. However, male dominance is seldom criticised. In this respect Meja made an unusual comment on the day of the *Maulidi* reading, a comment which indicates some degree of indignation.

After the *Maulidi*, a communal meal of *pilau* (pilaff) was served to all the participants. The rice and meat had first been given to the children and the few men present. After waiting for a couple of hours for new supplies to arrive, the majority of women got to eat. At one point Meja whispered to me that the food was already cold. Normally, in public gatherings, she would behave with extreme modesty and not make any sort of critical remarks. Her judgement about the cold food therefore appeared surprising to me. On reflection, I think it might not be a coincidence that her showing of impatience coincided with this celebration of 'development'. The event was explicitly organised for women, but they were served towards the end, as usual. Later, and on my prompting this time, she elaborated on her resentment at the fact that men were always served first during ceremonies. There is little meat left for women afterwards, she complained. She appeared to have had an overall feeling of indignation vis-à-vis such structures. However, during this particular event these asymmetric relations proved to be too much to bear. Meja has hopes of improvements in her life but she was disappointed with the way she was treated. An important question related to the development discourse and the effects of electricity's arrival is whether gender relations are modified in the process. As we shall see in the following chapters, there are signs of transformation that appear to strengthen women's position when appliances are in use. Their financial autonomy in the long-term is another issue and is also important to take into account.

The generation of money in Uroa

Figure 5.1 provides an overview of men's and women's monthly generation of money in Uroa. The figures are given in absolute numbers (US$) for the whole village.[1]

Figure 5.1 is informative in that it illustrates the extent of various types of cash-generating activities in Uroa. In addition to fishing and seaweed, we see the importance of governmental jobs (teachers, health workers and administrators) and tourism, which have come to contribute to male income and some female income. We should acknowledge that all types of income in rural Zanzibar, even governmental jobs, vary for a range of reasons. Also, as accounted for in chapter 1, interviews with some of the most deprived households were avoided for ethical reasons. In consequence, the results are slightly biased. Nevertheless, Figure 5.1 presents a rough picture of people's income in Uroa in 2001.

I do not have a similar range of data for 1991 but can deduce some aspects that have changed. The most striking transformation between the early 1990s and 2000 concerns the growing importance of money in the village. In turn, people's increased access to money makes it possible for them to invest in electricity. Both seaweed and tourism are new sources of cash, and the governmental sector is also expanding (as reported at the Uroa School). However, the increased income is not equally distributed. A

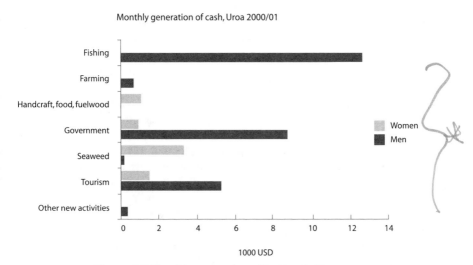

Monthly generation of cash, Uroa 2000/01

(bar chart with categories: Fishing, Farming, Handcraft, food, fuelwood, Government, Seaweed, Tourism, Other new activities; x-axis 0 to 14 in units of 1000 USD; legend: Women, Men)

1000 USD

Figure 5.1 Monthly generation of income in Uroa distributed according to type of occupation.
Source: fieldwork census 2000–1.

typical monthly income from fishing is US$37.50. Income from seaweed represents US$7 per month per farmer. In comparison people (mostly men) involved in tourism make US$65 a month on average and some make as much as US$130.

It should be noted that the income from tourism reflected in Figure 5.1 in most cases stems from people's jobs in one specific hotel in Uroa which is partly locally owned and managed, the Tamarind Beach Hotel. (Diving instructors and people directly involved with tourists tend to earn more than those employed as regular staff as housekeepers or watchmen.) The other, and larger, hotels in Uroa do not hire people from the village (apart from a few exceptions). This highlights the fact that in Uroa, and probably elsewhere in Zanzibar, joint ownership is a prerequisite for tourism to benefit the local population. This conclusion deserves attention at a high level in Zanzibar. It is important because tourism is the most significant sector in terms of the money-generating capacity of rural Zanzibar. Rural electrification accelerates the expansion of tourism. Rural electrification was also supposed to bring development to the rural population. Therefore, something should be done to help the rural population benefit from tourism to a greater extent than is the case today.

Changes in the village economy have also occurred in this period due to modified fishing and farming activities. First of all, men who have started to use new types of fishing technology make considerably more money than those who use the traditional canoe (*ngalawa*). In the latter case, work is organised in small, family groups. The new corporations, in contrast, are larger and are organised in a different way whereby membership is no longer dependent on the family network. When I asked Abdalla, a member of such a group, why his brother cannot come with them, he said that you have to provide your share to become a member. In other contexts Abdalla would often help his brother, though always with a focus on reciprocity and the expectation that his brother also make an effort himself. This balancing represents a general dilemma between looking out for yourself and helping relatives who need help. However, for Abdalla's modern fishing corporation the rules are clear. Each member brings in a certain amount of money, the group applies for a loan in town and then they buy nets, engines and larger vessels. Contacts in town are crucial for obtaining such loans (normally guarantees have to be given, which is impossible for most Uroans).

Secondly, after the introduction of a FINNIDA tree-planting project in the late 1980s, there has been a shift in the way land is used – including who has access to land and firewood. Shifting cultivation is common in this coral ragstone area. This is carried out by farming each piece of land over a given period of years (5–10), planting various vegetables (e.g., maize, tomatoes), roots (e.g., cassava, sweet potatoes) and fruit trees such as papaya and banana. Subsistence farming was, and remains, important. In 2001 it was practised by 40 per cent of households in Uroa who either have a *konde* or a *shamba*. Only a minor part of this production is reflected in Figure 5.1.

Here, the recent introduction of casuarina (*mivinja*) trees – and also lime trees (*midimu*) – has had a particular effect and also important repercussions in my view. These are valuable sources of income for the few entrepreneurs who have taken up this type of farming, though the income is always unreliable and there are no guarantees of profit. However, the new emphasis on tree-planting involves larger areas becoming privatised for longer periods of time. Individual ownership of land has previously (after the revolution, that is) mainly been associated with individual rights to coconut trees and the land on which these grow. Apart from this, anybody was free to ask the village leadership for permission to cultivate a given piece of land to produce their crops. Today the 'privatised' fields for planting trees imply that less land is generally available within a close distance from the village. It also implies that most women, in order to fetch firewood, must walk farther than they used to. They are not allowed to take wood from other people's fields. I never heard the issue discussed in Uroa. Seeing how tree plantations owned by a few individual men now surround the village, the effect is nevertheless quite striking.

Finally, the arrival of electricity (1990), tourism (1989), seaweed (1989) and the tarmac road (1998) represent developments that produce interrelated effects. In Figure 5.1, the category 'other new activities' sums up some of these. For instance, public transport has increased rapidly during the period. In 1991 there were small buses (*dala dala*) or lorries (*magari*) going to town twice a day. By 2001 they were running every hour, thus also stimulating Uroans to take up work in this sector. In addition, there are three new brick-producing enterprises in Uroa. Their leaders said they had been motivated to start these businesses when the road improved (they do not use electricity for manufacturing bricks). Furthermore, the Tanzanian telecommunications company, Mobitel, established a tower in Uroa in the period in question which would not have appeared without an electricity supply in the neighbourhood.[2] Electricity also provides opportunities for electricians, and the current is used for lamps to keep young chickens warm. In one case, a man makes an income from renting out freezer capacity. Finally, electricity is considered important to managers of a new type of shop that has appeared in the village. The reason for calling shopkeeping a new occupation is its new and profit-oriented focus. Again, transactions (purchasing goods for money) have moved from a network-oriented realm towards more impersonal relations where individuals seek profit.

In sum, the recent socio-economic changes imply that subsistence production is losing importance and this affects family relations in Uroa. The organising of farming and the pattern for sharing products often appear as family corporations. Some hire labourers but most commonly people rely on their own, and their relatives', efforts. This sector, which Figure 5.1 overlooks, continues to represent a significant share in providing households with necessary resources. Fishermen always keep some of the fish for their families and they are partly expected to share this with more distant relatives too.

However, women spend less time in 'land' fields than they used to. Their disappearance into seaweed production probably makes it less attractive for men to open up new fields. Men also farm less than before, apparently. 'The young do not want to do the hard work', Abdalla said, explaining why this is so. With the arrival of new jobs this sounds plausible. On a few occasions people expressed concern for what they perceived to be a tendency to abandon the production of edibles.

When one source of income fails, alternatives are crucial. Today, as in the past, Uroans often spread their efforts over various activities (cf. Anderson and Ngazi 1998). Therefore, the categories given in Figure 5.1 do not represent a picture of a population divided into separate economic realms. Most commonly men have at least two different types of work. Diversification of production activities is one of the Uroan strategies for handling economic uncertainty.

What appears as the most significant trend is the new extent to which monetary transactions characterise economic life. This makes people increasingly dependent on markets outside their locality. The unreliable market for seaweed is striking in this respect and we noticed Meja's vulnerability. This adds to the uncertainty produced by unpredictable variations in the natural environment, which fishermen also fear. Uroans always hope for a calm sea. The tourist market also has its ups and downs and the sector's impact on life is full of paradoxes. In addition to Zanzibaris' limited benefits from tourism and the way they must cope with the sometimes disrespectful behaviour of foreigners, their finances are closely intertwined with development in this sector. When the market is 'good' and foreigners keep coming to Zanzibar, the price of fish rises to the extent that Zanzibaris who do not fish themselves cannot afford to buy it. In 2005 I observed that many of my aquaintances in Uroa did not regularly eat this important source of protein as they had done in 2001. A man from Zanzibar Town explained the situation from his position as a governmental employee with three children to feed: 'nowadays, the big fishes [tuna and kingfish] are only for the tourists'. If nothing is done to increase rural Zanzibaris' share of the benefits (e.g., employment, ownership) provided by tourism, an industry that was conditioned by the arrival of a technology (electricity) intended to provide development in rural areas, the social and economic vulnerability of people in places like Uroa is going to increase. As discussed, electricity has so far had limited effects on people's means for generating an income.

In comparison, electricity has improved public services (water, health and education) in significant ways. In the final chapter I discuss this in the light of electricity's contribution to reducing poverty and providing increased well-being. In the remaining part of this chapter I treat Zanzibari and Uroan discourses of development and account for the ways in which these combine with the changes just described.

Education as an icon of development

Central authorities in Zanzibar regard education as a premise and a means for achieving development. This is definitely a view shared by people in Uroa. In the households interviewed, 95 per cent of boys and 93 per cent of girls (between seven and eighteen years old) attend school. This high attendance-rate is extraordinary in the Tanzanian context. The figures are also much higher than those Larsen indicated for Zanzibar Town in the early 1990s (1995: 70–1). In this comparative light it is also striking that Uroans find education equally important for boys and girls. Based on observations and interviews in other Zanzibari villages in 2006, this appears to generally be (or have become) the case in rural Zanzibar. The way adults in 2001 responded to the question about their own education indicates that the tendency is relatively new. Some 20 per cent of the men and 25 per cent of the women interviewed had never attended school. For the middle-aged and the old men in my material, nearly 40 per cent

Plate 5.3 School children in Uroa, 2001.

reported having never attended school. Among elderly women, non-attendance had been nearly 70 per cent.

The government's goal to provide free education to all has partly failed since the mid 1990s. Not only is a fee of around US$4 required (per child, per year in 2000). Notebooks, pencils and uniforms are also costs parents have to cover. Still, education is acknowledged as 'necessary' (*lazima*) 'in today's times' (*wakati wa leo*). Uroans do not question the need for children's schooling. However, opinions differ as to how early a child should start and how much education is needed after secondary school. A new nursery school (*nasari*) was opened in Uroa in 1999, improving the facilities for the education of children aged between four and six. In 2001, 33 per cent of children of this age attended nursery school, according to my data. Of a total of 136 pupils, 56 per cent were girls. The school also receives pupils from neighbouring villages. When Uroans label their own village as 'developed' compared to other places, they sometimes refer to the nursery school.

Meja and Khamis do not send their oldest daughter to *nasari*. They think this education costs too much and believe it would not put her at an advantage in later classes. In contrast, Silima's daughter attends *nasari* every weekday because her parents believe it is vital to provide her with the best start possible. They also have an older daughter who is about to finish secondary school. To prepare her for the final exams, which will determine her admission into successive schools in town, she receives extra tutoring several times a week from a private teacher. The daughter does very well compared with her mates but Silima wants her to be the best, he says. Therefore, she is excused from helping her mother fetch water, run errands, cook and help with the laundry, tasks other girls often do. As the young girl's parents see it, her future lies to a considerable extent within the education she gets.

Becoming educated and ensuring your children's progress in acquiring formal knowledge is a virtue in Uroa. Many would mention education as a criterion for girls and boys to obtain an attractive marriage partner. Education is also directly perceived to be closely connected with economic prosperity. Governmental jobs require formal education and you are required to master English before you can start working with the tourists. Without such skills one becomes excluded from many of the new job opportunities.

Adults who want to learn to read and write may face a dilemma. Meja (about 30-years-old) was practising letters and words when a senior relative of hers entered the house. 'First TV, now reading!' (*TV kwanza, sasa kusoma!*), the old woman exclaimed. She sounded as if she was making a critical remark and giving a compliment at the same time. Meja would show pride in such situations, but would also laugh and try to play down the importance of her material superiority and her efforts to become 'developed' by learning how to read and write. To her co-villagers, Meja aims to present herself as a modern person. However, she must not demonstrate her modern ambitions too openly, otherwise she runs the risk of becoming a social pariah (see TV dramas below). In her efforts to appear modest, she systematically tries to avoid demonstrating superiority vis-à-vis her relatives and friends. Claiming to be modern too emphatically may incur social risks. In contrast, attendance at modern health institutions poses no dilemmas for modest performance. People regularly go to the health centre for their infants' check-ups, for pregnancy monitoring, or if they have a problem that can be treated with pharmaceutical remedies. In 2001 they had to pay for medicine themselves. This is, yet again, a realm where the government's promises have led to disappointment. However, matters to do with health are sometimes defined as 'Swahili problems'. Therefore, modern medicine, rather than posing a threat to the norm of modesty if overdone, is simply irrelevant in many contexts.

Religious, modern Zanzibar

Religious education also has a central position in Uroa, as in Zanzibar at large. Most Uroan children are sent to Koranic schools (*chuoni*). They start at an earlier age than is the case for secular education. Parents emphasise the importance of receiving religious teaching for somewhat different reasons to those given for secular education. However, religiously and materially informed concerns are not incompatible. Both constitute important elements in the notion of development in Zanzibar where 98 per cent of the population adhere to Islam (McGruder 1999: 105).

Minou Fuglesang notes for Lamu that '[l]ocal discourses about '*maendeleo*' revolve around being 'modern' and still retaining one's identity as a Muslim in the context of a secular and Westernized Kenya' (Fuglesang 1994: 53). In Islamic Zanzibar there is less political tension between secular and religious concerns. People's Muslim identities are not under threat of usurpation by local, competing communities. In rural Zanzibar, the modern, religious discourse centres on what kind of societal changes can be accepted without preventing people from being good Muslims. Here, electricity provides an important means. The light is particularly appreciated for religious purposes, as I show in chapter 7. Furthermore, the new, extended use of tape recorders enables students of the Koran to listen to famous Arabic scholars. In this way electricity helps strengthen the ties between the local community and global Islamic networks. Privately, religious leaders (and secular teachers) are overrepresented amongst those Uroans who have electricity and TV sets at home. Compared to ordinary people, they are also more likely to have aerials that receive overseas channels. Islam in Uroa, as elsewhere, is a modern, global network. With the arrival of electricity Uroans increasingly experience their being part of transnational connections. In short, electricity is celebrated within the modern, Islamic discourse. However, in one particular realm, tourism, which I have so far mainly treated from its socio-economic perspective, the transformations produce unwanted effects.

Scepticism towards tourists arose in Zanzibar in the early 1990s (Parkin 1995). An Islamic fundamentalist movement, consisting of young men in Zanzibar Town, pointed to tourism as a threat and an enemy of Islamic values. David Parkin uses the term 'blank banner' to describe the movement's campaign. He maintains that criticism of tourists and the expressed anxiety for Zanzibari women's purity in reality covered-up for other dilemmas. Parkin claims that the young men's state of unemployment and exclusion from participating in a rising commodity market were the underlying causes. In Uroa the discourse is much more relaxed. Unemployment is seldom an issue due to the natural resources available. I met one unemployed, immigrant worker who said he could not go fishing because he does not know how to do it. His experience directly points to the way that practices in general, not only those recently introduced, require skills and competence. However, dissatisfaction with life and criticism of tourist lifestyles are not related questions in Uroan discourse.

It is primarily religious leaders who articulate a concern with the effects of tourism. They fear Uroans will start adopting tourists' improper behaviour in the long run. Children in particular are considered vulnerable when exposed to unfortunate influences such as tourists' dressing styles and drinking habits or the foreign films on TV. Among adults, people engaged at the hotels are considered to be tempted to lead life in an unacceptable way (see also chapter 7). These individuals themselves appear less worried about such influences.

However, as noted in the beginning of this chapter, ordinary people are sometimes rendered vulnerable in confrontations with tourists. At the same time, those who make a living from this industry have possibilities for income which others are excluded from. Among the young generation a future job working with tourists is a dream. What is more, young men in particular appear to adopt tourist styles deliberately. Some of them wear sunglasses and, in a few cases, shorts. In combination the longing for money and new styles, on the one hand, and the threat inherent in these foreign styles, on the other, appear to make Uroans re-work, negotiate and protect the boundary between themselves and the others.

Television Zanzibar (TVZ)

The drive for change and the emphasis on development is also encouraged by national and global discourses channelled through the media. The radio has for a long time been an important medium in this respect. However, TV has come to play a completely new role in rural areas since the arrival of electricity.

TVZ is an important tool for broadcasting the government's ideology. National development discourse(s) appear daily in Uroan living rooms. 74 per cent of men and 52 per cent of women state that they watch TV at least three times a week. On average they watch for more than two hours on each occasion. Attempts to improve people's living conditions are propagated in the daily emissions. The channel also tries to turn people into efficient citizens in a modern bureaucracy. News, trailers and debates often centre on educational issues, such as the importance of boiling water for drinking, attending health programmes for infants, forest preservation and voting procedures.

The Swahili dramas are particularly pedagogic. Extremely popular in the villages, these series are intended to teach people how they should live. This can be deduced from watching the series and was also explicitly explained to me by a producer from TVZ. Ever since Karume initiated the plans for colour TV in Zanzibar, educational purposes have been of central concern. For instance, one episode would contain the message that educated people will have success while the lazy and backward will lose out in the social competition. Education and hard work fits with Uroan

Plate 5.4 The TV set: a popular evening gathering point, Uroa, 2000. TV is considered an important source of education.

ethics. In addition, the producers want to make people understand that modern health care is better than Swahili remedies. As one producer told me: 'There is no relationship between Islamic and traditional medicine and ethics'. In this way the government tries to persuade people to reduce their engagement with the occult. Here we find a clear discrepancy between central discourses and those going on in the village. The same variation is found when people are advised to boil water during the rainy season or to not cut down living trees. People select the messages they find important. Other aspects are disregarded.

The series also treat the question of proper behaviour extensively. Viewers are warned against adopting Western styles. For instance, people who include too many Western words ('Okay, okay') in their performances are ridiculed in these series. So are people (always men) who appear obviously drunk. Losing control is such a contrast to the ideal of behaviour that it is easy to parody. What the producers have had great success in doing is in giving the dramas an appealing form. People, and particularly women, find them intriguing to watch and rate the dramas as the second most interesting programmes after the news, as shown in Figure 5.2. The television company is obviously aware of people's preferences for various objects. A new scene is often introduced with close-ups showing furniture, adornments and modern appliances such as freezers and TV sets. These items are admired and commented on in Uroa. However, perhaps more importantly, the dilemmas and interpersonal conflicts are raised within a setting comprised of human beings, spirits and material objects which gives enough room for ambivalence, interpretation and humour to become interesting.

Commercial enterprises also promote new kinds of objects as tools for living modern lives. Sportswear, electric water kettles, mobile phones and other commodities and services are displayed daily. There are also commercials for private schools and health clinics. Often, the moment of purchasing is put in focus. By presenting customers and merchandisers who look clean, healthy, materially successful and slightly more Arab than most people in the countryside, the viewers are encouraged to buy the products. Sometimes Western classical music is added. I also find it important that imagined customers often engage in the conversations with great confidence. They ask how things work, but their questions are always relevant and purposeful. To be modern is to be knowledgeable in a certain way.

This presented image of what constitutes modern consumer-behaviour is always linked with the life perceived to be going on in town. Life in town is in many respects an ideal within the development discourse. First of all it represents material opportunities. Sofas in particular are loudly admired. TV sets always appear in these living rooms. In addition, Uroans note what kind of mineral water a waiter puts in front of a couple who are chatting by a restaurant table. Life in town is portrayed as involving a graceful,

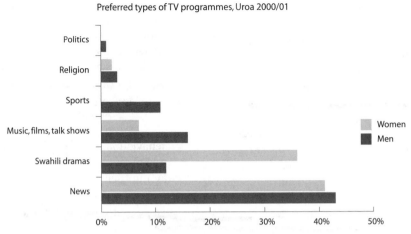

Figure 5.2 Uroans' TV programme preferences. Figures are given in per cent. 14% of men and 14% of women had no opinion.

aesthetic way of living, with no lack of material resources. At the same time, people in the countryside regard life in town as less marked by solidarity, equality and harmony. The ambivalence with regard to town could also reflect a more fundamental uncertainty inherent in how people relate to recent changes.

Towards increasing difference

When I asked Bi Mwatima, an elderly woman, if she had ever heard of the Internet, she started a vivid performance. She acted both parts of an imaginative telephone conversation: 'Hello? How are you? I am fine!' (*Allo! Habari za kutwa? Nzuri!*).[3] Reeling off numbers and talking rapidly and enthusiastically in a high voice, she pretended to live a busy, modern life. As other spectators and I kept laughing, I said I wished this could be recorded on video. She quickly retorted that she would let me do it on the condition that I brought her a TV set. However, Bi Mwatima's house is not connected to the electricity grid. She has never used a phone. New technologies and commodities are out of reach for her. Nor does she have the strength to farm seaweed. In her performance she had ridiculed people who used these appliances. The characters in the conversation were portrayed as being shallow. They were people who apparently had nothing important to talk about. A second later, though, Bi Mwatima showed her vulnerability: 'This is the time of TV. Everybody is busy watching. However, we have nothing, no money' (*Sasa wakati wa TV. Kila mtu anaangalia. Sisi, hatuna kitu, hatuna pesa*). Bi Mwatima's situation evokes Mary Douglas' interpretation of poverty (1982: 16). By not possessing these new objects, Bi Mwatima feels isolated and excluded from development, no matter how much humour she put into the task of answering the question.

What I have shown in this chapter is the significance of a range of socio-economic transformations that have taken place in the village. The gain has not benefited various groups equally. True, seaweed is open to all, but this is also physically demanding work. In addition the market is highly volatile and variations in the natural environment threaten to ruin a farmer's investments. We have also seen that new types of shops and fishing and farming enterprises may be profitable. However, getting loans for new technologes or starting up shops requires investment, networks and alliances. Similar exclusion mechanisms work within the tourist industry, where one's network is highly important. In addition the ability to speak with tourists is an advantage that few adults possess at present. In brief, people's various potentials for profiting from the current transformations depend on their position and capabilities, and these vary for a range of reasons.

We have also seen the way discourses of development initiated in central areas effectively make their way into the countryside. In many ways these serve to set the standard for what it means to live a modern life.[4] Educational institutions are important. Uroans fully support the value of children's education and the nearly 100 per cent attendance-rate speaks for itself. Elements within the central health discourse, notably, are adopted more selectively. Finally, the electronic media make a considerable impact on life in the village. The radio has been important for a long time. Television broadcasts now powerfully channel government rhetoric and present images of people and objects from elsewhere. These institutions and images, in combination with the increasing amount of money, the arrival of more shops with a variety of goods, and people's increased frequenting of town, affect not only people's everyday life, but also the criteria they use for evaluating progress and the good life in general.

That said, Uroans do not simply adopt central discourses. Rather, and in accordance with the general approach to social change employed in this book, people constantly negotiate the validity of various ideas and norms. Let me elaborate by specifying what 'development' means to people in Uroa today. To them electricity (*umeme*) is a sign of development (*maendeleo*, lit. 'moving forward'). In comparison with what has been noted in other parts of the Swahili region where 'recent times are worse times' (Caplan 2004: 5), rural Zanzibaris retain their hopes for development. Electrification is a sign of its manifestation. However, development as an emic term is also highly subject to change and its relationship to electricity is not static. As we saw in chapter 4, a person may use the term in quite shifting and quasi-contradictory ways. We also noted that, at the time of electricity's arrival, not everybody in the village agreed that electricity would bring development.

'Development' is interchangeably and contextually used and may, today, denote phenomena as distinct as access to electricity, piped water, education and lack of conflicts. This is an important premise for how they respond to central discourses of development. In short, they select what norms to adopt and what advice to follow. Such 'selection', notably, is not the result of some kind of voting system where everybody has an equal say. Rather it involves the negotiation of values between groups and individuals who are distinctly positioned. Here, the degree to which one is perceived to be modern becomes a criterion for judgement as I now will show.

Many people in Uroa, particularly younger men, would stress the importance of change and appear to be in agreement with central development discourses: 'Being modern means to get new ideas, to travel and learn'. Another person is quite moralising, even arrogant: 'Those without tapped water do not want development'. In both cases, my acquaintances celebrate the value of change, whether materially or at the level of knowledge and ideas. Simultaneously, discourses of development always entail processes of inclusion and exclusion. They would use the phrase *mtu anaotaka maendeleo* to denote 'a modern person'. Literally, this means 'a person who wants development', thus making direct reference to a conscious way of being.

However, categories describing people as modern or traditional are not clearly defined. No one would characterise himself or herself as a person of days-gone-by (*mtu wa kizamani*). Admittedly, when discussing this topic in the village I often felt that I was forcing my own categories on people. '*Mtu wa kizamani*' could be taken to denote 'a traditional person' but also 'a person living in the old days'. Nevertheless, everybody in the village, also Bi Mwatima, feels that she or he is part of a modern life to some extent. This is partly so due to the arrival of public goods and services, which everybody has a certain claim to. However, when constructing (or being asked to construct) differences between people and groups in the village, development sometimes serves as signifier for the relatively privileged. Zagu, for instance, provided the following classifications in English. First of all, there are the '*shetani* people' (lit. 'spirit people'), that is, those who are only concerned with spirits and the past. Then there are two groups of modern people. Some act modern by copying other people's patterns of consumption. The other class is the 'educated modern', that is, those who combine material development with new knowledge. This was, perhaps not surprisingly, where he would position himself.

Several people pointed out the importance of not copying (*-iga*) other styles. To copy implies to replicate without critically evaluating the consequences. In contrast, 'getting new ideas' (stated in English) or becoming educated in a broad sense (*-pata elimu*) is the legitimate way of modifying one's ways of thinking and behaving. The Uroan modern style thus implies the ideal suppression of impulses to copy unfortunate ways.

Discourses from the centre remain influential but modern styles also involve disregarding parts of the advice coming from the government. Judgements rest with individuals in actual situations. We may regard development as a battlefield of meaning related to what should change and what should remain as it is. In this process some groups are constructed as modern and others as ignorant (cf. Hobart 1993).

This phenomenon is not new. Various attempts to bring about changes in the past were spoken of in terms of development. The notion was actualised in Uroa during the days of electrification and has had its parallels during the introductions of the school, the health clinic and, already in the 1950s, the football ground. Conflicts are generally perceived to have followed. The use of occult forces is always highlighted in such accounts. Similarly, when certain individuals in the past are said to have been using new technologies, such as corrugated iron roofs in the 1970s and 1980s, they are described with reference to development. Significantly, these people also met social sanctions from co-villagers. The stretching of the limits for accepted financial and material behaviour appears inherent in the notion of development. The longing for change and the risks involved are not new.

Nevertheless, there are signs of a certain shift. I once asked a young man in Uroa about his views on development and the threats of sanctions that increasing differences may trigger. Hija, who had been working with tourists and had a higher income than the average Uroan man, replied: 'We, the young, do not listen to the old who threaten with witches if we get [too] much'. He also said that he would go and tell the elders that he will do exactly as it suits him. This quote is interesting because of the way he contrasts modern behaviour with the norm of modesty. Modesty, as mentioned before, is closely linked with the value of equality. Hija clearly plays on a modern style and opposes this with the sense of frugality that characterises village life to a great extent. In addition, despite his fear of elders who might be angry with him, he confronts them (at least theoretically). Here the battle over values has come to the surface.

Hija probably felt encouraged to share these views with me because I am a Western person whose background, he knows, is rooted in references other than those of the knowledge that encompasses the occult. He might therefore have expected my sympathy for this part of the story. However, the young man articulated a criticism of the norm of modesty that seems to be gaining increasing support. His use of the phrase 'we, the young' also signals that a generational conflict is involved. On behalf of a group Hija insists on the right to possess more than others. At the heart of this conflict lies the battle over how modern lives should be lived. Morally, individuals have had certain rights to decide over their own transactions. The present development discourse builds on this legitimacy, but the value of change is now openly celebrated. Together with the recent socio-economic changes and the increased focus on money, these dynamics fuel each other.

Increasing inequality, and increased legitimacy for such stratification, results. At the same time a shift apparently takes place towards a focus on individuals, away from the social networks they engage in. We have not scrutinised how electrical appliances are being used yet, and this will provide important material for the analysis. We may conclude, however, that the realm of production is losing significance as a realm for social interaction. Correspondingly, there are signs that indicate that the realm of consumption is becoming increasingly important for the negotiation of values and the creation of difference.

When I met Hija three years later he was troubled by evil magic and was spending large sums on treatment. His success in modern terms could not prevent him from feeling vulnerable vis-á-vis groups who possessed occult knowledge. What seems clear is that any kind of performance requires knowledge and capability. This was striking when we observed various customers' behaviour during the colonial period. It was also a significant trait of the way the Chairman performed during the days of electrification in Uroa. Today, too, people are positioned distinctly within, and negotiate, the norms for behaviour and success provided by central and local discourses of development. In the following chapter I examine how people deal with their role as electricity customers.

Notes

1. The data is based on interviews with 14 per cent of the 577 men and 14 per cent of the 689 women who resided in Uroa in 2001, and a factor of 7.14 has been applied to estimate the income of the whole population.

2. The construction of the tower was commissioned with an eye on increasing the tourist sector, one of the managers in the company told me. They also had expectations that local demand would grow in the future.

3. The English word 'Hello' (*Allo*) is only used when people speak on the phone and never in face-to-face encounters in rural Zanzibar. In commercials for mobile phones the word is endlessly repeated.

4. I have not been able to treat one of the important institutions in the village for channeling the government's ideas related to development, which is the local administration. This fact is linked to my exclusion from the relevant arenas since 2000 when the political situation in Zanzibar and Uroa became tenser compared to 1991, when I had full access.

Chapter 6

THE ELECTRICITY COMPANY
IN THE VILLAGE

An old lady had a wildly running electricity meter. On one of his regular rounds in April 2001, Baomar went to her house. I accompanied him on this round. The customer's meter stated that the consumption last month had been nine times (227 units) more than what an average household uses. The woman's arrears had risen to far beyond Tsh.100,000 (US$125). After Baomar had left the house the woman asked me, whispering, if I could explain this high use. She had five bulbs and used her freezer only occasionally, she said. When becoming a customer for the first time, she had not mentioned that she intended to procure a freezer. She had kept this information hidden from the company, she said, because it would have made them charge her more. I suggested she turn the freezer off for two months to see what the monthly consumption and cost would be then. Afterwards, I asked Baomar if the reading could be correct. He said it was probably not. Later he told me that he had reported the faulty meter to the company in order to have it replaced with a new one.

This case illustrates aspects of an electricity customer's situation which are of general relevance. The example points to how the utility company and its customers communicate, or avoid communicating. We also see the central focus on the meter. By scrutinising the organisation of electricity in Uroa I shall explore how rural consumers handle their role as customers. Bureaucratic, technical and economic aspects will be looked into. As social phenomena technologies are far from value-neutral. In addition, distinctly positioned human actors within a technological system differ in their concerns and interests. In our case, the relationship between the utility company and its rural customers is crucial. I focus on both the interfaces where the two distinct groups of actors meet and the technical system of which they form part. Baomar's visits to people's homes to register consumption provide an important setting for studying such interfaces. Another arena is the CCM party branch-office in Uroa where people come to pay their bills. I start by positioning electricity within the development discourses.

Linked to the developed world

Ten years after electricity's arrival in Uroa the current itself was not 'news' any longer, but was, rather, taken for granted as part of modern life. In the previous chapter we encountered governmental and local development discourses. Here, electricity is one of the most central markers of who is in and who is out. As an icon of modernity, people expect that everybody 'has a desire for electricity' (*wana hamu ya umeme*). However, differences persist and electric lighting has a powerful way of making them visible. I explore such effects in the next chapter.

Uroa was electrified as a common project. The relatively high number of private consumers in the initial phase meant that household connection soon became regarded as an 'ordinary' thing. I return to normalisation processes in chapters 7 and 8. At this point it suffices to establish that the installation of electricity is not regarded as immodest behaviour and does not incur sanctions.

In relation to various types of occasions where people are expected to provide each other with financial support, electricity belongs in the category of 'voluntary help'. In contrast to contexts in which it is expected that one contribute to covering expenses, such as weddings, funerals and healing rituals, electricity is associated with the realm where individuals (in theory) provide for themselves.

Of the 480 households in Uroa 159 (33 per cent) were registered as electricity customers by 2001. Some also used electricity without being registered, as we shall see. Of the 159 homes, 141 were connected at the time of fieldwork. Another ten were unavailable for meter-reading and interviews. Figure 6.1 provides an overview of appliances which were kept in the 131 remaining, accessible electrified households in Uroa. Such information enhances the discussion of customers' attempts to reduce their electricity bills.

The figures are given in percentage terms of the 131 electrified households that were visited. Electric light bulbs were obviously the first items to be provided. On average, people kept five bulbs. Electricity (*umeme*) is often used as a synonym for electric light (*taa ya umeme*). Radios were also common before the arrival of the electricity grid. Today people keep the radio on most of the day, in some cases even when the house is left empty. One day, when Adam was asked the time, he could not say because there

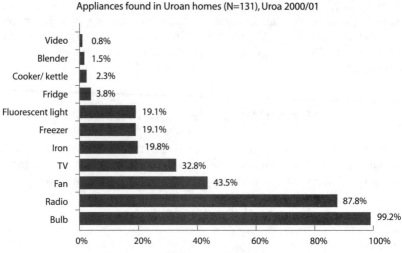

Figure 6.1 Electrical appliances in Uroa.

was a power cut (*sijui; hamna umeme*). Fans are also becoming common. The forty-three TV sets (found in 33 per cent of electrified houses) represented 9 per cent of all Uroan households.

When people relate to electricity in everyday life, their concern is, of course, with these appliances and the secondary objects they produce, such as light, information and entertainment. However, this chapter focuses on their consumption of electric units, meaning to say the commodity that conditions such attractive uses. To demonstrate a modern attitude one is also required to handle the purchasing of the current proper. People's capacity to engage as electricity customers remains our prime focus here.

Authorised installation

When a new customer, normally the male head of a household, wants to get connected to the electricity grid the standard procedure is to contact the electricity company (ZECO) in town. There are papers to be filled in and a fee to pay (US$8 in 2001) before installation can start. When this is accomplished the company sends an employee out who will do the necessary measurements and evaluate whether or not the house is fit for electrification. He notes the distance from the house to the existing grid, which is often the distance to the closest electrified neighbour. This distance determines the type and length of the line. The worker asks the new customer for what purposes the electricity will be used. From this information he registers the appropriate size of fuse, main switch and electricity meter. The customer may now go out and buy the necessary equipment on his own. Frequently it is purchased directly from the utility company. There is also a connection fee to be paid. In addition there is the wiring inside (works, leads, switches and brackets for lamps). Based on information from recently connected households in 2001, each had paid Tsh.100,000 (US$125) on average for connection. However, variations are significant (from Tsh.70,000 in one case to Tsh.220,000 in another), which points to the importance of one's network and thus one's chances of obtaining cables and equipment at favourable prices.

When men were asked about the costs of obtaining electricity and how these have varied over the years everybody said they are much higher these days. Those who played a central role during village electrification in 1990 put this down to the help and goodwill on the part of RUREL. Apparently, Uroans who had signed-on as customers at an early stage had only paid a modest amount of money to get connected. Meters and other equipment had been supplied at low prices, I was told. However, in real terms (as compared to the US$), the cost had not increased from 1991 to 2001 (Winther 2005). The average cost of installation had remained relatively stable during the period. It represented 3–4 months' income from fishing for an ordinary man (without accounting for how income from fish may have varied and regarding the US$ as stable during that period). By 2006, however, total installation costs had gone up to US$300. On top of this cost always comes the purchasing of electrical appliances and the monthly electricity bill. In short, Uroans spent and continue to spend an incredible amount of their resources on electricity.

Illegal connections

Upon returning to Uroa from town with my car one evening just before dusk, I noticed that somebody had recently dug a trench across the road. The earth and sand had been put nicely back in place and the traces were barely visible. Due to the rainy season at this time of the year the signs of the digging would have disappeared by the next morning. When I talked to the owner of one of these houses the following day, I cheerfully asked if the neighbouring house had finally obtained electricity. At first the owner acted as if he did not understand but then, realising that his wife had already told me the news, he admitted that he had helped a relative living next-door. This young man, whose father had died young, depends on my support, my friend told me. Therefore, when the relative had asked for electricity, he had felt obliged to help him. So they had completed the digging last night and were now waiting for an 'expert' (*fundi*) to make the installation. The selection of this time of the year was not accidental. It was crucial to cover the operation vis-à-vis the utility company employees, one of whom lives in the village. However, other co-villagers with bad intentions were also thought to be capable of reporting the case to the authorities.

Such unauthorised, permanent connections would not have been accepted by the electricity company, had they known. In most of the instances I was able to observe, installation was done by connecting the new user on the 'host-user's' side of the electricity meter. In this way, increased electricity consumption caused by the new user would be registered on the host's meter and, thus, paid for. In view of this, people involved in such arrangements do not consider it as stealing from the utility company. They do it to avoid the cost of installation fees and separate meters, switches and fuses. To those who were aware of the minimum charge system, this also provided an additional incentive for shared connections. The utility obviously loses income from this. They also warn against unauthorised installation for safety reasons.[1] Officially, such unauthorised connections are punishable with a fine (US$35 in 2001). The host connectee (the registered customer) is the one held responsible. Uroans, however, partly feel entitled to operate this way, for reasons I shall soon return to.

In contrast, utility company employees (and electricians) accept other types of unauthorised connections, as long as they are temporary. Weddings (one day), funerals (three days) and other kinds of ceremonies provide examples of such occasions. Therefore, it is very common for non-electrified houses to be temporarily connected to the grid. Authorised or unauthorised people simply use an extension lead from one house to the next to make the connection. The reason why electricity is regarded important on such occasions is first of all the quality of the light that it offers. It is considered appropriate to provide the guests with bright light (*mwangaza*) during the long hours they sit together after darkness. Food is always prepared and served and the number of guests may amount to more than a hundred visitors. Light is required for managing this efficiently at all hours. Furthermore, music plays a central role during weddings, both for the purposes of religious and popular songs. Electricity allows for the use of larger amplifiers and loudspeakers. In less affluent families (that is, the average Uroan home), a portable tape recorder suffices. In sum, the use of electricity merges with traditional celebrations (*mila*). In the same way as street lighting, it constitutes a common good in Uroa. It provides people in general with light and music when the occasion requires or allows for it. There is no longer any hesitation about the technology per se.

Entering private space

Baomar is a man in his early thirties employed by the electricity company. His job is to collect monthly readings of electricity meters in domestic and commercial buildings in Uroa and 5–6 other villages as well. He also runs one of the bigger shops in Uroa and offers services to one of the larger hotels in the area with supplies of fish bought at the Uroa fish market. The man has two wives and five children. They all live in his two houses in Uroa.

Baomar is very concerned with doing things quickly. He has bought a small motor bike (*piki piki*) as an effective way of getting around neighbouring villages. He also goes to Zanzibar Town where he reports his readings to ZECO. They call him for meetings once in a while. He considers it inconvenient to go by bus (*dala dala*) as the waiting can be tedious and would necessitate long walks to the bus stops. He is paid the same wage every month, despite the steady increase in the number of meters to check. The young man tries to complete the readings as fast as possible. He has time for a chat with people he knows well, but his style at work is less laid-back than what is usually the case in rural Zanzibar. Also, in contrast to most people in Uroa, he wears and uses a watch.

When approaching a customer's house, Baomar shouts 'Hello?' (*Hodi?*) and then knocks on the door. He does not wait for a reply before he enters the dwelling. Often the female head of the household would interrupt her cooking in the kitchen on the opposite side of the house to come and meet us in the room by the entrance. This is where the electricity meter is normally located. Small children would often appear and enter the house together with us. Often I had the chance to ask the hostess about the kinds of appliances they kept. However, sometimes there was nobody at home. In that case Baomar would quickly note the new figure on the meter and repeat it loudly to me, together with the meter number. On the way out he would tell me the types and numbers of electrical appliances in the visited household.

This way of entering a house (without the owner's invitation) is a new and important consequence of electrification in rural areas. There are no door bells in the village. After '*Hodi?*' has been announced in a questioning manner, one is normally expected to wait for the reply, 'Welcome!' (*Karibu!*), before going inside. The room into which one enters is the living room (*ukumbi*, see Figure 9.1 and Figure 9.2), and this indoor space is highly gendered. Only people with connections to members of the residing family would go further inside. Others would wait outside for the owner to approach them by the door. What we thus note here is that Baomar, on behalf of the governmental utility company, is entitled to enter the house and the living room without asking for permission.[2]

The dates for meter readings are never strictly predetermined, thus people do not know when Baomar will be around. Some have started to lock their doors when they are away, apparently because of a fear of theft in general. The new appliances people keep are said to encourage thieves to come and take things when the house is empty. However, I never heard of items being stolen from private homes in Uroa. People tend to keep valuables locked inside their bedrooms during the daytime. In any case, keeping the main door locked means that Baomar cannot read the meter. In consequence, the customer will not receive the bill for the current month, the next bill will be higher and this is generally seen as negative.

People seldom complain about having utility company employees visiting their homes. Such readings are considered necessary and as a condition for having electricity. This new practice nevertheless breaks with Uroan aesthetics, as referred to above. More concretely, some customers deliberately wish to prevent the utility company from knowing what appliances they keep. As the old woman expressed in the introduction to this chapter, they do this because they think charges (connection fees and successive bills) are dependent on the type of appliances they keep. If used regularly, objects that consume a lot of electricity, such as freezers, will indeed result in larger bills. However, the link comes through consumption and this is where the misconception lies. My concern here is the effect this has on how the monthly visits are perceived. To the few customers in question, these are moments that may reveal their 'cheating' with regard to what appliances they possess.

People who are critical of the government in Zanzibar fear being caught demonstrating their political affiliation. Everybody seems nervous about politics (*siasa*) in today's Zanzibar. However, those committed to the political opposition are, of course, most exposed to sanctions. The employees working for ZECO in Unguja effectively report activities considered unfortunate in this respect. By this they demonstrate some accuracy in suggesting that the electricity system directly serves the government's purpose of also controlling the population in a strictly political sense.

Furthermore, the continuous evaluation and social control of appropriate levels of consumption makes public-inspection sensitive. Here, the public is more related to Baomar's identity as a co-villager. His knowledge of what is to be found on the inside of houses poses a potential threat in this context of frugality. Decisive moments arrive when new possessions are obtained and become public knowledge. Visible increments in affluence may disturb others and cause sanctions. The local public-inspection may here provide the wrong people with vital information.

Moreover, the relationship between a utility company employee and customers may be particularly delicate. The encounters sometimes create situations where both parties are rendered vulnerable. Many stories of how illnesses and problems got started are directly associated with a meeting with a person or a spirit, such as this quote reveals: 'It was after he visited this house that my problems began'. The transfer of evil often takes place through physical encounters. For those who are not on good personal terms with the employees, the monthly visits directly result in customers' perceptions of increased risk. The meter-readers, on their part, try to balance their duties as employees with their role as villagers, and attempt to avoid dangerous encounters. I spoke with one employee who takes care not to enter three particular homes when the owners are present. This older man has recently been seriously ill and ascribed his problems to the 'witches' (*wachawi*) among his customers. As is generally the case, employees seem particularly exposed when they reach a relatively high level of affluence. In sum, this highlights the dilemma of holding a dual identity as a villager and a government officer simultaneously. Rituals of protection are the only remedies for resisting malevolent attacks.

Electrification has thus changed the norms and practices regarding who might enter which house and when. The corporation's regular access to domestic homes overrides the culturally informed aesthetics for visiting. However, in cases where he is directly involved in controversies, the meter-reader modifies the actions he is formally prescribed to perform. In sum, the government's entering living rooms constitutes a remaking of boundaries which, to me, appear to be more abrupt than subtle (cf. Lien 2003). The consequences are more complexly demonstrated, though. This is partly due to the fact that few people preoccupy themselves with this phenomenon. It is a voluntarily, chosen act to become a customer and I think this informs people's acceptance of the government's increasing control. The control is an aspect of the 'lock-in' that accompanies the customer relationship (Southerton et al. 2004; see also Akritch (1994) and the similar notion of 'scripts' in relation to electricity). However, there is little doubt that engaging in a relationship with the utility company implies being submitted to increased monitoring. In many cases this also implies increasing tension. When customers are cut off from their supply, as I show below, these are the moments that most strikingly illustrate the government's legitimacy and ability to intrude in people's lives. At such times the meter-reader experiences his split loyalties as particularly difficult. For now we shall study how an appropriate customer–utility relationship is inscribed in one of the objects that come with the electricity system, that is, the electricity meter.

Measuring proper behaviour

Electricity meters (*mita*) are designed to measure electricity-use. The device codifies and states the amount of units consumed, which is the reference used for billing the customer. The kWh-meter is widespread in rural Zanzibar. They are imported, often second-hand, from various parts of the world.

I find it useful to follow Madeleine Akrich (1994) and Bruno Latour (1994) in their way of scrutinising the materiality of technical objects. My purpose is to investigate the content of the meter as a 'black box' in the context in which it is used in rural Zanzibar (Latour 1987: 130–1). The authors keep a close eye on the networks of heterogeneous relations in which technical objects are developed and put to work. From its initial stages, an electricity meter is shaped in accordance with designers' ideas about potential future users. However, not only is the meter delegated the specific function of measuring consumption, norms for proper use also come inscribed in the artefact. It is in this sense that Akrich and Latour speak of artefacts as non-human actants. In their materiality, objects partly determine what people will do. This is why studying the meter's script is important for understanding the relationship between customer and utility, and in consequence, how the arrival of electricity has influenced social life.

To a lay person, the kWh-meter appears as a concealed, impenetrable box. A circulating wheel is displayed through a transparent plastic window on the front. When the wheel moves this signals that electricity is being supplied, consumed and measured. Below the wheel is a display which shows the registering of consumption in figures. Now, as expressed by representatives of the company as well as in the written conditions of supply (what Akrich (1994) labels 'pre-scriptions'): 'The Consumer shall

Plate 6.1 Electricity meter inside a private home in Uroa, 2000.
The device is connected to the main switch (to the left) and a fuse-holder (above). A card for recording the customer's monthly consumption is kept together with the meter (to the right). The sacred paper fixed to the lead (to the extreme left) is a charm intended to protect the house, the objects it contains and the people residing there.

not interfere or permit any person, not being an officer or servant of the Corporation to interfere in any way with the metering equipment'.[3] In sum, the meter presumes, measures, and evaluates the correct behaviour of each party. The supplier should provide current and issue correct bills. The customer should remain passive vis-à-vis the device and pay for the amount used. The device ensures a symmetric relationship.

The meter's configuration with other technical objects is also important. It is presupposed that meters are connected to switches and fuses. The current enters the building from the low-tension grid and passes through a main switch. From the switch, the current enters the meter. On the other side of the meter, the current passes through the fuse holder with a detachable fuse. Finally, leads are stretched to the various outlets in the house.

The task of surveying the safe use of electricity has been delegated to the main switch and the fuse. Without the latter, the circuit could blow. Customers who want to use electricity must adhere to rules of conduct. They must not open the meter and they must not remove the fuse. However, they do not have to be told by anyone how to behave. The materiality and configuration of fuse, fuse holder, and meter script such action tacitly.

An obedient customer who uses electricity awaits the reading while making his home available. He receives his bill, pays it on time, and performs according to the contract. However, the meter can also be manipulated by the customer. In this case, consumption might not be recorded at all. What now appears is a modified electricity meter which no longer represents a symmetric relationship. As a modified actant, the meter omits to accurately report consumption to the electricity company. Done cleverly by the owner, the meter may be disconnected and reconnected from time to time so as not to raise suspicion. A household known to be users of electricity would soon be revealed by a meter that reported zero consumption. Moreover, there is then the danger of being caught with a non-functioning meter at the time of the monthly reading, as will be seen below. In such cases the illegal configuration of the meter has immediate consequences for the owner who is held responsible (and who is subject to disconnection and/or a fine). The condition of the bodywork of the meter is thus the basis for judging if the device has been used in ways that conform to the norms it represented in the first place.

Payment time: humbleness and resistance

It was time to pay the monthly electricity bill in Uroa. As usual, customers (men and a few women and children) started to appear in the CCM party's branch-office located centrally in the village. One bill is issued per meter (thus some men receive several bills). Baomar collects them in town and distributes them in the village about ten days before payment is due. Either he gives the piece of paper to the residents of each house or he hands them out to neighbours or children who are to pass the bills on to the proper owner. The bills are produced by a computer, thus the paper's text is printed. They state the number of units consumed, the previous balance, the number of days used for reference, the VAT, the sum due for payment and also give some other information. Generally, invoices are considered an important means of communication between the utility company and the customer. In Zanzibar some of the text is written solely in English, an incomprehensible language for the large majority of the rural population. However, warnings to the customer are, notably, also stated in Swahili.[4] In this way the utility company expresses a certain degree of distrust in their customers, without displaying the capacity or willingness to render other types of information accessible. There is here a striking parallel to draw with the situation of the customer on 'the Other Side' in Zanzibar Town in the 1950s whom we encountered in chapter 2 and who could not read and write. Both situations point to a considerable degree of bureaucratic arrogance. Despite my attempts over the years to communicate the need to provide bills in Swahili, by 2006 ZECO had not made any steps in this direction. In any case, to return to Uroa and the CCM office, potential offenders now continued to arrive in the room with bills and cash. The queue grew longer and we sat down to wait our turn.

Two clerks from ZECO's office in town had arrived by car. They were ensconced behind a desk, ready to collect money and sign receipts. The man was in shirtsleeves, tie and a *kofia* (an Islamic hat for men), which he later removed. The lady arrived in a black veil (*bui-bui*), which she removed, and a dress. She did not keep her hair covered once inside, in contrast to Uroan women who always keep a head veil (*kanga*) on in cross-sex spaces such as this. The woman from town also wore golden earrings, necklaces and bracelets, which are objects out of reach to most women in Uroa. Both clerks had watches showing 'International time' (that is, six hours different from Swahili time).[5]

The aesthetic contrast between the people from town and the village residents coming to pay their bills was not only related to their distinct ways of dressing. Their different manners and styles were also striking. Customers humbly approached the desk and spoke in low voices. The seated clerks seemed to feel free to speak loudly, particularly in the case of a misunderstanding or insufficient payment from the customer's side. A couple of customers did not understand how much they had to pay and were simply told how much money they should provide.

Others demonstrated doubt as to the correctness of the stated balance. In these cases quiet conversations went on for a while, sometimes with Baomar intervening to explain. If the customers persisted voices would be raised. Such dialogues often ended with the customer having to admit that he would not be able to pay the whole amount. The parties then agreed

Plate 6.2 Mr Kassim Moh'd Ali 'Nondo' paying his monthly electricity bill at the CCM office in Uroa, 2001.

that he would pay a larger share on the next occasion. It is significant that everyone present witnessed such discussions. In this way the particular way of organising payment produces a new type of public space. This provides villagers with increased insight into each other's financial circumstances. Being a customer and arriving to pay without sufficient cash locks a person into exposing his situation to others.

It is perhaps not so strange that quite a few avoid coming to pay. On the other hand, people seem to have a relatively good idea about other people's income and expenditures in Uroa anyway. The intriguing question appears to be how some individuals of relatively equal material status as the others are able to make more than the rest. Perhaps the demonstration of one's inability to pay for electricity in fact provides a form of social safety. In Cairo, in contrast, Wikan observed that public exposure of a family's inability to pay their expenses, such as the electricity bills, put them in a situation of the gravest of shames vis-à-vis their social network (1996: 19–20). In Uroa people's feelings of disgrace in such situations seem more a product of their relationship to the utility company itself. They certainly want to perform well in their role as modern customers, and also in relation to co-villagers. In any case their shared, humble body-language and the results of their attempts to negotiate show that few of them fully succeed.

In contrast to most customers who turned up to pay, Rashid firmly took up his charges against the company. In appearance he looked very different from the clerks as he came in barefoot with filthy, torn clothes and with a battered straw hat. He is, however, a respected man who had come directly from his work in the fields. He also runs many additional projects. Like many other customers that day, Rashid had difficulties accessing sufficient cash. However, unlike most of his co-villagers, who expected critical remarks and hoped for mercy, Rashid started by announcing to the clerks that there was something he wanted to discuss. He complained about increasing tariffs and the corporation's failure to distribute bills on time. Then, with a clear voice, he explained his own situation. He presented a suggestion as to how he could pay a certain amount today and the rest later. The discussion went on and nearly developed into an argument ('Listen to me!' – 'No, you listen to me!' (*Sikiliza! – Sikiliza!*)).

By the time the negotiations were over they had agreed that, of the Tsh.70,000 (US$82) Rashid owed the company, he would pay only Tsh.5,000 (US$6). On his way out, Rashid shook his head. The event was in one sense a victory in that he had demonstrated his ability to discuss these difficult matters on equal terms with the employees and proven his powers of negotiation. However, the debt was far from serviced, and his discontent with the system remained. I later learned that his objections against the company are also related to the handwritten notes which may easily be fixed, according to the customer. He had more trust in the receipts one gets in town because these are produced by a computer (*kompyuta*). He thus regards machines as more reliable and neutral than employees who he suspects will try to benefit from their position.

One may describe Rashid as a villager who embodies more of an ability to perform as an electricity customer than his co-villagers. He does not hold a political position but focuses on the various activities that give him a considerable income in comparison to the average villager. The man emphasises the importance of education and speaks English. In a situation such as the above, he has resources at hand which indicate a considerable amount of knowledge.

Considering people's generally modest income in Uroa, the fluctuating markets and the unstable natural environment they depend on, it is not surprising that many customers have problems settling their electricity bills. However, most people somehow manage, if with something of a time lag which incurs an increment in debts. In April 2001 the monthly minimum bill was Tsh.1,680 (US$2). On average, the one hundred customers on this tariff in Uroa had accumulated Tsh.11,500 (US$13.50) in arrears to the company. This means that they were 5–6 months behind in their payments.

It might seem that ZECO purposefully keep their customers from becoming knowledgeable about the system. The use of the English language and the lack of efforts to explain to customers the invoicing and accounting system both point in this direction. Whatever the case may be, I shall argue that the incomprehensible system causes not only local frustration that could have been avoided. It also contributes in people's increasing distrust of the company. As a result, unauthorised connections become legitimised. This practice, in turn, results in the company losing potential income.

The consumption of electricity: a high awareness of the cost

Uroans in general show a strong concern for keeping their consumption (of electricity, but also of other fuels) as low as possible in order to reduce costs. In contrast to the 'folk units' customers in a Michigan study referred to when measuring their electricity use (that is, dollars (Kempton and Montgomery 1982)), people in rural Zanzibar speak directly of the (physical) units (*yuniti*) they use. Therefore, from their verbal expression of the matter, Uroans appear well-positioned to understand and control their own consumption compared to customers in Michigan. However, speaking of units is not synonymous with grasping how consumption is converted into monthly payments. The minimum payment here blurred the situation to a considerable extent. I return to this after showing Uroans' high awareness of how much various appliances consume. Rural customers are also very economical in their methods of using electricity.

At dusk lights are turned on in space occupied by people. The five bulbs in a typical household are seldom in use at the same time. Fluorescent lighting (9 W or 11 W) is said to consume less energy and give brighter light, which is in accordance with what a technician would say. Fans are put to work in bedrooms only in the hot season, and then only at the time when people go to sleep. Radios and TVs are used daily in every home that has one, but are considered to consume little energy (again, in accordance with the level of power they are stated to use).

Freezers tend to be turned on and off on a daily basis in order to save electricity.[6] On ordinary days the freezer would be put to work during the night and turned off in the morning with cool drinks and sweet ice (*malai*) ready for consumption. At Ramadan, the pattern is the opposite. Discussing and doubting the effect of saving energy in this way, I suggested to one family that they let the freezer run continuously for one month (I covered the cost). In this way we could compare the consumption of kWh for the two ways of using the appliance. Their theory proved to be right. The amount of units went up during the testing month.[7]

Finally, people's use of electric water kettles also shows their concern for keeping consumption to a minimum. In one family the procedure always started with measuring the quantity of cold water that would fit into a thermos flask (for tea). Then the appropriate amount of water would be

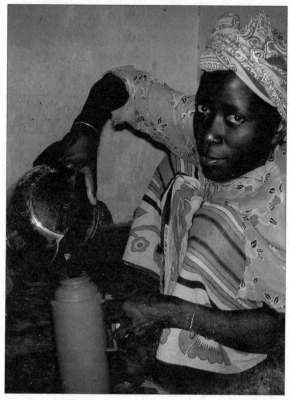

Plate 6.3 Ms Kazija Khamis preparing for tea at her home in Uroa village, 2001.

boiled in the kettle and, again, poured into the flask. In sum, people in Uroa are extremely cautious in their energy use. In the light of this, they also say that electric cookers are not used because they 'eat a lot of units' (*yanakula yuniti sana*).

These practices demonstrate that Uroans have extended knowledge of electricity consumption. Men and women know exactly which appliances contribute more to increase total consumption and which consume so little that they can be used extensively. In short, they know the relationship between an appliance's power (W), the amount of time it is used (h) and its resulting contribution to the total consumption (kWh). What tended to be misperceived, at least at the time when miminum bills were issued, was how consumption was linked with payment.

Problems caused by the accounting system

Many rural customers exposed their limited knowledge of the accounting system. The most widespread misunderstanding regarded the minimum tariff system. In 2006 this system had finally been abandoned and replaced by a fixed 'service charge' plus the payment for the monthly kWh consumption. Although I am highly in favour of the new system, for reasons that will become clear, the accounts of the days of the minimum bill system are worth recording.

I was puzzled myself when observing that the 'minimum tariff' in fact varied from month to month. The logic of the system was as follows: regardless of the level of consumption up to a limit of fifty units per month, a customer pays the minimum charge. The reference for billing is thirty days, and this is what complicates the calculation. These thirty days are what the amount of Tsh.1,680 refers to. However, Baomar and his colleagues would not read meters on the same date every month. Therefore, according to the intervals between two readings, the period could be longer or shorter than thirty days. In consequence, the minimum payment was perpetually adjusted.[8] Now, many customers (wrongly) interpreted these changing amounts as the result of their own varying consumption. In consequence, they tried to reduce electricity-use to a minimum to avoid high charges. When the monthly sum remained elevated (though changing each month), disbelief, frustration and distrust in the company resulted. On average, the households in question only used twenty-five units in March 2001. In other words, they could have doubled their electricity consumption without having to pay more than they already did.

From the perspective of sustainable development one could say that Uroans' modest electricity behaviour is in accordance with global discourses' concern for the environment. Keeping consumption low is an international goal which saves on the burning of polluting fuels and the construction of new dams for hydroelectric power. However, 'development' also constitutes a fundamental part of the notion. This was what the RUREL project was meant to bring to rural areas. What was so striking in 2001 was the target group's attempt to save electricity in everyday life without experiencing the benefits of such thriftiness. They could have kept the lights on for more hours without having to pay more, but few were, in 2001, aware of this. The consequences of this are best demonstrated by looking at a few extreme cases. Some of the points also continue to be relevant after the abandonment of the minimum bill system.

One man had reduced his electricity consumption from five units the previous month to three units in March 2001. This corresponds, in theory, to the burning of one single bulb (60 W) for one and a half hours per day (technical losses not accounted for). Still, and beyond this committed man's knowledge, he would nevertheless have to pay for fifty units. He did not show up on the day to settle his arrears. These had risen to Tsh.9,900 TSH at the time. The sadness of such stories lies in how people struggle to avoid economic hardship and yet how they fail to accomplish their goals. In addition, perhaps even graver, his omitting to show up to ask the company why his bills were getting so high indicates his state of disempowerment. It is difficult to initiate a dialogue with a party you feel indebted and subordinated to. Instead his debt is increasing, together with his fear of sanctions.

Another customer had been living in town for eight months and closed his house in Uroa. During this period he was charged the minimum tariff each month. His debt had reached the unique level of Tsh.139,969 (US$165) in April 2001. In such cases, a customer may go to ZECO in town to arrange for a temporary stop in supply (from 2006 the same applies in order to avoid accumulation of the 'service charge'). However, such regulations are very rarely known to people. The unfortunate result in this case is obvious.

A shopkeeper in a neighbouring village faced a rather different situation. The customer had paid Tsh.14,000 the previous month but, strangely enough, the company owed him Tsh.52,000. I first went to talk to the owner himself, but the old man said: 'I do not understand anything about units' (*Sifaham kabisa yuniti*). He usually sends his son to town to pay the electricity bill.[9] However, the boy has also had problems understanding the system: 'That son of mine goes to town to pay, but he too does not understand'. Speaking to the son, I learned that he had thought the figure at the bottom of the bill indicated the amount his father owed the company. Therefore he had tried to raise sufficient funds when paying bills the previous year; but the debt only seemed to increase every time. Finally, he had asked a cashier at the company about this problem. He was told that the company was in fact indebted to his father. The man did not show relief after having settled the problem despite the fact that he had 'received' a considerable amount of money on behalf of his father. He explained the story in detail so as to share with me how the misunderstanding had come about.

In sum, electricity customers in Uroa have a thorough understanding of appliances' consumption of electricity. However, the regulations and the billing and accounting system continue to be obstacles preventing people from feeling at ease in their role as customers. Regulations, such as the option for voluntary cuts of supply, continue to be poorly understood. The English language in bills has been noted and questioned. Few customers are able to check their own meters as to the actual level of consumption. Furthermore, we noted that the meters are not always trusted to do their job to ensure that a symmetric relationship is maintained. This results in yet further scepticism and accusations made against ZECO.

Disconnection

On 18 May 2001 it was time to cut off some of the bad payers in Uroa from connection to the electricity grid. When the last customer to pay his/her bill had left the CCM office, Baomar and the ZECO employees discussed the situation. While looking at outstanding arrears and those who had not come to settle their bills, the meter-reader gave his colleagues his opinion. One customer had paid the Tsh.8,000 stated on his bill. However, the local employee said he knew this man kept several energy-demanding appliances and that his bill should have been far higher. He suspected the man of disconnecting his meter from time to time, so as to have only a small proportion of his consumption recorded. The employees decided it was hard to prove this case as everything would probably technically be in order at that point in time. Instead they would start by visiting another suspicious house. Here, the electricity had been cut off several months ago. However, recently, the house had been observed with lights on in the evening. Below is an extract from my field notes, written after I followed the local employee and his three colleagues from town to check up on this customer.

> We passed along various paths in the village. The men walked fast, speaking together but not paying attention to the people who were watching us from their houses. There were no greetings when we passed people on the road. I soon started to feel uncomfortable. There was a possibility that people would look on me as belonging to ZECO, working for them, or worse, that I had misused their confidence. Now it could seem that I had been a spy for the government and the company all the time. To run off and get to the houses independently and before the ZECO staff was not an option. In that case I would have to warn the customer about what was going to happen and obstruct ZECO in doing its job. At the same time, I had wished to observe such occasions for quite some time. When we approached the target, the local employee gave instructions as to how to find the house. He went to sit and wait at another place. He did not want to be involved in the physical disconnection proper. 'He is too close' one of the other men told me, 'it is his relative' (*ni ndugu yake*).
>
> The four of us continued. They found the house. I realised it was where I had attended a wedding a couple of months previously. Neighbours were watching in silence. Nobody was greeting or smiling, as they normally would. One of the men went to the neighbour's house. The other two knocked on the door (no *hodi*) and went inside to find the meter. Inside there were some greetings between them and the young man who was present. Then there was silence. One of the men checked the meter. He wrote down the meter number and read the number of units on the display. Then he used his screwdriver and opened the small part down to the left. There, one wire was loose. They showed me this and said loudly in English: 'This is very bad'. The boss dramatically announced that the fine for this is one hundred thousand and if this is not paid, then the person will be taken to jail (*kamatwa*). Children who had entered the room smiled at first but soon understood that something was wrong, so they did not say anything.

The customer had been cut off before. At the time, ZECO had confiscated the fuse. The circulation of fuses makes them easy to obtain, however, and the customer had had one reinstalled himself. This time the meter was disconnected and removed to be taken to town. In addition one of the men climbed onto the neighbour's roof and separated the thief's cable physically from the grid by the use of a knife. At this point the customer's wife came home with a child in her arms. She looked straight-faced and showed no feelings or signs of recognising me. She stood in silence and watched until the operation was completed. I approached her by saying 'I am sorry' (*Pole*). She replied with a sober expression that this was no problem at all (*hakuna neno lolote*), which made me think that she was indeed concerned. However, she did not beg for sympathy or lose control of herself. When I later spoke with some of the neighbours, they suspected the owners now felt shame (*aibu*).

This intrusion into what used to be private space, and the violent way of stripping electrical gear off the house along with the threats of prison demonstrate the power ZECO possesses to punish disobedient customers. The incident was obviously not pleasant for the customer's wife. She had to face another moralising lecture from the employees and the curiosity of neighbouring witnesses. The huge fine they received probably made it difficult for the family to reconnect for a long time. In terms of Baomar's dilemma, the story speaks for itself.

By way of ending this chapter I shall sum up some of the ethics involved in various types of connections to the electricity grid. I discuss this in light of the customers' general lack of knowledge of regulations and the accounting system.

Striving to behave like modern customers

The ethics involved in various types of connections to the grid can be considered along a continuum. At the one extreme we find the ideal relationship between customer and utility, a relationship based on mutual trust, continuous supply and correct measurement, registering and payment. On the other side, we have incidents such as the disconnection described above. Here, the customer is caught in the act of an obvious and well-calculated theft. In between there are other types of connections which are not strictly legal. However, they have various degrees of moral support in the village as well as among utility workers and electricians.

Electricity is considered a necessity during weddings and funerals. An electrician commented on this practice: 'it is an expense for the utility, but we show humanity' (*ubinadamu*). In a way this gesture resembles the special tariffs during Ramadan that the British government occasionally provided during colonial days. However, where the colonial power appeared to make such offers after pressure from certain groups, the electrician expresses a more enduring concern. His reference to humanity says a great deal about how the relationship between people and electricity is currently perceived.

Then there are the unauthorised connections, called 'direct current' (*umeme direct*) or '*komba*' (lit. 'to spend other people's money'), such as the one my neighbour prepared for that evening. As long as consumption is registered by a meter, this is not condemned in the village. It is not preferred but may pass if somebody wants to help another person. A poor man would notably be met with more acceptances for asking somebody to help in this way than a more affluent man. The receiving party is expected to pay a little for the service. Quite interestingly ZECO staff said that such connections were acceptable, until recently, for one particular kind of household. Men with several wives living in neighbouring houses were allowed to make 'direct current' installations. The justification for such connections is that a husband with several wives should not have to pay the double (or triple) for connection fees and equipment. When practical circumstances allow for it, the morality is that one meter suffices per man. Apparently due to increasing emphasis on safety, utility staff members say that they no longer accept such arrangements.

People generally agree that non-registered consumption is bad (*bila mita; hile ndo mbaya*). This is considered to be theft. However, again, a consumer's possession of economic resources is relevant for evaluating his way of connecting to the grid. Similarly to the contextual judgements of 'direct current' connections, a rich man using electricity without a meter is judged more strictly than a poor man would be. This is linked with the non-determined character of Uroan social life. In addition this inconsistency when judging various types of electricity connection is related to how people perceive their counterpart, the utility company. In sum, we see that what constitutes 'stealing' is subject to local definition and may differ for a variety of reasons.

ZECO is a big player and is regularly accused in the Tanzanian press of cheating its customers. The utility company's authority and rural customers' subordinated role is demonstrated when ZECO enters households, during payment time and, thirdly, through the company's practice of disconnecting disobedient customers. At the same time the company supplies people with a commodity they 'long for'. ZECO also, of course, needs a return for their services in order to keep the company running. In general they have a huge problem collecting arrears from an increasing mass of consumers. Therefore, the parties are bound together in a long-term interdependent relationship (cf. the image of a 'married couple' in chapter 2).

The changing boundaries of the citizen–state relationship since the arrival of electricity are important and involve the fact that the state has got increasing control over the electricity-consuming population. Becoming a customer means being registered as an individual within the bureaucratic system. Subsequently one's consumption is measured and registered and one is asked to pay. This involves a multifaceted shift of the boundary between a person and the Zanzibari authorities. Through the new formal and financial connection the government's presence in people's lives is intensified. An economic bond is created which was not there before. Also, the physical boundaries as to where a person (the meter-reader) has the right to keep his body are influenced by the arrival of the electricity system.

To a large extent, rural customers in Unguja appear to accept the way they are subject to control and sanctions from the utility company and/or state. They have chosen to become consumers and acknowledge the package that comes with it. However, when noticing signs they perceive as evidence of the company being flawed, the anti-utility discourse gains weight. 'Signs' can be dysfunctional meters, handwritten notes, erroneous bills, failure to distribute bills, etc. Customers also use the sanctions they have available. Either they can make unauthorised connections. Such practices enjoy local legitimacy to a considerable extent. Alternatively customers can show dissatisfaction by refraining from servicing their debts. Such measures are, of course, also closely linked to actual inability to pay. Although non-payment has consequences for the utility company in the first instance, avoiding paying quickly backfires on the customer. Due to people's fear of generating debt to the government, a radically new phenomenon in itself, most try to avoid this. The threat of fines and prison are often spoken of.

I have also shown the significance of customer knowledge in this picture. Inadequate awareness of regulations and the invoicing system not only produces uncertainty and discomfort for the customer, it also results in increasing distrust in the company. The majority conclude that ZECO is not accountable. However, the majority also wish to perform in proper ways. Those who steal are exceptions. There will probably always be some degree of mistrust between the two parties. However, further adjustments could improve people's experience of how they 'perform' as customers. Today they are quite confident as modern consumers when they turn the TV set on. With a little more initiative on the utility company's side, this could also be the case (at least to a greater extent than today) when people go to pay their bills at the CCM office.

Plate 6.4 Ms Zuhura Salum Mchenga, of Uroa, explaining the use of appliances to people in Uzi village, Unguja, July 2005 (photo: Henrik T. Bentzen). In the background is Mr Makame Hassan Juma, who is also from Uroa and part of the team. The meeting formed part of an information project intended to improve the communication between ZECO and potential customers in villages to be electrified (see SUM 2005).

Plate 6.5 Audience in Uzi village watching and listening as Mr Ali Abeid Haji, from ZECO, accounts for the way electricity meters work at an information meeting, July 2005 (photo: Henrik T. Bentzen).

Plate 6.6 Mr Omar Khamis 'Baomar' reading the electricity meter at a shopkeeper's house in Uroa, 2001.

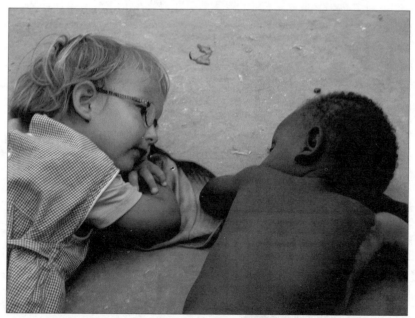

Plate 6.7 Anna and Sele getting to know each other, Uroa, 2000 (photo: Henrik T. Bentzen).

Plate 6.8 Girls in Dikoni, Uroa, fetching water after school, 2001.

Plate 6.9 Dikoni, Uroa, by night, 2005 (photo: Henrik T. Bentzen).

Notes

1. ZECO staff hold that unauthorised installation increases the risk of short circuits and trouble with earth connections. Fire may result from poor installations. This is why each house should have its own main switch.

2. ZECO's Conditions of Supply, #14, states: 'Authorised officers of the Corporation are entitled to enter a Consumers [*sic*] premises at all reasonable times for purposes connected with the supply of electricity to the premises'.

3. ZECO 2001, Conditions of Supply, #16.

4. The sentences 'Balance of previous payment' and 'Payment received – cash – thank you' are not given in Swahili. In contrast, reminders of the importance of paying are, e.g., 'Please settle your bill before the due date to avoid disconnection' (*Tafadhali sawazisha bili yako kabla ya tarehe ya mwisho kuepuka kutatiwa umeme*). Also in Swahili is: 'Please ensure that your meter reading is correct' (*Tafadhali hakikisha kuwa somo la mita ni sawa*).

5. In Swahili time, the first hour of the day (*saa moja*) is when the sun rises (seven o'clock). In everyday speech in the Swahili language people refer to Swahili time. Those working with governmental institutions and tourists tend to adjust their watches (if they have such things; very few do) according to 'International time'. When speaking English 'International time' is used.

6. Of the twelve 'freezers in the census sample two did not have a freezing capacity and would, in English, be better described as refrigerators. In Uroa the difference between a *friza* and a *friji* is related to their distinct shapes. A *friza* is placed horizontally on the floor while a *friji* is standing and can be opened in the same way as one opens a door.

7. The family said they had not otherwise changed their use of electricity for other purposes during this month. They were just as interested in the results as I was and only kept relatively low-consumption appliances (light, TV, radio and a fan) apart from the freezer.

8. Thus with a period of twenty days between readings the minimum tariff would be Tsh.1,120. Periods of forty days would make the minimum amount Tsh.2,240.

9. ZECO does not come to collect payment in this village as they do in Uroa. Thus customers must go to town once a month to settle their bills.

Chapter 7

UROA BY NIGHT

At night-time, if you were to return to Zanzibar and observe the east coast of Unguja from above in a plane, there would be long stretches of nothing but darkness. Depending on the moon, and with the help of kerosene lamps indicating human settlements, you might be able to make out the coastline. What would not escape your attention would be the halogen floodlights that light up a number of hotels along the coast. Tourism is certainly visible at night and demonstrates its influence in this indiscrete manner. However, not far from the hotels, you would also see several villages lit up by electricity. They are more modestly equipped. However, here and there, there are stronger points of light placed in lines, indicating street lighting. The sight tells you that these places have changed.

This way of introducing a discussion of electricity's symbolic significance in Uroa might seem a little odd. The above passage is seen through the eyes of a travelling individual and, in the present economic circumstances, he or she is unlikely to be a person from rural Zanzibar. One may thus rightly ask for whom electric light has come to have the particular meaning I have indicated above. We are, however, in a position to say something on this point. To Uroans electricity is associated with development and is synonymous with progress. They strive to be electricity customers but they are quite content with displaying their icons of modernity. In Uroa electricity and artificial light reflect and produce prestige. Therefore, Uroans would share the view that such 'enlightened' spots in the landscape are markers of significance and, also, difference.

At the same time Barbara Bender reminds us that human encounters with time and landscape are characterised by untidiness and contradictions (2002). The meanings people attribute to place are not unequivocal, they are multiple and shifting. People and their physical surroundings mutually create each other and these dynamics occur within matrixes of power relations in which one's position is crucial (ibid.). Perceptions of Uroa as a place are likely to be unsettled. By way of narrowing down the topic, I start by touching upon the materiality of electric light.

A universal feature of light is that it attracts the eye. The stronger the beam, the more attention is given to it. At least this is the case up to the point where it becomes uncomfortable, such as when watching the sun. Bright light can render one incapable of seeing anything at all. In addition, light is relative – the stronger light will usurp the weaker light. Therefore, objects positioned near to a strong light source are less visible than they would be without the neighbouring 'star'. From the aerial perspective, the beams from Uroa cause neighbouring villages to momentarily disappear. Given electricity's conceptual significance and the way electric light reconstructs physical space at night, my first interest lies with the way people's use of electric light outdoors produces and reflects differences.

Secondly, perceptions of space and time are closely interwoven. I point to some significant changes in the way artificial light transforms the difference between night and day. The consequences are treated in relation to how these combine with Uroan sociality. I follow Wikan who says that the meaning of place is best captured by following people in social space as they encounter multiple pressures and injunctions (1990: 47). This is partly what we did in the previous chapter when focusing on interfaces in the utility–customer relationship. In the present chapter I shall continue to follow selected people in their footsteps and account for the way daylight aesthetics are modified after darkness.

Furthermore, and important in this context, electric light causes a rebounding of another relationship, namely that between people and spirits. I show how artificial light affects space shared by humans and spirits and thus the relationship between them. Then I treat Uroan demography and account for why and how this is changing. Finally, I provide a discussion of how the arrival of electricity has affected the pace of life in Uroa.

Light as a marker of power

'Now we have a town here!' (*Mji hapa sasa!*), Hija exclaimed to his friend the day street lighting in Uroa returned in 2001. The lights had not been working for years. Now, the change made people talk about the effects that were produced. I also asked people for their reactions and views. An old man said he would not have been outside at this hour (nine o'clock) had it not been for the light. He was about to visit a friend. The road and paths in the village are far from even, thus elders are often afraid to stumble and fall when moving about in darkness. A woman was also outside, beating sand out of dried seaweed close to her house. She would not have been able to do so without this particular light, she said. Sitting in another place, young boys were playing cards and exchanging pictures of their international football heroes. In brief, there was more life outdoors after the lights had returned to Uroa. The artificial light remoulds the distinction between day and night. Uroans are able to continue working or relaxing in different ways with the arrival of light.

The arrival of electricity and the lighting of public space in Uroa are perceived as rendering it increasingly town-like, in comparison to the earlier situation. Uroa's status is elevated. The use of electricity during weddings and funerals marks the same phenomenon. However, people living on the fringes, in more ways than one, sometimes raise critical voices. One of the women who expressed dissatisfaction during a census interview (see chapter 1) is situated on the outskirts of the village, beyond the reach of the public lighting that exists today.

As we know there are distinctions within the village as to private consumption. First of all, houses connected legally to the grid make up a network of significant modern actors. At night-time one can easily trace this 'community within a community' by looking at which houses have lighting. Those with unauthorised connections rely on others' mercy and do not seem to be fully members of this club. This is signalled in the way they must take care to use their light secretly. My neighbour, for instance, never turns her bulb on before nine o'clock. At this hour she assumes that unwanted observers will not show up and sanction her 'direct current' consumption (see chapter 6). In short, this type of electricity user is restrained in her display of a modern life.

In contrast there are institutions and private consumers whose use of electric power vividly signals their superior status in the village. The visibility of mosques, the school, the residence of a former politician, and the house of a young tourist guide are striking. They represent the powers of Islam, education, the ruling party, and tourism, respectively. Below, I sketch how these units appear at night.

The mosque

A greenish radiating light escapes the sacred room through the windows and doors and illuminates the space outside. The light is produced by long fluorescent tubes inside. It is reflected on the white ceiling and turquoise walls and reappears as a colour which evokes associations of purity. Lights are left to burn all night and welcome people who wish to read and pray after the last common prayers. Particularly during Ramadan, some men do come at night. Other physical attributes of the holy building also bear evidence to the power of the institution. The building is about four-times the size of a normal house. In addition, and contrary to ordinary houses, the walls are plastered and painted. Carpets cover the floor and there is a

Plate 7.1 The mosque in Dikoni ward, Uroa, 2001.

water tap on the outside of the building. Just before dawn, men, and sometimes a couple of older women, approach the mosque to attend the day's first prayers. Naturally, there is a practical benefit in seeing clearly where to go and where to wash your hands and feet when the sun is not yet up. On another level the materiality of the building radiates an aura of purity and authority. It expresses Islam's continuous presence and moral superiority in the village.

The school

The Uroa primary and secondary school has a central location in the main village. Fluorescent tubes are fixed on the outside of the building and inside classrooms. The illuminated building reflects education's importance in this society. However, we earlier noted the Zanzibari government's problems in fulfilling promises of free education. In 2001 six classrooms did not have roofs and were not in use despite the lack of classrooms. Moreover, in 2003 the government ceased to cover expenses for electricity used in Zanzibari schools. Now schools have to gather money themselves or the current will be cut off. As a result the nursery school in Uroa has been forced to continue without electricity. Teachers here said that the most severe setback is the long distance they must now carry buckets of water. The water pump at the nursery school does not run without electricity.

The ordinary school, in contrast, has managed to organise many people to help with the task of providing money for electricity through collective effort. Teachers and pupils farm, collect and sell firewood in order to have sufficient money to keep the electricity running (among other things). Therefore, at night-time, it is likely today that the lights are turned on. In fact, they have started extra classes at night for age groups that are about to take exams (Standard 9 and 11). After the evening lessons, which go on until midnight, teachers and pupils sleep in the building until it is time to go home for breakfast. Afterwards, they return for the morning shift. There is little doubt as to the Uroan conviction that electric light benefits children's learning opportunities. The illuminated school building expresses what teachers were proud to tell me: 'In Uroa, we want the best pupils'.

Electric light provides opportunities for learning that are morally acceptable, welcomed and immediately realised though the establishment of night classes. Uroa is not alone in its way of organising night classes. When, in 2006, I visited Makombeni and Kitogani villages, where electricity had been available for only a couple of months, night classes for girls and boys were already in operation. Teachers also highlight electricity's significance for education in other ways than by the mere access to light. At the Uroa School there was, by 2006, a functioning laboratory. Furthermore, the school uses three personal computers (PCs), a printer, and a photocopying machine, which are all valuable items, for the administration in particular. During interviews with teachers in other villages in 2006, the topic and importance of access to PCs was always brought up. Some villages, also in Pemba (but not yet Uroa), have an Internet connection. The consequences of information access doubtless merit an independent study.

The politician's house: power and privacy

At one point along the road you see a spectacular sight. Blue, red, green and yellow bulbs illuminate the wall of a house and give the promise of something special. There are also planted, blossoming trees by the entrance, which is quite unusual. This domestic residence belongs to a former MP and is considerably larger than most private buildings. In the same manner as the mosque and the school, the walls are smooth and painted.

Commonly, Uroans give priority to indoor lighting. Light would appear from the inside and exit through the open windows (glass is rarely used). The light source would either be a bulb or the greenish/bluish light from a TV set. In this way elements from life inside slip outside and become observable from the street. In some cases people place their TV set outside the house so that neighbours and relatives can watch. At the MP's house, on the other hand, what strikes you first are the multi-coloured bulbs on the dwellings outside. The light appears as decoration (*pambo*) designed to attract the sight of others.[1]

Secondly, the house's interior is hidden from the street view. The living room in which the family spend their evenings is carefully concealed from inspection. This goes for visual observations, but neither do sounds easily escape from the enclosed brick construction. By 'reading' the exterior of this house (cf. Moore 1996; see also chapter 9), we thus see a demonstration of power, on the one hand. On the other, there is a stronger focus than there normally is on the boundary between the family and the outside world.

The owner's position distances him from his co-residents. People admire what he has accomplished. His house would tend to be mentioned when men and women were asked which dwelling in Uroa they considered to be the best. They speak of the building and its accessories as 'a town house' (*nyumba ya mjini*). The use of coloured light bulbs marks the crown of the house and resembles what Veblen labelled 'conspicuous consumption', with the obvious purpose being to attract attention. Only during weddings would such a demonstration of openly competitive signs normally be tolerated. The owner possesses knowledge and resources and performs in a style distinct from that of other villagers. His material demonstration can also be seen as a comment on resistance against the norm of modesty. By doing what he does, he states that he is not afraid of, and can cope with, jealousy and social sanctions. However, he does this whilst at the same time turning inwards to protect his boundaries.

The tourist guide's house: optimism and openness

On the other side of the village another residence stands out from its surroundings. Here, you need only to throw a quick glance through the windows to observe that the evening's TV show has started. Plenty of people, particularly children and adolescents, are gathered in the generously-sized living room, sitting on sofas, chairs or on the floor. Again, luminous space attracts the eye. The bright, fluorescent light inside blends with and hides the characteristic colours coming from the TV set. The light and noise speak to the passing observer of a central meeting place. Compared to other households with TV sets, the visitors who enter are not only those who are close relatives and friends of the hosts. The half-public, half-private setting is emphasised in that snacks are sold to the audience. Before the shows begin the hostess prepares tiny plastic bags of frozen lemonade and cookies. During the show she sells them for Tsh.10 each.

Again, plastered, coloured walls, furniture and decorative items make the house different from the average house in Uroa. During the years when tourists were numerous Hija, the owner of the house, earned good money. However, as this market declined, he took up a range of other activities. Hija is one of the young men quoted in chapter 5 who most clearly articulate the value of 'moving forward' (*kupata kuendesha*), that is, 'reaching development' (*-pata maendeleo*). We also noted his opposition vis-à-vis elders and their use of occult powers to obstruct progress. Hija appears willing to take the risk of confronting values that he does not approve of. This is also interesting in view of the spatial organisation of his house. He emphasises transparency and opens up the house for inspection. Other people would be more reluctant to let just anyone enter due to the threat that they might pose to the house and to the people living there. The young couple do not try to hide their wealth but express a confidence in displaying their things and thereby their modern identities. They clearly regard themselves as representatives of a new generation of Uroans.

The symbolic power inherent in electric light has been noted in many historical contexts (Schivelbusch 1988; Garnert 1993; Nye 1990). In Zanzibar we saw the relevance of such links when treating various governments' ways of including electricity's applications in their policies in chapter 2. In the sketches above there are similar connotations between institutions and people in power and their demonstration of such through electric light. Strategies somewhat varied for the two private house owners, though. One tended to enclose domestic space and the other demonstrated openness. In the case of the institutions, the continuous power of the mosque served merely to enhance the evidence of decay at school, but only temporarily, however. Teachers and pupils rediscovered development together. By 2003 the illuminated school building stood as an icon for Uroan's hopes for a better future.

We can discern these relatively enduring aspects by scrutinising the significance of the physical objects in the social context. Electric light has a tremendous effect on aesthetic and moral expression. The analysis has so far centred on showing the signification of electricity as a marker of difference and authority. Now I turn to the dynamics of social forms and explore how these appear after sunset.

The aesthetics of darkness

Meja does not like to walk on her own in the village, at least not without having a particular purpose. On the occasions when I told her that I would go for a walk in the evenings, she always offered to come with me. During the daytime this was not an issue. She led me tacitly to understand that, after sunset, it is important, also for a European woman, to walk together with somebody.

Meja would wrap the two pieces of her *kanga* on top of her dress and her head, as usual. Her red plastic sandals were searched out. She would not walk barefoot as she normally does during daytime. In darkness the rough, coral path is a challenge. Also, possible animals, indefinable objects and puddles of rainwater would be unpleasant to step on or in without shoes. Meja would quickly tell her husband what our plans were and then leave the house. When walking with her I understood that I had to learn a whole new set of greeting rules for approaching people in the darkness. Contrary to the daylight ritual of greeting thoroughly, asking for news about family members, making jokes and so on, the same people now seemed more like strangers to each other.

On our evening rounds in this ward of Uroa we would mostly meet older women relaxing on benches (*baraza*) outside their own, or their neighbours', houses.[2] They would be sleeping, sitting together in silence or chatting in low voices. If the moon was not up we might make them out in the light of a bulb or we would not see them at all. When we approached a group, their conversations would fade away before we reached them. If words were exchanged at all, we would always wait until we had arrived at a closer distance than what would be the case during daytime. Significantly, it would be we, the walkers, who started the greeting. Furthermore, the conversation would be briefer: 'How was the day?' (*Za kutwa?*). 'Fine, and at your place?' (*Nzuri. Za huko?*). In this way, without ceasing to walk, and with soft voices, we exchanged these words which would have been too short to be polite during daytime.

The change of aesthetics between daytime and night-time is connected to two important phenomena. One is linked to respectability and the other concerns people's relationship to spirits. First of all, darkness reduces the possibility of controlling people's behaviour. Uroans adore to tell stories about lovers who secretly meet at night. A lady wandering about alone in darkness could easily put her reputation at risk. Men are also limited in their mobility at night. However, they would not be condemned for spending leisure time outdoors at night-time which is what they have normally been doing together with their friends. The other reason for people's changed behaviour at night is their fear of meeting spirits.

Security light

Darkness represents increased risk to humans. Uroans would often start conversations about darkness by describing how scared children are of it. This is why it is common to leave kerosene lamps (*kibatari*) burning all night in the rooms where children sleep. If electricity is available, however, the lights are turned off completely when sleeping. The light is considered too strong to sleep in. Kerosene is not used in electrified houses at all, except when there is a power cut.

People would also give mention of the unpleasant surprises darkness can bring. An insect in a bed in a dark room, for instance, is nasty. If you are unaware of it when you lie down, suddenly feeling it may terrify you. Eating in the dark is considered bad for the same reason ('*Si vizuri kula kwenye kiza'*) because you would not know what you were eating. One of my assistants from town remembered from her childhood that her parents always told their children not to eat in the dark. When one day there was a sudden power cut, the whole family immediately stopped eating. My assistant was not sure what exactly caused the parent's obvious anxiety. Perhaps it was because they feared spirits, she said with a twist of humour, but she also left the question open.

Finally, the accounts would point out the danger of larger animals (*madudu*, also used to denote spirits) and evil spirits themselves (*mashetani*). The supernatural beings may live anywhere and they may appear as humans or animals or as spirit-like creatures. The uneasiness caused by not knowing what a given spirit would look like is reinforced when people find themselves in dark or unfamiliar space. The spirits' actions are unpredictable and even brief encounters may be devastating. The description above of how greeting patterns change in darkness demonstrates how people's anxiety materialises. A stranger who approaches someone might be a spirit. This is why the walkers should start the conversation and reveal themselves. Those sitting outside a house are most certainly known human beings. Also the low voices and brief greeting codes are linked to people's concern for avoiding disturbing anyone, human or non-human. In sum, darkness is linked with uncertainty and danger.

The question remains as to the extent to which the arrival of electric light has influenced these social forms and the fears that inform them. People certainly move around outdoors after darkness more than before. However, Uroa is not flooded in light despite the arrival of certain bulbs, thus the place is not radically altered in this respect. Jan Garnert speaks of the way shadows disappear with increasing amounts of light (1993: 109–10). With one light source shadows are significant, but in 'flood light' they vanish. As for outdoor space at night in Uroa, as people pass from one point to another, the few bulbs make objects shift between being illuminated, reflected as shadows or disappearing in darkness. The walks taken with Meja reflected the high degree of darkness that remains. Some confirmed (after I had suggested it) that people greet each other more on the street now than before electricity's arrival because faces are easier to recognise. Such changes have been very difficult to establish by observation, however, and village space remains a grey zone, not completely dark and yet not clearly lit. An aesthetic of darkness, as distinct from that of daylight, remains.

At the same time, loud noises reach the ear outdoors at night. Music, news, religious programmes and the voices of crowds gathered inside slip outside. The few who keep TV sets outdoors also follow the practice of turning up the volume quite high. Correspondingly, the sounds from waves in the ocean and of insects fade away. The noises produced at large contrast the low voices people continue to use when occupying space outdoors. It makes one aware that the disturbing effects of various noises are not random. The high volume of noise coming from any modern medium generates little reaction. People's voices, however, have a particular social relevance in which co-villagers' concern not to evoke fear in each other seems crucial. Furthermore, on the inside there is also often laughter and an apparently freer atmosphere. Outside, control and considerations for others must be maintained.

Spirits are thought to be around more after darkness because they do not like to be detected. An important question in the present context is whether electric light transforms space in a way that affects spirits' whereabouts. Older men in particular tend to label electric street lamps 'security light' (the English term is used). A young electrician claimed that these men did not know what is meant by the expression. True, they may have adopted a Western-informed concern for the theft and robbery that surrounds the hotel business. There are many possible ways this notion may have come to be adopted. However, when elderly people in Uroa speak of 'security light' and simultaneously stress that spirits do not like it, the notion has quite a specific meaning. Of concern is the way light is thought to reduce the threat of any kind of evil. Electric light thus also protects people against spirits. The shift is not radical but the barrier against malevolent attacks is strengthened with the light. There is a visual emphasis on the way spirits are detected. The visual is also what is modified with the light.

Upon reflection, Kirsten Hastrup notes for rural Iceland how the disappearance of certain supernatural beings coincided in time with electricity's arrival in the area, some ten years before Hastrup conducted fieldwork (1998: 69–70). The *huldufólk* ('the hidden people') did not vanish, but they began to keep themselves more to the forests outside human settlements. Hastrup suggests that the two phenomena might have been interrelated. This is also what we could see the signs of in Uroa. Spirits are thought never to be present in the mosque because they would not have enough power in this sacred space. Neither are they perceived to be around during weddings, a fact which I believe is related to the way many people's effort and energy provide strength (*nguvu*).[3] Therefore, because spirits do not like light, they are more hesitant to visit spaces lit by electricity. In this sense too Uroa, as a place, is modified. It is safer. However, some people are intrinsically bad and evil magic will continue to be around. Moreover, spirits have not vanished. These things are too uncertain for anybody to make conclusions concerning the consequences of the arrival of electricity and how this affects spirits.

Demographic changes, men, and their houses

Uroa is constantly adjusting its geographical position. By night, electric light roughly reveals its demographic structure. Map 7.1 and Map 7.2 provide a sketch of the village in 2000. They show that the density of houses has increased compared to 1991 (cf. Map 4.1). The village stretches in a long, narrow line from south to north along the coastline. There is a dark area which splits the village into two parts. Here lie the remains of the first hotel established in the village (the Uroa Bay Hotel). The land used to be a graveyard before the Italians arrived. Today the place is only used when people are crossing from one part of the village to the other. Due to this limitation in the south and a graveyard in use to the north, expansion of the village is heading inland, away from the beach. Between 2001 and 2004, thus after the maps had been prepared, the number of houses increased from 480 to 550. Most of these new houses lie by the new tarmac road which comes from Chwaka in the south and continues to Pongwe in the north. Two of the six shops in Uroa are also located here. They stay open until late at night. Bright fluorescent light and TV sets are purposefully switched on to attract customers and make men stay for the evening. Women only come to buy things (preferably during daytime) and quickly leave. During Ramadan the road is crowded with men who like to sit on the smooth, still warm, surface after sunset and the family meal. It was one of the goals of electrification to make people stay in the countryside. In Uroa this appears to be the case. Many Uroans hold that the place is attractive for young people. They also say electricity is one of the reasons for this.

As for new houses, bricks and cement tend to be chosen as the materials. Bricks are now also locally produced and cheaper than the alternative – limestone and chalk. Depending on a range of factors, the cost of constructing a house varies from Tsh.300,000 to Tsh.2 million (US$375–2500). Uroan men agree that limestone is of a finer quality and will last longer – up to 30 years or more. In contrast, concrete tends to dissolve after twenty years. Limestone and chalk are the traditional construction materials in Uroa but have become expensive to produce (due to a reduction in their availability in the natural environment and demanding labour costs). There is a flavour of nostalgia in such comparisons of building materials. Things were more solid (*madhubuti*) in the past.

Houses by the tarmac road tend to be larger than in other wards. Some of them also have a new type of entrance. Constructed as separate entities, the purpose of these is to make registering of the electricity meter possible without someone having to be at home. The front door can remain locked and the device is accessible, yet shielded from rain. In addition, many of these houses have plastered walls, like the two domiciles described above, and electric light and appliances.

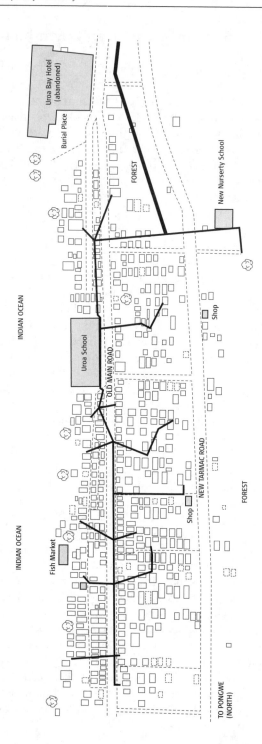

Map 7.1 Sketch of the village of Uroa in 2000, northern part. Produced by Mr Hamid Ussi Mnemo of Uroa.

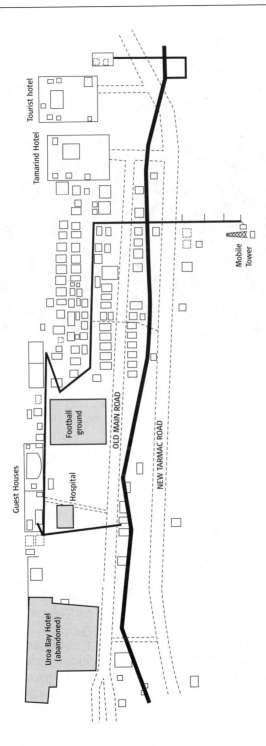

Map 7.2 Sketch of the village of Uroa in 2000, southern part (including Dikoni ward). Produced by Mr Hamid Ussi Mnemo of Uroa.

Plate 7.2 Households with electricity and TV aerial (to the left)
and household without, Uroa, 2001.
House constructions change and social differences increase with domestic
electrification. Note that the electrified dwelling has no natural ventilation in
constrast to the traditional house covered with palm leaves.

The increasing emphasis on houses and their materiality is of general
relevance in Uroa. To an increasing extent, domestic dwellings are
becoming the measure of men and their status. People told me that in the
past a man's wealth was linked to the number of children he had. Today,
having many wives and many children may invite mockery. This is notably
so if one's material resources are particularly scarce. It is regarded as
irresponsible to marry a second or third wife if you are unable to provide a
satisfactory standard of living for them. Here we touch on one of the
fundamental consequences of recent developments in Uroa. A 'satisfactory
standard of living' is not what it used to be. Electricity's normalisation, in
the sense that a 'nice house' (*nyumba nzuri*) should contain electricity, has
raised the stakes for entry into marriage. Young men explicitly state that
they must wait to marry until electricity is installed. One of my
neighbouring bachelors remained unmarried for the whole year I resided
in Uroa. He was striving to equip his house with doors, concrete floors and
to obtain an electricity connection. He would often speak of the moment
when he would finally be ready to marry a woman he knew of.

If a man is married to several women, Uroans find it important that he treats them in equal terms emotionally and materially. Quarrels easily occur due to jealousy among co-wives, they say. If the first wife's house is electrified it is important to provide the same asset in the second home. This should at least be done before equipping the first wife's house with expensive appliances (such as a TV set or a freezer). In the previous chapter we saw that some men solve this problem by connecting the two houses (if neighbouring) with a 'direct' connection. Now, if the utility company imposes sanctions against such arrangements it will become more expensive for these men to provide satisfactorily for their families. For everybody, however, expectations for material objects are not the same as before. They have risen immensely. This is the reason why old men with little monetary and material resources are ridiculed for having many wives. In today's Uroa, they have bitten off more than they can chew.

There is also an environmental factor related to electrification that appears to be forgotten in development projects. This concerns the link between construction techniques and electricity consumption. Consideration for electric installations provides incentives for changing construction techniques. Utility regulations in Zanzibar say that roofs should not be thatched with palm leaves (*makuti*), this in order to prevent water leakages. Therefore corrugated iron sheets (*mabati*) are increasingly becoming the norm. In this way the former natural ventilation of air is replaced with airtight buildings which do not let the breeze inside. In consequence, cooling becomes a challenge in the hot season. We noted earlier that as many as 43 per cent of households with electricity kept a fan in 2000. It is presumably only a matter of time before more affluent families start using air conditioning, which is not uncommon in Zanzibar Town. Electric appliances at work (lights, TVs, etc.) also produce heat. Thus we can see evidence of a pattern of spiralling consumption. This could have been avoided if effort had been put into the task of providing waterproof houses that also breathe. Bi Asiya described how she perceives the various seasons in relation to the sealed house she lives in:

> In the cold [rainy] season, we close the windows and doors at night [both wooden]. We sleep wearing a dress and a *kanga* in order not to get cold. In the hot season, we open the windows, using mosquito nets if necessary. With iron roofs, it gets so hot (*joto sana*). We use the fan by the bed at night. Brick roofs (*vigae*) are better, but expensive.

Electric lights' capacity to make space visible should be considered when people shield their houses. Many people also close their windows in the hot season because they do not want people to be able to watch what goes on inside. The politician's house is a case in point.

Speeding up life – consequence and ideal?

We have now seen electricity's impact on Uroa's spatial dynamics. The chapter ends by focusing on how electricity affects people's perceptions of time. The two are interlinked.

In rural Zanzibar distinct time references exist simultaneously. They are made relevant according to quite particular circumstances when people act, interact or do nothing but sleep. In order to explore the way electricity's arrival affects people's uses and perceptions of time, it is useful to draw on Bender. She speaks of the way 'different times nest within each other and draw meaning from each other' (2002: 104). I also follow Bender in that 'clock' time is not necessarily neutral or 'event-less'. What clock time shares with many other time references is that, when used, it is located in space and linked with wider networks.

Electricity has had a fundamental impact on the distinction between day and night. With their new-found liberty people have to decide what to do at different hours of the day and this constitutes an experiential transformation. While cognitive psychologists or philosophers might be better equipped to grasp the full implications at this level, our evidence from practical life demonstrates that the change is significant. Instead of ending the evening after the seven o'clock prayers, a meal and relaxing in same-sex groups, Uroans now continue with a range of other activities. The day is not twelve hours any longer but, in theory, twenty-four. Therefore, a considerable part of the Uroan population has come to exercise more control over what they do and at what hour. In this sense they now master or, rather, overcome some of the limitations produced by nature.

They still depend on natural cycles. For fishing, seaweed and land farming, people continue to relate to the tides, winds and rains, which follow the cycles of the moon and the sun. People tend to plan their activities one day ahead when they know how the tides will be the next morning. What electricity provides, however, (though again, not for all) is an increasing flexibility as to when to do other necessary tasks.

Another significant time is the clock-time which government institutions (and tourist enterprises) follow. When people are preparing to send children to school or are in need of a health worker's advice, they relate to this Tanzanian public hour. The clock-time also corresponds to the Islamic structuring of the day. Here electricity provides the authorities in question with a means of making people adhere to religious rules. Loudspeakers magnify the calls to prayer to the extent that the show-up rate in the morning has increased. Khamis said, half-jokingly, that now 'we wake up even in this place' (*tunaamka mpaka hapa*). His reference to 'place' could have a double meaning, the first being that of his house's geographical location on the outskirts of the ward. However, with his laughter and his awareness of my knowledge of his rare attendance in the mornings, he could also have meant that now even those less committed to Islamic rules would have no excuse for not attending prayers. A situation I witnessed confirms that electricity and loudspeakers have effect in this respect. In 2000 the speakers in the mosque in Dikoni ward, Uroa, were stolen. After they had been replaced the imam told me that thirty-seven people now regularly attended the half past four morning prayers (*Alfajiri*). In contrast, only twenty people had appeared on the mornings when calls were made without loudspeakers.

We encountered Baomar's hurried manner at work and his wearing of a watch (which he also uses). Watches and clocks inside people's homes are frequently displayed even though they sometimes do not work. This, I think, points to some sort of status inherent in clock-time. A person's type of job influences which type of time s/he is most attuned to. However, all Uroans relate to all these time references. Our interest lies in how these work together and how electricity influences people's balancing between various references relating to time.

Uroans at work in hotels seem particularly split during Ramadan. Serving food and drinks (even alcohol) at a time when one is not supposed to do so results in a dilemma. Due to their interest in keeping the job and keeping tourists satisfied (whilst continuing to earn money), employees tend to let job concerns come before religious duties. In other words, those employed to serve foreigners have already chosen a life of religious compromise. Religious leaders appear flexible towards people's priorities for work, though. Tides cannot be controlled. However, even so, Fridays are for religious reasons not working days for men at sea. Zanzibaris employed by the government only work a half-day on Fridays and have Saturdays and Sundays off, as announced in the public, Tanzanian calendar. Here we see the compromises that are made to make the various systems fit each other. Or more precisely, we see how these compromises enhance people's management of different times simultaneously. Various times provide contexts for each other.

In addition to the three references related to time and how to measure its passing (and their wider references in Tanzanian and global public life, Islamic global networks, and nature), there are a range of other mechanisms for structuring time (often interrelated with these three). Bus timetables, eating hours, bodily cycles, celebrations, healing processes and political elections are examples of the variety of heterogeneous references Uroans use for thinking about time. This variety is not new and is bound to provide people with daily dilemmas. I suggest that electricity's arrival has reinforced some of these conflicting concerns. Gradually, more negotiations result from people's increasing preoccupation with not 'losing time' (*potea time*). Time is speeding up because the extended days directly provide people with increased freedom to pursue their goals. Simultaneously, increasing flexibility has a conceptual consequence. It makes it more demanding to optimise the balance between various activities (including rest). In short, Uroans' exploitation of time has become a more complex task. It is significant that the word for electricity (*umeme*) denotes something fast or quick (*haraka*) in Swahili. Electricity comes quickly when turning on a switch. This is how people explain this meaning of the word. However, electricity's speed can also represent the various ways in which electricity speeds up life. As mentioned, this is partly due to the expansion of 'daytime' resulting in more choices of activity and also people's consciousness of such choices. Moreover, electricity's way of producing a faster kind of life is also linked with changes in how people perceive of and spend their leisure time. This is to be treated in chapter 9. Finally, I show in chapter 10 that the speeding up of time in Uroa now makes women cook fewer meals per day than in the past. I demonstrate how this is linked with the arrival of electricity.

Uroa transformed

In this chapter we have seen how Uroa as a meaningful place is perceived and reconstructed at present. In relation to town, Uroa has moved closer with the arrival of electric light. We may say with Edwin Ardener (1987) that people in Uroa perceive of themselves as less 'remote'. Compared to non-electrified villages, Uroa's visibility at night marks its higher rank. With the notion of remote areas, Ardener captures the social meaning attributed to place and the hierarchical, but also complex, relationship between remote and central areas. From central areas, the remote is considered to be backward. As seen from the remote area, the distinction is different. To them, the centre is approachable but they are also vulnerably positioned. I complete this discussion in chapter 11 when we know more about what it means to live in the place called Uroa.

Also, within Uroa social boundaries have become more striking with electric light. Light represents social power and those left in the shadows can do little but watch how differences increase. The physical structuring of space at night is modified with the artificial light. However, the social aesthetics at night-time remain committed to extreme modesty and control. This is so despite the discovery that space has, indeed, become safer with electricity.

I have shown how village demography is changing at present. The spatial reorganisation is partly linked with limitations on space, with building materials and with utility regulations. However, these changes are no less the results of the socio-economic changes and the great momentum of the development discourse treated in chapter 5.

An important finding is that the pace of life is becoming faster due to the new, blurred distinctions between night and day. In another sense, everybody in Uroa wants to move ahead, which is what development, to them, is about. However, people do not agree as to the manner and pace at which such movements should take place. Inherent is the quest for a better life. What a better life involves and how its assets should be distributed remains a delicate question.

Notes

1. *Pambo* denotes small items which have a decorative effect, such as a nice, home-made tissue for putting the TV on.
2. The *baraza* is attached to the house and is made of limestone or bricks and concrete. It is an extension of the house outdoors. It lies open to observation and judgement from people passing on the path or road. Women use the *baraza* more frequently than men. During daytime as well as in the evenings most men prefer to meet other men at their *maskan*, that is, their gathering spots. These are often constructions made of concrete, sometimes with a roof. Or they can be a log on the beach or a bench outside one of the three mosques. The *maskans* are located at a distance from the houses where women stay.
3. See Winther 2005: 113–21 for a discussion of 'strength' and the importance of many people's presence during healing rituals.

Chapter 8

INTRODUCING OBJECTS OF DESIRE

Women and men in Uroa give quite specific answers when asked why they have obtained electricity, lamps, freezers, TV sets and so on. For example, they want to be able to read at night, to do business (e.g., produce frozen, sweet ice) or to get information and entertainment. Some also refer directly to the importance of 'moving with the times', thus linking electrical appliances directly to the development discourse. We have come to understand how this discourse gains impetus in the present and why current processes lead to an intensified focus on the objects in question. First of all, 'electricity is there', as Rashid pointed out. Availability is the first condition, and this is far from a trivial fact. The presence of infrastructures such as electricity matters. The second driving force towards new objects relates to money. The increased amount of money in circulation adds to some groups' range of choices as to how resources should be allocated and consumed. In short, people possess increasing amounts of money with which appliances can be bought.

Thirdly, I have shown the particular ways national discourses of development come into play in the village. The medium of TV provides an important driving force for new commodities by displaying these in commercials as well as in Swahili dramas. Such programmes, and notably peoples' interest in and admiration for what they see, also produce an image of the town as an ideal. The politician's 'town house' in the village is a local showroom in this respect. Furthermore, the virtues of education have been demonstrated, including people's convictions about the benefit of electricity for such purposes. I maintain that after more than a decade with electricity it is people's own experiences with the new technology that constitute the most important driving force for further use. The time has come to scrutinise the manner in which appliances are introduced into peoples' homes. I seek to show how electrical appliances are made room for in the social matrix made up of individuals, spouses, and larger networks. I also account for why women do not own electrical appliances. By focusing on people's strategies for obtaining material objects, I seek to show how people take care not to provoke those in their social surroundings. As we shall see, such provocation may cause serious harm.

Strategies for obtaining electrical appliances

In order to understand people's financial priorities it is vital to grasp the distinct moralities embedded in various transactions. I focus on various types of expenditure and the degree to which people expect these to be shared. By 'expenditure' I refer to the notion's standard meaning in English, that is, the spending or using of money or other resources. This general term contradicts emic distinctions between various kinds of transactions. In rural Zanzibar people speak either about spending money (individual focus) or about ritual gifts (necessary) or about 'kindness-gifts' (voluntary). The three are perceived as distinct realms which each have their own organisation and logic. As a result, the actual economic unit shifts between the singular person, the spouses, the kin group and the extended family (or other types of constellations). Figure 8.1 provides an overview of various, important types of expenditures and the extent to which Uroans expect these to be shared. I emphasise that the various categories constitute norms of behaviour.

Each exchange is linked with a particular morality, and it is by studying their interconnectedness that we begin to grasp the dynamics in economic life. People in Uroa often refer to what matters more when explaining why certain kinds of expenditures are shared and others not. Economic resources are also scarce. To understand how expensive and enduring artefacts are introduced we have to compare a person's various types of expenditure, which may be in the form of cash or objects.

Reciprocity characterises the types of occasion that involve a high degree of sharing. During ceremonies (weddings and funerals) and during healing rituals, members of the kinship network are supposed to contribute and help each other. Here it is important to note that the reciprocal aspect is linked more to demonstrating mutual concern for each other than to keeping tabs on each member's material contributions (Winther 2005: 113–21).

Transactions that reflect and produce asymmetric relations pose greater dilemmas. Here, the 'surplus' type of occasion, to be explained below, is of particular interest for the present discussion. This is qualitatively of a different kind compared with the other categories (and is thus marked in italics in Figure 8.1). In all the other types of situation, it is the occasion that induces the obligation to share/give. For 'surplus', it is the giver's

Degree of sharing	Type of occasion/ investment/ expenditure	Social bond between giver/ receiver
High degree of sharing	Healing (possession rituals)	Kin, in-law (reciprocal)
	Funerals	Kin (reciprocal)
	Weddings (gathering resources)	Kin (reciprocal)
	Weddings (exchanged in the gifting proper)	Kin, in-law (strictly reciprocal)
Some degree of sharing	Support the poor	Kin, in-law (asymmetric)
	Surplus of resources	*Kin, in-law (asymmetric)*
Individually acquired (men)	Providing houses	
	Installation and consumption of electricity	
	Purchasing electrical appliances	
	Purchasing tools and other personal belongings	
Individually acquired (women)	Providing non-electric kitchen utensils	
	Purchasing clothes and other personal belongings	
Individually acquired to provide for the household (men)	Purchasing/supplying household everyday necessities including food, clothes, school fees, etc.	

Figure 8.1 Various types of expenditure in Uroa and the extent to which these are expected to be shared.

relatively large amount of resources that triggers the demand for sharing. I explore some aspects of how this is handled in practice.

Transforming resources into non-divisible forms

The claims for distribution of surplus vary according to the quantity of resources a person possesses. Such demands for sharing are also related to the type and shape of resources involved. Products from fishing and farming are the most common types of resources that are expected to be distributed. The catch is, to a great extent, sold and is also consumed within the household but it is good manners to share some of it with your relatives. For example, Meja may catch an octopus one day. Rashid has just started harvesting maize from his large field. Both would be expected to give some of this away. Meja would distribute cooked octopus to her mother-in-law, her cousin and also to her best friend. Rashid, who in these sketched-out cases obtains a larger quantity than Meja, would provide his relatives with maize that day. However, he will also have to judge how much various people should have, how much he should store and how much he should sell. To Rashid and to those who observe him, there is a grey zone here when quantifying the amount he is justified in keeping for himself. What is generally the case is that natural products are shared, at least to the extent that relatives get a taste of what someone has obtained.

Purchased items such as kerosene, rice and flour bought in larger quantities would also trigger demands for re-allocation. The claims for sharing could help explain the fact that groceries and similar objects for immediate consumption are normally bought in small quantities.[1] For example, people without electricity tend to buy kerosene for lighting on a daily basis. Children are normally sent to the closest shop in the village to purchase a quarter of a gallon. When I asked about this phenomenon, people confirmed my suggestion that the lack of stocking-up on groceries and kerosene is related to the pressure to share. Nobody would directly admit that they have such intentions when buying in small quantities. However, when talking about other people and in general terms, such strategies were thought to exist and critically judged: 'They don't want to share' (*Hawataki kugawa*).

In view of this, it is also worth noting that fish is rarely kept in freezers in Uroa. The exception is when freezing capacity is rented out to commercial partners. Here, the stored fish belongs to people external to the household. In general people often highlight the possibility of freezing fish but in practice they seldom do. I suggest that people's avoidance of storing fish is partly related to the expectations concerning sharing edibles. (When treating food and taste in chapter 10, I provide some further reflections on the separation of freezers and fish.) In the same way that stocks of groceries become the focus for needy relatives, one is likely to meet requests for fish if this is known to be stored in the house.[2]

Theoretically money is easily divided too. In Uroa it does not seem any more impolite to ask a relative for money than it does for groceries and fresh products. Accordingly, people keep their stocks of money closely hidden from inspection. This is also sometimes the case in relation even to one's spouse. My friend, Amina, upon being asked what her current salary was, did not want to reveal it in her husband's presence. Only when he left the house could she share the information with me. However, how much a person earns is often a relatively well-known fact. This is particularly so for money that derives from the production of natural resources. During census interviews husbands and wives were often able to state what the other earned. They would also be free to state their income in a neighbour's presence. The most sensitive information lies in how much is accumulated. It is significant that wives tend to be unaware of the fact that their husbands keep bank accounts. In 2001, 26 per cent of men did. This topic appeared to be the most secretive aspect during these interviews. In contrast, people would freely tell me that they 'secretly' (*ya siri*) worked for the government as informants to report what goes on in their neighbourhood.

In contrast to these kinds of resources that may be divided, solid, enduring objects cannot physically be split into smaller parts without becoming useless. This implies that people's aspirations for electricity/ appliances can be seen as (partly) being motivated by the desire to avoid sharing. In turn, investments in appliances may be considered as strategies for accumulating non-divisible wealth. This is so because the more resources are transformed into the form of processed and exclusive objects, the less claims can be made on them. I do not say that avoiding sharing is the Uroans' prime motivation for investing in appliances. Nevertheless, there are signs that people manoeuvre so as to obtain increasing space to handle their economic affairs individually. The drive for new appliances encourages people to use such strategies without which they would not be able to purchase expensive objects. In consequence, when resources finally become bound up in these objects, they serve to prevent the social network from making demands on one's resources. In this way resources that could have been shared end up in particular houses as icons of development. However, one important part of the story of how they get there remains. It is difficult to manage large investments on one's own. I start by accounting for how brothers help each other accomplish such tasks.

Brotherly cooperation

Amina had helped her husband, Jadidi, with money to buy a packet of cement for his maintenance project. This had been an act of voluntary help (*msaada*) and indicated to me that they keep their finances quite separate. Jadidi had also received help from his brother on previous occasions. The brother helped him provide all the electrical equipment at the time the house had been connected, including the meter. The value of this gift was, thus, considerable. Jadidi has also provided his brother with help in return. However, with regard to more help for the maintenance project, Jadidi hesitated to ask again. Voluntary giving involves careful judgements of when it is appropriate to ask.

Amina generally finds it inappropriate to ask for help in obtaining 'big things'. Included here are electrical appliances and sewing machines. Significantly, costs involving health matters are the first thing she mentions when stating what one may ask for. Also food can be requested 'if you have little money'. Furthermore, it is important when she says (on behalf of her husband) that help to maintain the house is an accepted purpose in this respect. A wish to buy clothes, in contrast, is not a legitimate reason for asking somebody for money. This indicates that there are differences in what men and women may ask from others.

Judgements about the aptness of making requests are also related to who is asked, as well as the ego's ability to return similar gifts. Significantly, more affluent individuals with a relatively equal standard of material living help each other obtain what Amina finds it inappropriate to ask from others. Silima and his brother are among the relatively affluent men in the village. They seem to enjoy a close relationship. Silima gave me a recent example of how he and his brother help each other out:

> My brother's TV set broke down and he asked me to lend him 250,000. When he had returned 50,000, I said it was okay. I did this because he is my brother. I also would have had all his children in my house every evening.

Silima and his brother regularly exchange financial support of this kind, but notably not at the same time, which would seem meaningless. The point is to help the other when it is mutually judged as 'needed'. Neither do they make detailed calculations in order to sort out who has contributed more than the other. However, the relationship (beyond being brothers) is still dependent on a strong sense of reciprocity. With the purpose of investigating what is communicated through such exchanges, I provide a partly constructed, but probable, account of how the degree of symmetry was evaluated and maintained in this case.[3]

When Silima's brother asked him for a loan, he had knowledge about Silima's current resources (they are involved in the same business). He probably also interpreted the balance of their past transactions. In addition, he had some idea of Silima's own interpretations of their previous exchanges (cf. Carrithers's notion of 'higher order intentionality' (1992: 58–60)). When Silima considered the request, he evaluated the state of his own resources and his brother's need (and, apparently, also the consequences of having his brother's children coming round every evening to watch TV). In addition, for Silima too, interpretation of their past exchanges was of relevance. The previous balance was probably in favour of the brother who has had a high income for some years but who does not now have that particular job. Therefore Silima might have felt some degree of obligation to help. However, through the act of providing the loan Silima also told his brother that he wants to keep a good relationship with him. The voluntary and communicative aspect became particularly clear when he decided to turn the loan into a gift. By this he showed that he is not only willing to help his brother in an acute situation, but that he appreciates him to the extent of not making claims to a direct return of the gift. Silima does not exchange gifts of similar sizes with his other brothers even though they are also relatively well off.

Two points are important. By founding the gift on brotherhood ('because he is my brother') the investment (on the TV) is shifted slightly away from the principally individual realm and becomes the result of brotherly cooperation. The acquisition now resembles ceremonial exchange (for example, healing rituals) with its emphasis on shared expenditures. It is therefore significant that mutual help for larger investments is primarily provided by brothers. Men engage in friendships with non-relatives too, and reciprocal gifts are quite common. However, for larger investments and issues regarding the house, such as in Jadidi's case, it is much more common for male relatives to help each other. Electrical appliances can here be seen as extensions of the house and therefore as of concern to the whole family. Fathers also sometimes help their sons with similar projects. Following the direction of inherited property, such donations are asymmetric without threatening any balance. 'I gave him support for the roof because he is my child.' As with mutual help between brothers, the exchange expresses a concern for the well-being of a close relative and, in turn, the future of the family.

There are cases where brothers choose not to give each other support to this extent even if they could in material terms. Relations have to be good for such exchanges to exist. Furthermore, with limited resources and the general experiences of unreliable sources of income, the most obvious advantage of exchanging gifts in this way should not be underestimated. Without mutual help between brothers, investments are very hard to make at all. Makame originates from Pemba and does not have relatives in the village. When he found himself in considerable economic difficulty, he complained that he had nobody to turn to: 'They go in as family'. Without a network, a person's opportunities for investments (and means of production, see chapter 5) obviously become poorer. Bank loans are not an option as they require collateral security. In hard times people like Makame do not have the economic and social back-up that is so important for people in this area. His financial marginalisation is congruent with his socially excluded position.

The second point regarding brotherly cooperation relates to the types of object that may be obtained by this method. I would hold that their voluntary collaboration provides greater room for experimenting with what to buy. Both brothers evaluate the need for an item before a decision is made. In this way, mutually, they provide future investments with acceptance and legitimacy. It is important that this 'certification' is issued before the item is actually obtained. As we shall see timing is crucial for how those in the social surroundings perceive a new acquisition. Furthermore, the two brothers together obtain more strength to face potential jealousy. In consequence, they become better positioned to obtain objects of desire without having to consider so carefully the reactions these may produce. Their common effort and evaluation is also important in light of the general pressure for sharing surplus with relatives of less affluence. Within the total flow of resources they help each other transform assets from a state where they should be shared with the wider group to a form in which they become untouchable for distribution. Finally, cooperation blurs other people's insight into how an object was actually financed. In consequence, the purchasers are more protected from accusations of immodest behaviour. In sum, this strategy makes the purchase and display of extraordinary objects possible and safer than it would have been had an individual accomplished such an acquisition on his own.

Women's wealth

Once in a while I asked women farming seaweed on the beach what they would do with their money. Most showed great pleasure at the thought of soon obtaining a considerable amount of cash. However, few had, or were willing to share in a public place, their plans for purchasing in this respect. An income of US$10 would represent nearly half the price of a small cooker. However, if I suggested 'What about an electric cooker?', they would either make a joke about it or simply remain uncomprehending. The question, intended to provoke a discussion, appeared a bit crude and broke with the social aesthetics of the situation. The place was not the best one for revealing dreams of what to spend money on, given the great care people take to keep secrets from one another. However, the content of my question was also beyond relevance. By 2001 women in Uroa did not own electrical appliances apart from radios, and certainly did not own electric cookers.

This is not to say that women were uninterested in electric devices. In electrified households, they use such objects to a greater extent than men. However, as to the purchasing of such items, which in turn defines ownership of them, men dominate the scene. To grasp the way women and objects are associated, we must look at the gifts a woman receives at her first wedding. These items constitute a large proportion of her total stock of belongings in the years that follow. As Subira put it when we were on our way to such a ceremony, 'it comes at weddings' (*inakuja harusi*). Figure 8.2 shows a woman's belongings and how she obtained them.[4]

We see the quantitative and qualitative importance of the gifts a woman receives at her first wedding (later weddings are common but involve few, if any, transactions of gifts). Female in-laws provide her with clothes, beauty objects and sometimes money. A woman needs *kangas* for concealing and adorning her body. Her purity and beauty are of central concern to her in-laws who include her in their descent line. Possessing many *kangas* means being able to choose a suitable pair of cloths for each occasion. *Kangas* should be new, that is, unused, during ceremonies. If not, this is connected with great shame (*aibu*). I met women in Uroa who said they could not participate in celebrating the end of Ramadan because they lacked proper, new clothes.

Furthermore, the kitchen utensils mark her new identity as a housewife. Such tools equip her to cook food for her new family. It is important that it

Types of objects	Clothes and objects of beauty	Kitchen utensils (non-electrical)	Beds, big things
Possessions before marriage	4 *kangas* 3 dresses 5 bracelets (aluminium) 2 earrings (not gold) 2 pairs of shoes		
Received at first wedding from in-laws (the assembly of gifts is called *sanduku*, lit. 'suitcase')	12 *kangas* 2 dresses 4 pieces of material 1 pair of shoes bracelets (not gold) 1 necklace (not gold) earrings (not gold) 2 chains of plastic pearls to wear around the hips oil incandescent powder body soap coconut oil for the skin		
Received at first wedding from own lineage		2 clay pots (now broken) 4 ceramic cups (2 broken) 4 tin plates 1 big tin plate 1 wooden spoon 3 plastic buckets (now broken) 1 strainer for coconut milk 1 *kawa* for covering cooked food 1 ceramic teapot	
Bought after marriage	*Kangas* Dresses Underwear *Bui-bui* (black veil) 2 aluminium pots	4 tin plates 4 clay pots (*chungu*) (1 broken) 1 wooden spoon 3 plastic buckets 5 thermoses aluminium spoons, a knife	Bed Mattress
Self made after marriage		1 *kawa* for covering cooked food	Mats Prayer mat Decorative cloths (*pambo*) for TV, table, bedroom door

Figure 8.2 A woman's belongings and how she acquired them.

is her female kin who provide these items. First of all, she has quite a pragmatic need for such items to fulfil her role as a wife and mother. Secondly, in chapter 10 I will show how closely food and cooking processes are linked with questions of fertility in a wider sense. In this way cooking utensils become objects that provide the family (both the bride's own kin and the new family she is about to establish) with strength (*nguvu*).

The two types of wealth a woman obtains at her first marriage articulate cultural codes for how a newly wedded woman's position is to be perceived. The bride's in-laws emphasise the importance of purity. Her own kin stress the importance of fertility. Furthermore, both types of transaction belong to the long-term cycle and reproduce relations that transcend the individual (Parry and Bloch 1989). Wedding gifts can thus be seen as things which objectify cultural values and the moral order in general (cf. Weiner's notion of 'inalienable wealth' (1976)).

The way wedding gifts are interwoven with processes that concern the reproduction of the larger kinship group appears to make wedding gifts resistant to change. For weddings, it is not a woman's prosperity as an individual that is emphasised but her particular position *within* the larger group. On the other hand, we have noted that wedding practices in rural Zanzibar include the use of new objects such as electric light and loudspeakers. Such adaptations do not alter the wedding institution's strong elements of continuity. Mark Johnson (1998) has treated wedding practices in the (Islamic) Philippines. He shows that the balance between two distinct styles (a 'modern' and a 'traditional', respectively) is debated and in flux, also in the context of weddings. However, women more than men, are expected to wear traditional clothing at weddings because of their position as carriers of 'cultural purity and authenticity' (Johnson 1998: 219). In rural Zanzibar, however, families who can afford it provide the bride with a Western-style white dress. The groom always wears the Islamic *kanzu* (a long white robe). I think this indicates a certain degree of undeterminedness in regard to what kinds of styles may be adopted within the wedding institution.

Moreover, in middle-income families in Kerala, India, Harold Wilhite observes that electrical appliances are becoming an increasingly important element of what the bride receives from her family at the time of her wedding (Wilhite 2006; Wilhite in press). Defined as a 'dowry', the flow of such wealth goes principally from the bride's family to the groom's. However, as is the case in Zanzibar, the bride's family has a concern with their relative's future well-being. Wilhite argues that one of the reasons why electrical appliances are introduced as wedding gifts in Kerala at present is that the groom's family might not so easily take control over such wealth as compared to money, a car or land.

There are a range of differences between the Keralan and the rural Zanzibari context, perhaps the most important being that the degree of normalisation of such appliances is much higher in Kerala. Almost every home there has a TV set and an electric cooker. On the other hand, there seem to be no vocalised restrictions in Uroa as to the quantity and nature of what, in principle, a woman may receive at her wedding. When asked if a bride might be given so much that people would become envious, women laughed and said: 'No, others will just want to give more' (*Hapana, wengine wanampa zaidi*). In this way, and with an element of acknowledged competition, the items and money given to a bride pose no challenge to the norm of modesty. Such competition has also been noted elsewhere in the Swahili region (Le Guennec-Coppens 2004).[5] In the light of how women in Uroa cherish electrical appliances and their families' concern for their well-being; how is it that they are not provided with electrical appliances at this point in life, when they make their most considerable leap forward in terms of possession of wealth?

I think that explaining the continuity in wedding gifts solely by referring to these objects' central role in reproducing kinship relations would constitute a sort of reification of the argument. The Kerala case indicates this. Rather, there also appear to be quite mundane factors that, taken together with what vaguely and situationally is defined as 'appealing' in rural Zanzibar, prevent electrical appliances from becoming women's property. One point relates to the spouses' distinct finances. This is generally important, but particularly so in the wedding context. We have seen that men are responsible for paying the electricity bill. In consequence, it is likely that a groom would be discontent if seeing his bride receive objects which will increase his future costs. A marriage is the creation of an ideal liaison, where the parties' equal standing and shared future are celebrated. Conflicts are avoided. If one of the parties became dissatisfied, it would threaten the new relationship from the start.[6] In sum, due to electricity's particular organisation, the spouses' separate finances and the concern for avoiding friction when a new relationship is established, it is unlikely that wedding gifts constitute a realm where women will start becoming proprietors of electrical appliances.

There is also another factor that may account for why women do not receive or purchase electric devices. This is related to whether the norm of individual ownership of objects also applies in practice.

A new, integrated cupboard had been installed in Hija and Zawadi's home. When being asked who it belonged to, Zawadi said: 'It's his. It doesn't leave' (*Ya yeye. Haitoki*). Women leave the house in the event of a divorce. Physically integrated objects stay. However, not only fixed objects may remain. Kassim elaborated in English: 'If there is a divorce, big things must stay in the house'. He gave the example of a large, electrical stove. According to this view, it becomes less relevant who first provided and owned the item. Its physical shape influences the degree to which it will stay. Furthermore, over time, objects may be regarded as a part of the house and thereby become irremovable.[7] Most people contest this idea and say that a woman has the right to take with her every item she had acquired. However, many would also add with regret that this is not always the case. If there is a conflict and the man is angry, he might just 'throw her outside' (*anamtupa nje*). Implicitly she is forced to leave her 'big things' behind under such circumstances. The inherent uncertainty in what a woman can take with her – probably a locus of conflict in real cases – could also be relevant to the discussion of why they do not become owners of big, electrical appliances. Indirectly, however, they contribute to the purchasing of such devices.

During fieldwork, nine women were asked to keep a record of everything they bought, earned, gave or received for a week. All of them reported having spent money on food and other items to be consumed in the household. For example, on 14 May 2001, Bi Mashaka sold seaweed for Tsh.3,067 and bought rice, sugar, and milk and a *kanga* for her sister (in all Tsh.3,000). When Subira received Tsh.500 from the hotel she works in, she spent two hundred of this on loaves and washing-up powder. The women's husbands were also requested to present their corresponding income, expenditures and gifts. A pattern based on this modest sample fits with my general impression. Husbands provide rice, beans, flour, potatoes and fish. These constitute staples, the basic ingredients for everyday meals. Women (apart from Bi Mashaka, who also bought rice) mainly spend money on spices, tea, tomatoes, onion, garlic, oranges and bananas, personal items (clothes, shoes), soap, things they need for generating income (needles and thread, fabrics, colour and sugar for making sweet ice) and often also children's education (school fees, uniforms, pencils and notebooks).

In general terms people seldom acknowledge women's share in supporting their households. They would instead tend to highlight the norm that a man should provide for his family. In concrete situations people would label a wife's contribution of food as 'gifts' or 'help'. However, in contrast to the gift Amina gave her husband (cement), food is required every day and the voluntary aspect of the gift becomes of less relevance. The US$7 women in Uroa make on seaweed per month are not stored in bank accounts. True, women travel more than before. They also buy themselves a bed if they do not have one. In addition those with husbands who are able and willing to cover most of the household expenses probably buy more *kangas* and dresses than before. However, the majority of women in Uroa are daily concerned with providing sufficient and proper food and the other items needed in the household. At the same time their husbands make considerable investments in enduring objects, such as electricity and appliances. What this shows is that women contribute to paving the way for electrical appliances.

Explaining women's exclusion from the ownership of appliances

Electrical appliances are uniquely purchased and owned by men. In view of women's increasing income and the pervading individual focus, it is important to account for this fact. As in many contexts elsewhere, wealth is gendered in rural Zanzibar (Weiner 1976; Johnson 1998). Electricity's male association is first of all linked to the male inheritance rules of descent and the ownership of houses. In consequence, as we saw in chapter 6, men handle the installation of electricity. They are also primarily the ones who engage in the customer relationship with the utility company and who must settle the monthly arrears. Electrical appliances, in turn, consume the current which it then falls to the person responsible for the electricity to pay for. In this way electrical appliances become linked to men's wealth, that is, to the house, in 'naturalised' ways. The script of the technology produces obstacles for women when it comes to making decisions about what to buy.

I have also shown that the gifts women receive at their first wedding are of great significance, both conceptually and materially. Women's wealth appears as a category which is incommensurable with electric devices. I partly accounted for this by showing the significance of wedding gifts in defining what women's wealth should be. Therefore, in addition to the technical constraints, there are social and cultural constraints on what a woman should possess.

In addition there is the current uncertainty as to what things a person might take with them in the event of a divorce, which is itself more easily obtained by a man than by a woman. In most cases it is the woman who must leave the house. Again, Islamic law seriously limits women's chances of becoming financially independent. In sum, the barriers reduce both women's possibilities and also their desire to purchase and own electrical appliances. There are, nevertheless, negotiations going on in the realm of electric stoves which we shall see in chapter 10.

Paradoxically, women are financially heavily involved in the shift towards a growing range of electrical appliances in the village. They earn a considerable amount of income at present (chapter 5). They provide the housekeeping expenses for foods and other purposes, which in theory is the man's responsibility. They also become associated with objects of the household and they are as exposed as men to the risks involved in purchasing things they desire to have.

Putting yourself at risk

A person's well-being in rural Zanzibar is dependent on family support but, as in any social setting, relationships can also be very troublesome. In Uroa open or latent conflicts are often linked to the distribution of goods within family networks. By turning to 'dangerous acquisitions' we re-enter the realm of occult knowledge which we encountered at the time when electicity was introduced. By 'dangerous acquisitions' I include situations where people purchase or otherwise obtain objects that implicitly or explicitly are thought to trigger envy and sanctions. Dangerous acquisitions have the potential of creating imbalance. Whereas collective effort is emphasised during weddings and healing rituals, contexts in which large expenditure poses no conflicts (Winther 2005); dangerous acquisitions occur in situations where individuals push accepted standards for what one can obtain.

In 1998 Khamis had saved money in a bank account for some time and decided to buy a TV set. None of his brothers possessed such an item. He went to town and bought the item with his own money (Tsh.150,000, approx. US$200). Three months later he started to feel an ache in his arms and legs. He felt he had needles in his skin and went to see a healer who diagnosed his state. The doctor told him that a bad person had become upset with Khamis's latest acquisition. By the use of evil magic (*kijicho*) he had succeeded in harming Khamis. From the doctor's description of the person and where he lived, Khamis deduced the bad person's identity. A male relative living in another ward was doing him harm.

The treatment at the doctor's place in town was less elaborate than what would have been the case had a spirit been involved. Khamis brought a chicken, paid a modest amount of money and did not bring relatives or in-laws. He covered the expenses himself. During the possession ritual the doctor pulled out Khamis's pain by sucking the evil out of his skin. This was manifested as snails. Towards the end the doctor used a feather with which he touched Khamis's tongue. Out of his mouth came a kernel and the healing was over. The objects used were a ceramic basin for burning incense, a plastic bowl with water in it (into which the snails and the kernel were thrown) and the chicken feather. Khamis was cured and balance was restored.[8]

To Khamis this incident confirmed that TV sets are dangerous to acquire. The fear of sanctions from envious observers and the pressure to share material goods create an atmosphere of frugality and secrecy. Despite women's fewer investments in valuable, enduring objects than men, they are no less subject to envy and sanctions. In the little story that follows I became involved in various strategies for keeping a particular acquisition secret.

Meja longed for a sewing machine. With this item she would have more flexibility in providing clothes for herself and the children. Also, she thought, she might earn some money by making dresses for others, if she became good enough at it. However, with a price of Tsh.70,000 (US$82) Meja considered this out of reach. As a farewell present I wished to give her a sewing machine. I presented the idea to Khamis and asked him to help me with the purchases in town. However, my idea of surprising Meja was soon replaced with a different plan as to how to proceed, a plan that was orchestrated by Meja herself.

As intended, we arrived with the item after darkness when few people were outside. I drove the car up to their front door from where Khamis and I carried the device directly into one of the unfinished bedrooms. These non-electrical devices, imported from China, are integrated in a table and are therefore quite heavy. As usual, many children were watching TV in their home. Meja did not show any signs of emotion but simply told us where to put the machine. As soon as we could talk privately she instructed me on what 'we shall tell them' (*tutawaambia*), that is, what the public story would be. We were to explain to everybody, including her best friend and her mother-in-law, that I had only helped with the transport. Officially, the sewing machine had been borrowed from one of her relatives in town.

Before obtaining a device its type and value are evaluated against perceptions of what other people consider appropriate. However, the manner in which things are obtained also matters for how one is judged. Gradual indications of an increase in wealth pose a lesser risk than sudden ones. In the case of Meja's sewing machine she used a double set of strategies for avoiding sanctions. The public story maintained that she had borrowed the device from a cousin. Still, we had to arrive in darkness and try our best to hide the object. It was probable that her closest circle of family and friends would start suspecting that the machine in fact belonged to her. However, if ambiguity regarding the ownership remained, Meja seemed to suppose that the question of how she had obtained the item would become less critical as time passed. With time an item becomes less 'news' and more something 'we have become used to' (*tumeshazoea*). Sudden news has the potential to provoke reactions. What has been known for a long time is relatively safe. In addition it is possible that her strategies were related to a wish to keep the sewing machine from being associated with me. When we were in public she often played down her acquaintance with me.

The moralities articulated in such cases reveal the cultural emphasis on material and social egalitarianism. Inherent is the following message: 'Do not sing your own praises among equals, but share your surplus if there is one'. However, the references vary as to how equality in performance is evaluated. First of all, a person's gender is of relevance. Men's wealth represents at least ten times as much in monetary value as women's possessions. The difference in, and the magnitude of, the types of objects that men and women are associated with, point to gender differences in how a person is evaluated. While keeping this in mind, members of a household can also be regarded as a unit with which their total stock of objects is associated. Wives, parents or children are sometimes said to undergo pain because of jealousy or open disputes between a man and a second party. In this way acquisitions that may appear individually centred are also related to members of the entire household.

Moreover, we found that voluntary gifting and help between brothers can be seen as a strategy for making individual purchases appear to be legitimate extensions of family cooperation. Therefore, moving from the individual's gender to household relations and to the extended family, there is great variation in the possibilities of links that exist between objects and people. The actual unit for measuring equality in performance is correspondingly unclear.

Finally, rural Zanzibar has not historically been a class-divided society in economic respects (Middleton 1992). I have shown that this increasingly seems to be the case. In consequence the reference for judging the appropriateness of acquisitions also depends on your financial and social standing in the village. A sewing machine is probably too much for Meja's league. None of her in-laws or close friends in the village possess such a device. In the same way Khamis is better off than most of his relatives, and when he stretched the limit of what is common among his equals he became vulnerable. Wealthier men seem less exposed to threats when they make similar acquisitions, partly because people have become used to their level of affluence. The open admiration for the politician with the coloured light bulbs is a case in point (chapter 7). This apparent acceptance of the politician's high standing is a paradox when we consider the generally held view that the affluent are more exposed to risk than other people. Here, ambiguity remains due to the multiple purposes for which occult knowledge may be used. Wealthy men are not only thought to protect themselves in a defensive way. They also, apparently, use occult forces to accumulate wealth. They possess power (*nguvu*) both in its economic and occult sense. In brief, they remain in another category for judging financial behaviour to that of ordinary people.

In everyday life sanctions are most likely to come from relatives who expect you to behave as their equal. It is within the family network that the anticipation of sharing is strongest. By demonstrating attempts to make a move 'upwards' or 'away' one increases the risk of experiencing trouble. The sources of such difficulties lie less within the groups situated higher on the social ladder – and even poorer groups unrelated to ego – than with the protagonist's own friends and relatives – those left behind.

Partly due to the predictability with which they occur, wedding exchanges pose a contrast to the realm of dangerous, or potentially dangerous, acquisitions. Wedding gifts entail little ambiguity. They clearly express cultural conceptualisations. Conversely, dangerous acquisitions are unpredictable in their size, type and timing. Moreover, the item in question is most commonly (at least as it might appear to others) purchased by the man who also becomes the owner of the object. To those witnessing such an acquisition, it might appear to come out of the blue and take them by surprise. Dangerous acquisitions are markers of difference and morally ambiguous.

I stress that it is not the purchasing itself that puts the owner in danger in such cases. Objects in Zanzibar are not endowed with inherent and possibly evil qualities like those objects Birgit Meyer describes for Ghana (1998). In Uroa the significant moment appears when the object is displayed in the village to become appropriated (rejected or approved) by various people in the social environment.

Now, many of the objects that trigger desire and anxiety, such as TV sets, freezers and sewing machines, are elements within the development discourse. Moreover, these objects have been imported to Zanzibar. This could indicate that perceptions of 'globalisation' have relevance in this context. In Ghanaian Pentecostalist discourse imported goods are particularly dangerous due to their origin in the West (Meyer 1998). According to Meyer this discourse 'problematizes the alienation which consumers experience *vis-à-vis* foreign commodities' (ibid.: 768, original emphasis). She speaks of 'alienation' as people's feelings of inability to control the processes by which objects are produced, marketed and consumed (rather than being simply a result of people's limited insight into such processes, as Appadurai uses the notion).[9] For rural Zanzibar I think one should not exaggerate the implications of where objects originally come from. In contrast to the way in which they enter caves, stones and forests, spirits in rural Zanzibar do not possess commodities. Neither is there a general discourse about the need to appropriate foreign appliances with modesty. Islamic leaders voice their critique of Western styles in relation to proper conduct, and they find certain TV programmes to be sources of negative influence. However, as I have already mentioned, they are overrepresented as owners of electrical appliances and give no general warnings against acquiring such objects.

The appearance of dangerous acquisitions 'out of the blue' speaks of the fact that they have not been produced or even purchased in the village. However, rather than focusing on 'alienation' in the way people relate to the objects in question, I think the issue of ambiguity is more meaningful for our purposes, and in a very social sense. To observers, secrecy and ambiguity surround the whole process of acquisition. On one level the uncertainty concerns how the money was raised, how much the item cost, its type and the manner in which it was bought, and finally how the object was transported and put into place. On another level unexpected acquisitions and the display of valuable objects raise suspicion of occult forces having been at play. In brief, buying an item in town which, in the village, breaks with the social aesthetics (cf. Carrithers 1992) involves a high degree of ambiguity and mystery with which the acquisition is associated.

Normalisation: balancing equality and difference

The study of people's acquisitions of electrical appliances in contemporary rural Zanzibar provides a good case for exploring normalisation processes in general. Elisabeth Shove treats two distinct types of models that, in combination, may account for the way in which novelties become normal (Shove 2003: 43–57). The first group is labelled 'models of coherence' (ibid.: 53). Inherent in this perspective is the expectation that items, habits or practices should match, or at least contribute to, some meta-order. In this view consumption patterns and lifestyles come as 'packages'. Shove gives the example of someone in a contemporary Western, hot country who lives in a large house, has a high income and keeps several cars. Such a lifestyle would be seen as 'incomplete' if the house did not have air conditioning too. Here, it is the concern for coherence that drives the demand for the air conditioner (ibid.: 53). In our case, as the novelty of existing devices transforms into ordinariness, we might expect that the politician's house (chapter 7) will continue to be equipped with new objects, so as to preserve the image of a certain lifestyle. Coherence as a driving force for increased consumption is also relevant with regard to the way elements within larger technical systems 'lock each other in' in particular ways (Shove 2003: 53–5). Here, the sealing of houses, which is triggered by electricity's materiality, is a highly relevant example. As shown in chapter 7, the lock-in results in increasing electricity consumption in order to maintain a certain level of comfort. On another level, a preference for maintaining men's and women's wealth as complementary categories could inform the way changes are likely (or not) to occur.

Secondly, there are theories of 'difference' for explaining how novelties become normal (Shove 2003: 48–9). Building on Mika Pantzar Shove here identifies three steps (Pantzar 1997, Shove 2003: 50). Initially the things are objects of desire; secondly, their acquisition is legitimised in rational or functional terms; and thirdly the objects become so ordinary that their acquisition needs no justification.

In rural Zanzibar new objects of desire are clearly dangerous (cf. Shove 2003: 50). Khamis's problems when he acquired the TV set point to the fact that this device is not an ordinary thing among his equals. Khamis probably had a concern with his social prestige and personal advantage when he decided to buy the appliance. Such intentions would be in accordance with the value of 'difference' inherent in the Uroan development discourse.

When Khamis and other people in his situation have lived through the sanctions produced as a result of their acquisition of novelties the meaning of objects like TV sets gradually changes. They start becoming the norm for what a man or woman should possess. This process is speeding up at present, a fact which becomes clear when we look at how the meaning of

TV sets has recently changed. In 1998 such an acquisition caused sanctions. By 2004 this was no longer perceived to be the case. The device has become 'an everyday thing' (*kitu cha kawaida*). This change of meaning is probably linked to the fact that between 2001 and 2004 the number of TV sets in Uroa increased from forty-three to seventy-four. This implies that 13 per cent of households now keep a TV. I emphasise, though, that the question of normalisation is not only linked with quantities but is also a highly social matter. What is normal in one family might be very different in another. Another striking trend pointing to the normalisation of television sets is that, in 2001, the common sequence for the acquisition of appliances was to obtain light and radio first and then gradually expand electricity's uses. In contrast between 2001 and 2004 seven men obtained TV sets at the time of their connection to the grid. TV sets continue to be objects of desire in Uroa but they are no longer dangerous. They have reached Pantzar's third step in the process and have become normal.

The tension between modesty/equality and difference is not thereby put to rest, though. People's rewards for investing in modern identities by acquiring new objects of desire have their counterparts in painful punishments for not acting as equals. As new objects continue to be introduced, so they will go from a state of being ambiguous and dangerous towards being 'everyday things'. In the 1980s corrugated iron roofs had the status of being ambiguous and dangerous. In 1998 this was the case for TV sets. Perhaps a similar shift from 'dangerous' to 'normal' has occurred for the status of mobile phones. Only three had been obtained in Uroa in 2001; twenty-two were reported in 2004; and 'everybody has one' in 2006. Mobiles have not been the centre of concern, but I argue that I have shown some of the dynamics of how new devices are introduced in rural Zanzibar. Objects are obtained within a complex field of conventions, moralities and social relations. In order to understand how ideas and practices have been modified since the arrival of electricity we also need to see how people make use of the services electricity provides. This is the topic to be explored in the next chapter.

Notes

1. The exceptions here are the most affluent families, where the network seems to have either acknowledged that some families keep larger stocks or that they all have a similar and relatively good standard of living. Also, it should be mentioned that the poorest part of the population is unable to buy anything for future consumption having to concentrate daily on getting something to eat.

2. In other cultural settings people's use of freezers is quite different. In northern Norway people appear obsessed with maintaining large stocks of edibles (Lien 1987: 49). Some keep up to four large freezers per household just for storing food for private consumption. Now, there are a range of factors that differentiate Zanzibar from Norway.

One of the significant differences in this respect lies in the way material life in Zanzibar often concerns a balancing on the edge just to sustain a living. In the North, and in light of the global distribution of goods, consumption patterns appear conspicuous. Seldom do people in this privileged region of the world receive visitors who feel hungry. In Zanzibar they do. Nevertheless, some Uroans still manage to obtain expensive appliances which is our present object of study.

3. The relationship between the brothers is mostly treated in light of their exchanges but is in reality, of course, constituted in a much more complex way. I also knew Silima much better than his brother and only got his version of how this loan came about and how it was transferred into a gift. However, the argument is also based on other people' judgements of what one may ask from others.

4. The list of objects is not necessarily complete but is based on what one woman clearly remembered seven years after the wedding. The types of items and the level of affluence correspond to the situation of a typical woman in Uroa. I observed exchanges of gifts at five weddings during fieldwork.

5. The Comoro Great Marriage (Le Guennec-Coppens 2004) has stronger competitive focus than the rural Zanzibari equivalent.

6. 'Bridewealth' (*mahari*) is the third type of gift exchanged during weddings in rural Zanzibar. This money, given to the bride's parents, is also a social confirmation of the relationship initiated between the two families. Here, there is a moral danger that the 'bridewealth' become excessive. If the size of the gift is too high, the groom might start thinking that he 'bought' (*nunua*) the bride. Correspondingly, he could start treating her badly. This would transfer gifting into the realm of bartering and commodity exchange which in Uroa, as often noted elsewhere, is a morally distinct realm (Appadurai 1986: 11–12; Parry and Bloch 1989: 4–6).

7. The use of 'big things' (*vitu vikubwa*) and 'small things' (*vitu vidogo*) is sometimes expressed as the opposition 'heavy' (*zito*) and 'light' (*epesi*). The notions' meanings are very context-dependent. Generally what is 'big' is connected to size and weight, consisting of things such as beds. Freezers, fridges, cookers, TV sets (and everything fixed) tend to be classified as 'big' too. 'Small' appliances are irons, blenders, radios, and table fans. In practice, though, all these items are owned by men, apart from radios, which women in some cases also obtained before electricity's arrival. I do not have census data on the rate of divorces in Uroa. I would estimate that 30–40 per cent of marriages end in divorce. Many people remarry several times.

8. The healing ritual described was repeated some years later when Khamis's problems returned, apparently due to his success with fishing. This was when I observed it. The healing procedure on the two occasions was said to be identical.

9. Appadurai holds that a double set of illusions are at work in the present transnational context. 'Production fetishism' involves the masking of where and how objects have actually been produced. This generates alienation in Marx's sense of social distance, but also spatially. On the other hand, according to Appadurai, it is also the 'fetishism of the consumer' who is falsely taken to be the seat of agency (1996: 41–2).

Chapter 9

REORGANISING INTERIOR SPACE

Relaxing in Uroa

The opportunity to relax or rest (*pumzika*) is emphasised in rural Zanzibar as part of the 'good life' (*maisha mazuri*). Resting is contrasted with work (*kazi*) and the oscillation between the two conditions makes up a particular rhythm. The repeated articulation of these opposing notions does not imply that their contents and meanings are unequivocal. People's use of 'rest' and 'work' rather reflects a relative comparison of two distinct states of being, often involving a shift from one to the other. In the forest, for instance, the expression 'let's go home' (*twende zetu*, lit. 'let's go to our place') indicates a shift from working (collecting wood) to resting. Some would explicitly state that it was time to relax. At home the women would immediately start to cook, sweep the floor or fetch water. For those coming from the field such chores do not appear as work, but they might do once undertaken. Consequently, when asked about their views on electric cooking, many women mentioned the 'hard work' (*kazi kubwa*) involved in traditional cooking. Furthermore, in informal talks some said they would wait and 'relax' a bit before having another child, thus implying that giving birth to and nursing an infant is the opposite of resting. This contrasts with how women in everyday life often 'relax' and take care of children at the same time.

Work and rest are situationally and relationally defined. In addition, although highly cherished, relaxing should not be exaggerated. This would render a person lazy (*mwivu*) in the eyes of others. Women in town are said to be lazy, thus not balancing work and reward properly. Women in the countryside, with their large burden of tasks, here seem to take pride in contrasting themselves to town women.

When same-sex groups gather to chat, as Uroans love to do, there is little doubt that what they are doing is relaxing. Socialising is a virtue in Zanzibar. Therefore, relaxing is not only related to what you do. It also matters who you share your non-working time with and how rewarding such occasions are perceived to be. Here are some of Silima's views on the phenomenon. He works in the tourist industry and speaks English.

Tanja: What does it mean to relax?
Silima: There are differences. You go outside [abroad] on holiday to relax. We don't have places where we can go, we can't afford it. ... Relaxing is sitting with friends.
Tanja: What is more relaxing, to watch TV or being outside with friends? [Silima has a TV set.]
Silima: It depends. In Uroa, sitting outside is more relaxing. TV, only when good movie. ... It depends on how you are sitting there. You are trying to get good stories. This is relaxing.
Tanja: Can you relax alone?
Silima: Alone you are thinking about many things, how to get food and so on. It is not relaxing.
Tanja: Is sleeping to relax?
Silima: When going to sleep you are tired, so you don't relax.
Tanja: Is going to a wedding relaxing?
Silima: A different way of relaxing. For men, weddings are not important. You relax when you are really happy. When you are happy, you relax. For women, they are happy at weddings. It is relaxing for them.
Tanja: What about funerals?
Silima: You don't relax. You are in grief.

A great deal could be said about how Silima begins his account. By referring to Western ways of relaxing he could be implying that going abroad would be his choice too if he could afford it. As an Uroan working with foreigners he somehow appears torn between different ideals of how to live the good life. I let such aspects rest here.

Silima expresses the shifting and gender-relevant aspects of what it means to relax. It is significant how he links relaxing to happiness and social circumstances. His comparison of TV watching and sitting outside is also relevant for our purposes, but here he appears somehow atypical. Most Uroans show a desire for watching TV and many explicitly link this activity with relaxing and living the good life. What I intend to show is the way people's extended use of the new media, combined with the arrival of electric light, transforms indoor space and affects people's visiting and sexual patterns. People's new ways of relaxing appear to take over important social functions. In the process the notion of relaxing and its evaluation against work also become modified. The consumption of objects related to electricity is a driving force for such changes.

The home as a stage

Relationships are created in space. The meanings of distinct types of spaces, thus their 'senses of place' (Feld and Basso 1996), are determined by the nature of the relationships they host (see also Wikan 1990; Moore 1996; Bender 2002). In Zanzibar a distinction between public and private space bears meaning. People are varyingly exposed to judgements from others in distinct contexts. One spot's particular characteristics, for instance the degree to which it is 'public', depends on the kind of interaction it hosts at a particular moment. The Swahili term *hadharani* captures this situatedness. The notion literally means to 'act in front of people'. When asked to explain what *hadharani* means, people say that this is where and when a person 'cannot tell secrets' (*hawezi kusema siri*). Therefore, shifting, and also influenced by the ideal and practice of sexual segregation, the qualities of space must be contextually investigated.

Nevertheless, there are certain continuities as to how various types of spaces are perceived in this respect. The boundary between the inside and outside of a dwelling is relatively stable. When Rashid was to call Khamis with whom he had just started a shared project, he stopped by the front door. He shouted 'Hello?', and waited outside for Meja to come to the door. In contrast, relatives (male and female) and other people closely associated with the household would be received inside. In chapter 6 we noted how the government officer (meter-reader) when entering living rooms by the front door sometimes caused a break with such aesthetics. However, in general, and due to the types of relationship the space in question normally entails, it is relevant to say that the inside of domestic houses has a more private character. Space outside is more public. To a considerable extent, the front door represents a boundary between front-stage and back-stage (Goffman 1959).

A central finding in the present research is that the arrival of electricity and television has radically altered people's use of household space. Today women and men frequent their relatives homes much more and for longer periods than before. Men who possess TV sets themselves have started to spend their evenings at home. These are issues to be explored. Before I treat the restructuring of living rooms in which the new practices take place, a quick look at various rooms in daytime is in order.

Rooms and their various faces

According to Mary Douglas, the room where visitors are received 'is the face of the house, which speaks composedly and smiles for the rest of the body' (1996 [1970]: 162). In daytime in rural Zanzibar, it is primarily women who occupy indoor space. Therefore, they are also the ones who receive guests. In the course of one day Meja would receive several short visits from her mother-in-law, sister-in-law, cousin and her best friend. These women would shout 'Hello?', and would then freely enter the kitchen or the living room, according to where the host was located. They feel at home. They may touch things. In addition, host and guest constantly tease each other. Information is also exchanged, often also of a practical nature, as they engage in shared activities.

Some women have started producing and selling sweet ice cubes (*malai*, lit. 'angel') since the arrival of freezers in their homes. They would, like those who sell spices from their homes, also receive female guests not so closely related to them. These women would be received in the living room and behave in a much shyer way. Polite exchanges of words would occur, but often no further conversation.

Women seldom visit each other in groups. In Zanzibar Town women are said to entertain each other for longer periods in the afternoon (Larsen 1995: 65). This is not the case in Uroa. Here, women are forever busy doing various tasks. If they have some time to relax, they prefer to sit outside on the bench, but only for short periods. Men's visits are even briefer. They remain standing on the inside of the front door if related to the housewife and tend to come with a specific purpose. An exception in Meja's case is her brother-in-law, who often shows up in the kitchen and spends some time chatting with her.

Therefore, although houses belong to men in an economic sense, indoor space is primarily female territory in everyday life. Olsen observed that it is embarrassing for men to stay inside houses, and this also has relevance in Uroa (Olsen 1999: 35). The living room is the first room people enter and the primary 'face' of the house. During the daytime, the kitchen is an important female arena for interaction with one's closest female network. However, the living room is where all types of guests are received.

Another significant group of guests are the relatives who travel from elsewhere to stay for a few days at a time. Staying overnight, these visitors (often the mother or step-mother, aunts, female cousins or siblings of the hostess) receive the best bedroom, that is, the one that the husband and wife normally sleep in. This space is explicitly perceived as female. Silima said: 'It is her room more than mine'. Furthermore, bedrooms (*chumbani*, lit. 'in the room') are commonly said to be the most important room in a home.[1] When Bi Asiya explained to me why this is so, she significantly pointed to the judgement of travelling relatives: 'If a guest says: "Oh, I went to the home of my friend, it was dirty!", it is not good. It is important to keep the room in order and clean it'. The 'public' nature of bedrooms is also expressed in the way the hostesses of relatively wealthy homes have them decorated with handmade tablecloths and mats. Such display is clearly not only intended for the eyes of husbands. Moreover, a bride-to-be will sit on the bed inside a female relative's bedroom during parts of the ceremony. First she is with her own kin and then women from the line she is marrying into will enter to make sure she is carried to the bathroom for a cleansing ritual. This seems to be the moment when bedrooms reach their most public character.

At the same time bedrooms are highly concealed from inspection by guests in everyday life. This aspect more resembles descriptions of the privacy connected with bedrooms I have come across from other contexts.[2] In Uroa bedrooms are also often locked during the day, as mentioned. Olsen did not once enter her hosts' bedroom (personal communication) and guests to Meja's and Khamis's house seldom got access to theirs. The space serves to hide potentially dangerous acquisitions, such as Meja's sewing machine (see chapter 8). In everyday life this is also where personal items such as clothes, adornments, praying mats and, during daytime, electrical appliances are kept. Those who have ceiling or table fans always keep them by their beds. Such uses are linked with the hosts' expressed longing for comfort but might also directly serve as signs toward visitors.

In sum, bedrooms are places where people prepare themselves for exposure, but they also provide space for crucial moments of evaluation. The dual characteristic of bedrooms is important for understanding consumption in the village. In a way this space can be seen as a buffer between household members and their audiences. Allowing for temporal solutions to unwanted display, keeping things secret but not for long, this space offers a postponement of judgements. Ultimately the room itself and the items it temporarily hides become exposed. In contrast, living rooms can be read as more plain statements of the owners' aspirations.

The physical transformation of living rooms

The current, physical transformation of living rooms in Uroa illustrates the importance of treating the processual nature of 'the house' (Carsten and Hugh-Jones 1995). With analogies to the human body, the authors advocate the view that houses and their inhabitants should be regarded as part of 'one process of living' (ibid.: 37). Below, I provide two sketches which show the configuration of two distinct ways of structuring household space physically. For the sake of simplicity, I shall call the first type 'traditional' (Figure 9.1) and the second 'modern' (Figure 9.2).[3] As the figures indicate, a major difference between traditional and modern houses is the size and the shape of the living room.

When I was received by my host family in 1991, all meals were served in the long and narrow living room (Figure 9.1). Here, male and female acquaintances occasionally came in and sat down on the floor for a chat. Children would also hang around in this room, waiting for a bite to eat or for something exciting to happen. The radio was usually on, either as

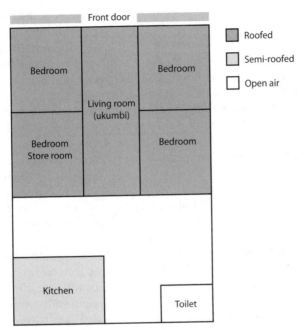

Figure 9.1 The traditional configuration of household space.

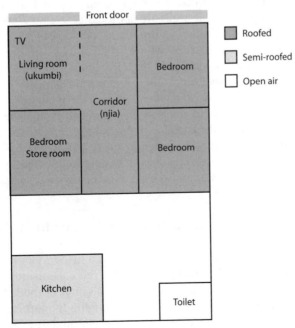

Figure 9.2 A 'modern' type of house where the living room is extended.

background noise or in the foreground when something interesting was going on. Death announcements and news were paid utmost attention to, and heated discussion followed the broadcast of the news of the coup against Gorbachev. When the husband came home to have his meals, visiting neighbours and children would leave. After a meal, the host usually stayed in the same position on the floor reading.

In 2000 I visited more than one hundred households connected to the electricity grid in Uroa and some seventy houses without such a connection. Many houses were found to be similar to the one described, also for those who used electricity. However, a considerable proportion had a different sort of living room than the former 'path' type. Significantly, the new type was to be found among houses along the tarmac road and generally in houses which contained a TV set. Figure 9.2 provides a sketch of the new type of house which is increasingly appearing in Uroa.

The extended living room may be framed by a fourth wall containing a door, left half open with a short 'bar' for people to lean on (as indicated in the sketch), or be without a fourth wall at all. In any case, the effect is a room with at least three walls that provides people with more space for socialising. It is also a space which is more concealed in its nature compared to the former type of living room. This part of the house is the second to have its floors covered with concrete, after the toilet. Living room walls are often also plastered in contrast to other rooms (apart from relatively affluent households where all walls are plastered).

What was previously known as the living room (*ukumbi*) is now also called the 'path' (*njia*). This space, which I shall also be referring to as the 'corridor', is used less for socialising than for going from one part of the house to another. The earth floor often remains unchanged. This means that one has to move up one step when entering the modern living room. When visitors enjoy meals in one's home, men and women tend to eat separately. Women eat in the corridor and men in the modern living room. However, Meja and Khamis eat together every day in the living room, from the same plate. The corridor is now mainly frequented by children (who eat and play there) and is also used for keeping water containers.

Reorganising space and social relationships

New houses today are always constructed with a living room of this sort. When Khamis was asked why, he replied: 'To relax. Husband and wife.' (*Kupumzika. Mume na mke.*) The spatial reorganisation of the living room might well be influenced by the expressed longing for furniture. Sofas, armchairs and tables are watched in TV dramas and advertisements. These objects are highly admired and, if obtained, obviously require space. Some of the relatively wealthy men in the village have purchased and installed such items (see chapter 7). I was invited to dinner at Baoma's place one day. After finishing our Cokes sitting on the soft furniture we slipped down onto the floor to have rice and soup. In Uroa meals are eaten sitting on mats on the floor. Furniture is reserved for other types of occasions. Both eating and otherwise relaxing are important for living a good life, but they are not mixed. However, very few houses contain furnishings of this sort. I do not think that the aspiration for acquiring such objects in the future is the most important explanation for the spatial reconstruction. Neither is it likely that Uroans would start building larger houses simply because this provides them with prestige.

I argue that the enlargement of living rooms is primarily and generally correlated to electric light and to the desire to watch television. The normalisation of electricity, the increasing number of TV sets and the widespread watching of news and shows are relevant explanatory factors. In addition, whereas TV sets may fit into traditional living rooms, large audiences do not. The re-dimensioning of living room space is made out of a concern for whom to watch with. In the few cases where traditional types of houses contain TV sets, one would sometimes find that the appliance had been moved outside in the evenings for people to watch.

In chapter 5 I showed which type of TV programmes people prefer to watch. People were also asked the broader question of why they had

Plate 9.1 TV set placed on top of decorative cloth and table, Uroa, 2001.

obtained a TV set. Many expressed a common interest in the programmes and a wish to get news and ideas from Zanzibar and elsewhere. Other people referred to their desire to relax, often combined with a wish to watch Swahili dramas. Thirdly, some also said they obtained the item so as 'not to have to go to other people's homes'.

For electric light, people often referred to the particular quality of this light compared to that provided by kerosene. Electric light is said to have, or perhaps bring, a particular atmosphere that is valued: 'Its environment!' (*Mazingira yake!*) Electric light is 'bright and strong' (*kali*). Fluorescent tubes are considered even stronger, and thus better. The latter light sources also have the benefit of being cold (*baridi*) in a concrete sense, thus rendering the room less hot than ordinary bulbs. Some women pointed to electricity's lack of smell and smoke compared to kerosene lamps. In sum, as many as 33 per cent of women emphasised that electric light has a particular value in regard to its quality. Men would not disagree on the particular character of electric light, but only 7 per cent brought it up as the primary reason for obtaining this technology. A range of other reasons were also given. Of the forty-one replying men 46 per cent said that it was cheaper (*rahisi zaidi*) compared to kerosene. Of the women, 19 per cent gave the same answer. In addition, whereas 19 per cent of women said electricity was easier to buy than kerosene, which is often bought on a daily basis by women, this

Plate 9.2 Incandescent lights are kept by 99 per cent
of electrified households, Uroa, 2001.

Plate 9.3 People prefer fluorescent lights for their bright light, Uroa, 2000. They are aware of their modest use of electricity but, due to higher installation costs, they tend not to choose this technology.

was only emphasised by 5 per cent of men. Furthermore, 11 per cent of the women and 19 per cent of the men said that electric light is easier to manage. A few of both sexes mentioned the importance of electric light for being developed and 'going with the times' (*kwenda na wakati*).

By now treating electric light and the watching of TV at the same time, we obtain a perspective that takes the whole room as its object for study. It is not always easy to separate the drives for and effects of light from those of television shows, since such use and consumption often go hand in hand. For reasons that will become apparent, it is vital that we treat such practices in combination.

Styles for relaxing: aesthetics and the morality of space

In Bi Mashaka's house I found her, one evening, in the traditional living room, together with a female friend one evening. The sun had gone down and the two were seated close to one another on a mat on the floor. A kerosene lamp had been lit and placed between the two women. Their faces were glowing in the yellowish, lively light which threw shadows of their silhouettes on the wall above. Apart from their bodies and faces, little else in the room was illuminated. The two held a quiet conversation and the radio was off. Apart from my 'Hello?' and Bi Mashaka's response of 'Welcome!', the voices were quiet as we exchanged news and continued the conversation. Her husband and children were all out watching TV and were not expected back until ten o'clock, her husband even later. Upon my asking, Bi Mashaka showed me the couple's bedroom, where the youngest children also sleep in their parents' bed. She lit the lamp inside on the floor. In the modest light that appeared she now explained in whispers how the room was used. She indicated that since electricity and television's arrival in the village there was less intimacy for spouses. Her low voice brought us close to one another and excluded her friend in the room outside from being privy to what was being said. The darkness of the room itself seemed to invite a social form of privacy as well.

Before returning home, I passed by Meja's and Khamis's house. The noise from the TV commercials reached me as I approached the house. At the door I had to shout 'Hello?' quite loudly for them to hear me. Inside the evening guests had arrived and the 40 W ceiling bulb without lampshade was lit. Having returned home early and before the evening prayers, Khamis had brought the TV set out from the bedroom.[4] Now it was placed on the adornment material on a table in the living room (new type) as usual. All the people present were glued to the screen and the programme that was about to begin. My entering the house was met with a cheerful 'Sit down' (*Kaa kitako*), and everybody continued to watch. The children were seated closest to the TV set (see Figure 9.2). Next to them, and also in proximity to the appliance, Khamis's mother was in her favourite spot with her back against the wall. Other women were also seated on the concrete floor but a little further back in the room, leaning against the half-wall. On the other side of this, Khamis's older brothers were standing on the earth floor. They were, therefore, less inside the living room than the women. The hosts, for their part, were sitting close to one another on the earth floor in the corridor. However, they were situated so that they could see the screen through the gap in the half-wall. In this position they could also watch the door when new visitors arrived or someone left. Clearly, this was a time for relaxation.

The contrasts to Bi Mashaka's house are many. First of all, the physically larger and partly concealed living room provides an arena where the extended family can sit together. Secondly, electric light from the ceiling bulb renders visible the frames of the room. In this way, to the eye at least, light renders space larger in volume. There are no boundaries between darkness and light since the whole room, with its protecting walls, is there to be seen. Its source, a radiating ceiling bulb, resembles a torch that reveals everything in its path. Garnert has pointed to the shifting aspects of space according to various types of light sources ('*rummets förendelighet*'), which are also relevant here (1993: 77–8). With electricity, people sit further away from each other but remain able to read each others' body language.

Light enhances communication. With light and the greater distances, people also use louder voices that in darker contexts would appear inappropriate, particularly in Zanzibar (cf. the discussion of aesthetics of darkness in chapter 7). Also, on entering a visitor immediately joins the audience. The standard greeting ritual is reduced.

At the same time, light exposes immoral behaviour. In few other contexts would men and women be located in the same room as they are when watching TV. In the secular school and at village meetings, they do occupy the same indoor space, but these two settings are highly public and therefore morally safe. The inside of a household is, by contrast, ambiguous and morally dangerous. As we have seen, space and its internal boundaries are largely shifting according to the types of interactions they host. What is male, female, public or private has always been recreated to some extent to produce boundaries that articulate proper distances between the sexes. It would, for instance, be unthinkable (or strongly condemned) if Bi Mashaka entertained male guests or a mix of men and women in the evening. The traditional solution to the moral danger of mixing sexes inside is that men seldom spend time there except when eating, washing, fixing the house or sleeping.

Carsten and Hugh-Jones point to the frequently found variable and complex gendered associations of 'internal' and 'external', and they question Bourdieu's inside–outside homology (1995: 40–1). Bourdieu concluded for the Berber household that men tended to 'exit' houses while women 'entered' them. From this he pointed to the close link between women and inside space, on the one hand, and men and the outside world, on the other (Bourdieu 1977: 90–1). In Zanzibar, the associations between gender and space should be considered carefully. However, with television, men have definitely 'entered' the house to an extent and in a manner that is completely new. When I asked a Zanzibari NGO worker in town who has worked with various communities in rural Zanzibar what he saw as the main impact of electricity on everyday life, he answered: 'Men have come home'. My findings support his observation.

Interestingly, the potential threat of impurity within households providing TV in the evenings seems to be compensated for by the particular light that accompanies it. The revealing character of electric light reduces the risks – and suspicions – of improper conduct, where women and men come together. In truth, I did occasionally observe homes where people were watching TV without the lights on. If nobody was reading or working while the TV was on, Meja and Khamis would sometimes choose to turn the lights off to save on costs. However, among the more affluent and, in their own eyes, thoroughly Islamic oriented families, the lights would always be on.

Also, the particular distribution of people in the room represents a strategy for maintaining the moral and social aesthetics. At Meja's and Khamis's place each person occupied the same place every night. Similarly, more space (in terms of square meters, but also visibility) means that women and men may sit at a distance. Two opposing concerns – the desire to watch TV and the importance of respectability – are thus solved by reconstructing a microcosm of gendered space within a living room. Electric light contributes in making this reconstructed order visible and acceptable.

Ending an evening: whose space is it?

Bi Mashaka would wait for her younger children to come home and then go to bed at around ten or half past ten. Had the children not been out, she said, she would have called it a day at nine o'clock. This corresponds to the time when women in non-electrified villages say they go to bed. In contrast, in Khamis's and Meja's house hosts and visitors became tired as the evening turned to night. The children would fall asleep one by one where they were sitting. If not members of the household, they would be woken and told to go home. Grown-ups would start to leave after the Swahili drama at around half past ten or stay a bit longer. Meja would claim to be tired and retreat to her bedroom with the youngest child at some point. However, it is significant that Khamis would stay up until all the guests were satisfied and had returned home.

It is generally acknowledged that people stay up later since the arrival of TV. School teachers often complain that children become too tired during the day because of their new habits. In addition, people who do not watch TV (less than 10 per cent of the population) would sometimes blame their neighbours' marital quarrels on their staying up late to watch shows. The Muslim daily rhythm continues to require (in principle) that people attend the half past four morning prayers. The arrival of loudspeakers in the mosques has increased men's attendance in the morning. With 53 per cent of the women and 74 per cent of the men watching TV at least three times a week, often late into the night, it is clear that they also sleep less.

It might not be the task here to investigate all the implications of modified sleeping patterns. However, I shall focus on one particular dilemma expressed by some of the people I met, one that apparently constitutes a general problem. It relates to electricity's way of affecting sexual patterns. Bi Mashaka complained that she seldom saw her husband before going to bed. And as shown in Khamis's case, men who provide relatives with access to TV shows are expected to stay up until the programmes are finished or everybody has gone home. A consequence of this is reduced intimacy with their wives. The couple would go to bed at different hours and anyway be too tired. Nevertheless, these men seemed uncomprehending when presented with the idea of asking guests to return home when it suited the host. 'They would not like it. I can't do that.' In this way, and in addition to the lack of sleep both spouses may suffer from, the relationship between husband and wife is diminished in deference to what the extended group expects. In turn, sexual patterns are changing. Garnert (1993: 107–9) has proposed a general correlation between lighting technology and birth rates.[5] In Uroa, the watching of TV in the evening could very well have the effect of reducing the birth rate. In addition, as I have also pointed out, the normalisation of electricity represents a financial constraint that may also influence a man's number of children.

Khamis's and Meja's house is crowded every evening with relatives wanting to watch the evening news and shows. Being a social centre represents prestige. They all rely on Khamis paying the electricity bill. The audience's dependency on him is powerfully demonstrated when either he or his wife fetches the TV set from the bedroom. His wife also enjoys high esteem and plays her role by leading the commentary on what is diffused from the screen. She seems to have the right to speak more often and to be louder than female guests. In other people's homes she would display far more modesty. Here, she is at home. I earlier described her female relatives as appearing to feel 'at home' in this space during the daytime. In the evening the same room somehow appears more public and more private at the same time. It is definitely not the place for revealing secrets, thus it has a public character. On the other hand, the way the two of them sit together as a host couple along with their control of the situation strikingly marks the space as belonging to them. Then again, it is not only theirs, however. Despite their providing the infrastructure for watching and having the right to mark the space as theirs, the other people present also have influence on the hosts.

In an early phase, I wondered if the guests' arrival every evening would accumulate into some kind of debt to the host. I had heard of one case where the hosts received payment from viewers who came to watch videos. Furthermore, in chapter 7 we met the tourist guide and his wife. They did not charge the guests for coming, but offered them snacks for sale. In this way, perhaps, they put an obligation on the many guests to buy some of these products.

For ordinary families and how they watch TV together, the conclusion is rather the opposite, or at least is more complex to capture. Khamis's relatives seem entitled to have their share of his wealth and development by watching TV in his house. As we have seen, it goes unquestioned that a host stays up until everybody is satisfied, even if he would like to spend some more time with his wife. Apparently he owes them this by being their son, brother, nephew or friend. Denying relatives the possibility to watch the evening show is unthinkable and would signal deep interpersonal conflicts. Breaking with the norm of sharing might be devastating. The problems Khamis encountered when obtaining the TV were a strong reminder to him of what envious or dissatisfied relatives are able to do. In one sense, he can be seen continuously to be paying the price for this purchase. I am not saying that owners of TV sets walk around with a fear of what would happen if they did not include relatives when watching the evening shows. However, most Uroans are thoroughly committed to their larger family networks and want to be on good terms with them. In offering 'viewing time', Khamis and Meja confirm their ability to show family solidarity. However, we also have to bear in mind the solitude experienced by men when they face the electricity company and the monthly bill. In short, they are (primarily) alone in providing the good but are expected to share the use of appliances.

Encapsulating the family

In sum, watching the news and TV shows is a social event and is expected to be so. Through their new ways of relaxing together men and women reproduce ties within the family network, but not without modifications. Neither is the marital relationship unaffected, as I elaborate below. There can be no doubt as to most people's desire to 'consume' TV programmes. However, as I have aimed to show, it is the study of the manner in which the transformed practices occur that provides the flesh and blood of our social analysis. The way household space is reorganised after the arrival of television is by no means arbitrary. It is the result of specific and interrelated cultural, social and material processes. To further understand why the presented solutions occur as opposed to others, I turn to Henrietta Moore's treatment of household space among the Marakwet of Kenya.

One of Moore's analytical premises is that '[s]pace considered as text does not take as its object real social and economic conditions, but rather certain ideological representations of the real' (1996: 160). Therefore, when the author observes changes in household organisation (that is, square houses instead of the traditional round ones) she is concerned with the ideologies that produce such transformations and how such representations continue to be maintained in the reorganised spatial order. Using an interpretative approach, Moore appears to open up various readings of space as text (representations). However, through her treatment of the links between interpretation and representation where, in practice, there is a limited range of interpretations of the organising of space, the author concludes that: 'favoured interpretations are those imposed by the dominant group' (ibid.: 205–6). For the Marakwet the dominant representation concerns gender relations, placing men above women. The author thus concludes that the modern type of house with a less overt representation of gender conflicts only camouflages such tension and still reproduces the dominant representation. At the core of the Marakwet dilemma lies the ideology of male providers and its incommensurability with the actual, but not openly admitted, interdependence of men and women.

The gender dilemma is also highly relevant in rural Zanzibar. Earlier we noted men's superior status and rights compared to women's. We saw that the ideal of the male provider is sustained despite considerable changes in reality, and even though some critical voices are heard. As long as they are married, women are identified with the homes provided by their men. Therefore, when a husband procures an item, such as a TV set, at the same time he supports his wife and children (cf. Moore 1996: 160). In addition, this act of providing for one's family is repeated every time the appliance is turned on for the wife, husband and children to watch. In this way, the dominant gender representations are reproduced.

However, the ordering of space also shows some tendencies that appear to open up alternative readings. Meja's position beside her husband is important. In other public spaces where the spouses are present at the same time there is a systematic segregation of the sexes. In addition male superiority tends to be demonstrated spatially and materially. We saw Meja's disappointment at being served cold food during the *Maulidi* ritual arranged for women (chapter 5). This reaction of hers is important in the present discussion too. Women make a similar claim to development as men. They do not own appliances even though they contribute with money that leads to their materialisation. However, concerning the use of such appliances, they are just as eager as men and gain a considerable degree of admiration from surrounding people when they behave in a modern way. In addition, the way they are positioned in the room contributes to the interpretation that they are also in power.

In contrast to their place in the shadows during communal ceremonies, at home, in this context, they are rewarded for being modern. To draw on some of Moore's recent work, being rewarded when taking up a particular subject position makes one invest in this identity (Moore 1994: 64–5). By sitting next to her husband, and often being the one to decide when to turn the TV on, she appears to be on equal terms with him in this particular context. The significance of this experience is linked to the fact that there are witnesses to these performances. When guests visit on other occasions, the sex-division immediately becomes an issue. For instance, we saw how spouses avoid eating together when guests join them. We heard how men are entitled to eat in the modern living room, while women eat in the corridor. However, for the evening show this is different. A general division of sexes (guests) maintains the purity of the place. The host couple have their own shared place. Their position, enabling them to watch the door and the television at the same time, marks the fact of their being in control. Therefore, what a male guest experiences here is that men's same-sex relationships do not come before that of Khamis and his wife. Each person in the audience witnesses and, from his or her position, experiences how the modern occupiers of the house perform. Though they have a claim on sharing the 'goods' and feel welcome to do so, they remain subordinate to the two.

Therefore, in contrast to Moore's conclusion for the Marakwet, I suggest that living rooms in Uroa provide opportunities for multiple readings. In Miller's terms, this way of reorganising material culture also constitutes a means for recreating values, identities and power relations (1994, 1998). There is little question as to the continuity of an overall ideology of male superiority in Uroa. However, in the particular situations I have treated, the texts do not appear simply to camouflage 'real' power relations. I have accounted for why the TV-hostess's relatively high position in this situation is significant. Due to the way this reworking of space is interlinked with processes in which people create meaning, there is also a potential for more enduring transformations. This, I hold, is linked to the particular circumstances in the village where life is speeding up, where the source and level of many people's incomes have changed, and, finally, where new technologies have recently become available. Uroa is reconstructed in important ways.

Correspondingly, a transformative potential is emerging (Lien 2003), possibly also in the realm of gender relations. For people's use of electrical appliances and light, I think it is central for the marital relationship we have encountered that not everybody in the village possess these items. Due to the fact that they are markers of difference and attractive icons of modernity, a woman may gain power and prestige when possessing the capacity to perform in a modern way, which other people are excluded from.

In 2004, with the number of television sets in Uroa having nearly doubled since 2001, living rooms had become further reorganised. Two tendencies could be observed. On the one hand, there were couples who now spent their evenings alone in front of the television. In contrast to what was the case only three years ago, there were few evening guests. Husband and wife now had the space of the living room all to themselves. Furthermore, due to the arrival of a new channel (Star TV), they frequently switched between programmes. In addition, and what is also a striking contrast to 2001, the hostess did not know exactly when the Swahili dramas were on. A producer at TVZ explained the purpose of one of the main shows that year, a drama called '*Mbio*'. The morality tale, he said, was designed to make people understand that disagreement in political matters is quite acceptable and no hindrance to the maintaining of peaceful, social relations. In Uroa, apparently, despite the social intrigues on which the dramas continued to be founded, this did not trigger much interest. Alternatively, the cause for the change was related to the perception that TVs are 'not new' (*sio mpya*) any longer. This was suggested as one of the reasons why neighbours and relatives now appeared to prefer to relax on their benches outdoors in the evening. Finally, the couple's endless switching of channels could also have made the guests less interested in watching television.

The other type of living room that appeared in 2004 was marked by consisting of same-sex gatherings. I encountered these on 4 July, the night of the European Championship football final (*fainali*). As the teams from Greece and Croatia were about to clash together on a field far away from Zanzibar, I was invited into one of the houses in Uroa. It was packed with men. The match was being broadcast on TVT (Television Tanzania). In the neighbouring house women were seated watching and listening to the Sunday *Taarab* concert on TVZ.[6] Thus we get a glimpse of a reorganisation of space that represents the ideal of sexual segregation in its more common form. Men's great interest in football, and the extraordinariness of a European final, could account for the same-sex gatherings on that particular night.[7] However, I was informed that due to the genders' distinct preferences for programmes, this pattern had become quite usual. Men and women's distinct preferences were noted in 2001 too, thus it is likely that the increased number of appliances and channels contributed to the new tendency.

I shall be careful not to draw conclusions as to how these various signs of further reorganisation of living rooms could be interpreted. For gender relations, the change could indicate that a women's 'moment' of increased status and power has already faded. In the next chapter we shall see tendencies to the contrary, though. What the latest observation shows us, however, is the dynamic ways in which space is socially and meaningfully constructed. Human beings with their desires, concerns and habituses, on the one hand, and technologies with their illumination, images, remote controls, floors and doors, on the other, make up this space together. I think the data from 1991 and 2001 have provided a good point of entry for grasping the shift from pre-electrification to post-electrification. For the latter period, it is significant that TV sets were still novelties in 2001. The signs of change in 2004 were linked with the normalisation of such objects; television sets appeared in greater numbers and were less of a (social) novelty. This shows the importance of including the use of objects, and not only their acquisition, in studies of consumption (cf. Shove 2003).

Finally, it should be mentioned that some individuals in the village are excluded from watching television for a range of reasons. They are, nevertheless, affected by their co-villagers new habits. Makame said that when people put their TV sets inside he does not feel welcome to ask to watch with them. For him, placing the appliance outside is the sign that people want others to come. This practice seems to be vanishing, however. We saw that some people said they wanted their own appliance so that they would not have to go to other people's houses. This either speaks of relational friction, or it simply means that people feel more comfortable being the host on such occasions.

If we consider men in the village at large, their evening gatherings outdoors had, by 2001, become disrupted. Due to the fact that the spatial reconstructions indoors and outdoors at night were so remarkable, it is likely that men's internal relationships also became redefined. When some of them went home to watch TV, they were ignoring their obligation to socialise with co-villagers. Perhaps this is what they sought to balance out when some houses, three years later, were reserved for football matches with friends. Silima, whom we met in the introduction to this chapter, said he prefered to exchange good stories with his friends. He obviously enjoyed this, as did other people in the village. However, he had the choice of what to do and possessed the important capacity of being able to perform in a modern way. Men like Silima demonstrated their superior position and articulated new perceptions of what providing for a family had become about.

When, in 2001, Khamis one day covered the windows of his house, this did not only have the effect of protecting the house against rain and wind. The wooden cover remained in place long after the rainy season had ended and turned out to be a permanent installation. By withdrawing to the increasingly concealed house to relax with his wife, family and selected neighbours and friends, he recreated and reinforced the boundary between the inside and the outside world. Perhaps, in 2004, the couple's apparent solitude indicated that they perceived this process to have gone a little too far. Alternatively, maybe the neighbours' interest will reappear. What is clear is that having the ability to withdraw to one's own living room to relax forms part of living the good life in modern, rural Zanzibar.

Notes

1. The standard Swahili notion for a bedroom is '*chumba cha kulala*' ('sleeping room').
2. Eva Londos (1993) provides an ethnological account of Swedish homes in the last century. She regards the bedroom, in contrast to the living room, as having being concealed from inspection by guests, and thus of having a distinctively private nature. In rural Zanzibar, this division is less clear cut.
3. Both types are common in present Uroa and this categorisation is not used by Uroans themselves. The chosen labels denote that one type has been introduced more recently than the other.
4. Khamis would return later on those days he had been in the fields until late. On such occasions, Meja would bring the TV to the table in the living room. Normally, both would pray at half past six, he in the mosque and she at home in the living room. The guests would start arriving after seven o'clock in the evening.
5. Garnert (1993: 107–9) proposes a general correlation between lighting technology and birth rates. In the case of Sweden he refers to the fact that before the arrival of electricity more (legitimate) children were born in September and October, that is, nine months after the darkest period. Today more Swedish children are born in March and April. He proposes that with electric light (when differences between summer and winter, and between day and night became reduced), people started reading and doing other chores in winter time (that is, December and January, which is much darker and colder than summer time in July and August). The consequence of light was definitely that people went later to bed. However, couples also possibly had less sexual intercourse than before. Garnert further registers that nine months after a period of rationing of electricity in Sweden in the first quarter of 1970 the birth rate shot up. Finally, he refers to the director of Tanzania Publishing House who, in 1987, is said to have stated that electricity

would be the best contraceptive remedy (making people read more instead of making babies).

6. Taarab originated in East Africa where it today remains as a popular music genre. In Zanzibar, *taarab* is also common during wedding celebrations. The female audience tend to participate in the dancing, and this aspect is of great interest to the women in Uroa who watch the concerts on TV.

7. The Uroan football team had changed its name in 2004 (by fusing the two existing teams in Uroa, one of which had previously been labelled the 'Uroa Argentina Sport Club'). The new name is 'Uroa Star'. The change of name was said to be inspired by the arrival of the new television channel, Star TV.

Chapter 10

NEGOTIATING TASTES IN FOOD

Cooking with electricity

One of the two families in Uroa who keep electric cookers (coil element type) agreed to show me how the appliance is used. I was to visit this house regularly for a month and watch Asha cook. In return, I would pay the electricity bill for that period. Her husband Muhamadi was present during our initial conversations and he was the one who answered most of my questions. Here is an extract from one of our first talks. The three of us were sitting in their living room (corridor type) and the front door giving on to the road was closed.

Tanja: How did you obtain the cooker (*ringi*)?
Muhamadi: I bought it in town in 1993 for three thousand shillings [US$10].
Tanja: Why did you buy it?
Muhamadi: I wanted to make cooking easier (*rahisisha mambo ya kupika*). Wood is hard to make dry in the rainy season so this is the time best-suited for using the cooker.
Tanja: Who decides when to use it?
Muhamadi: Since I am away most of the time, she decides when to use it. [Asha nods.]
Muhamadi: We are both very aware of its costly use. I notice that the meter wheel is going around fast when the cooker is used, so we try not to use it too much.
Tanja: Why do you think very few people in Uroa keep electric cookers?
Asha: It is just because they are afraid (*wanaogopa tu*). [Muhamadi nods.]
Muhamadi: Electric cookers are so dangerous that one needs things that are difficult to get, such as gloves and shoes for insulation. It is also important (*lazima*) that children are kept out of the room and that only wooden sticks are used for stirring since metal ones become too hot.

[Here there was a pause while we talked about something not directly related to the topic.]

Asha: [quietly] I am also afraid (*Mimi pia, naogopa*).
Tanja: Oh, if you are afraid of using the cooker I shall not ask you to do it!
Asha: No problem (*Hamna matatizo*). [Smiling and shrugging her shoulders.]
Muhamadi: Yes, it's okay. She manages. (*Sawa. Anaweza.*)
Tanja: Okay, but please tell me if you want to stop cooking in this way.
Asha: No problem.
Tanja: Do you do other things to protect yourself, such as reading the Koran, taking medicine (*dawa*) or closing the body (*funga mwili*)?
Asha: I read every night.
Tanja: Does reading also keep evil spirits (*mashetani*) away?
Asha: Yes.
Muhamadi: Yes.

If I had anticipated that Asha and Muhamadi would cite financial reasons for why most people do not keep electric stoves, or bring up the issue of development, I would have been wrong. Neither did they mention (at this point) that the taste of food is of relevance. Instead they showed profound concern for the danger involved. The means of protection ranged from physical measures to spiritual kinds, though the latter was also linked with general precautions for obtaining a good life.[1]

When I turned up to watch Asha cook, it was not her but a younger sister residing with them who was in charge of the operation. Asha had once got an electric shock (*shoti*) touching the mains in the living room. Since then she had refrained from using the cooker. Now, the appliance had been collected from the bedroom and had been placed on a wooden table in a special room in the inner part of the kitchen area (a quite unusual type of construction).[2] Asha watched her sister clean and cut garlic, tomatoes and onion. Without using gloves, but wearing rubber sandals, the sister inserted the plug into the electric outlet. She started to fry the vegetables in oil in an ordinary aluminium pot (*dishi*) on the cooker. She held on to the pot by means of a cloth. Afterwards, spices, lime, and water were added while stirring with a wooden spoon. The sauce was left to simmer for half an hour with somebody around to watch that the children did not touch anything. Then the sister cut the power. On the next occasion, the sister was again doing the electric cooking. However, after some days they told me that that particular electric outlet was out of order. So our little project ended.

Asha is not alone in her fear of electric cookers. 88 per cent of women and 66 per cent of men stated in the census interviews that cooking with electricity is dangerous. Men's sense of danger was less for those living in electrified houses (62 per cent with electricity versus 71 per cent without). For women, the feeling of unease with electric cookers remained on a similar, high level. The gravity of such danger was often expressed in faces, voices and the typical statement: 'very dangerous!' (*hatari sana!*). When I asked specifically for a comparison, no one hesitated to point out that electricity is the most dangerous technology. In 1991 my hostess described the difference in danger based on information she had heard on the radio: 'By touching the fire you may get hurt (*utaumwa*). Electric cookers can make you die (*utakufa*).' In 2001 Meja and other Uroan people said the same. Contrary to what my husband and I concluded from our own, regular experiences with electric shocks in Uroa, the danger was never said to be related to the artefacts' poor condition or bad installation. The hazards were quite directly associated with the cook's unsatisfactory skills or misuse of the device: 'You may make a mistake' (*Unaweza kukosea*). Compared to the three-stone hearth, electric cooking technology is seen to require a different type of knowledge. Some hold that it is a matter of learning: 'Everything you are not used to is dangerous. Afterwards it is okay.' Mwanajuma, who has been living in rural Zanzibar all her life, had a more essentialist view on the topic: 'For people in the countryside, it is dangerous to cook with electricity' (*Kwa watu wa shamba ni hatari kupika kwa umeme*). On the other hand, Mwanajuma's statement can also be read as a positive declaration of the taste of traditionally cooked food. Alternatively, she regards electric cookers as so irrelevant to people in the countryside that they will never become used to them.

The increasing practical experience many people have had with electricity since its arrival has not diminished people's general concern for the physical dangers involved. Cookers are considered to be the most hazardous types of device. Or rather, it is the electrical appliance which most strikingly demands particular knowledge and that no mistakes be made on the user's side. The 'script' cookers come with is perceived to require a range of precautions. A table, a waterproof ceiling, sandals; these are all extra measures and investments compared to what the hearth requires. In addition, keeping children away is perhaps the most constraining consideration. I will return to cooks and their concerns after having discussed the issue of taste, which will take us through an analysis of food, gender and kitchen technologies in rural Zanzibar.

Zanzibari tastes

Tastes in food (*ladha la vyakula*) were often brought up in conversations about electric cookers in Uroa. Men in particular stressed their preference for food cooked with firewood. Their emphasis on taste in explaining why electric cookers were not in use awoke my interest to explore the meanings inherent in cooking processes. The absence of electric cookers in the village points to food processing and eating as a more static realm of life than, say, how and where people spend their leisure time. TVs are embraced, electric cookers are not. The chapter seeks to illuminate this fact by going beyond economic explanations. Cooking practices and preference for food are often said to be conservative aspects of human life. Enduring, limited access to ingredients and technology may provide elements of continuity (Goody 1982). The structuring of meals and table manners imbues the consumption of food with formality and stability (Douglas 1999 [1972]; Goody 1982: 151). Furthermore, eating habits are learned from early childhood through 'rituals of family living ... [a]s a consequence, their staying power is great' (Goody 1982: 151). Bourdieu's concept of habitus is applicable and he says: 'it is probably in tastes of *food* that one would find the strongest and most indelible mark of infant learning, the lessons which longest withstand the distancing or collapse of the native world and most durably maintain nostalgia for it' (Bourdieu 1984: 79, original emphasis). Therefore culinary practices and people's perceptions of taste are thoroughly incorporated and resistant to change.

Should we then be content with attributing the preferences for food cooked with firewood – and the non-use of electric cookers in Uroa – to the conservative nature of such practices? Obviously, I think the topic deserves a more nuanced investigation. Transformative aspects of cooking and eating patterns have long been noted in anthropological studies (e.g., Goody 1982; Lien 1987; cf. also Mintz and Du Bois 2002: 100). In rural Zanzibar people acknowledge and describe how the culinary repertoire of today differs from that of the past. For example, noodles constitute one of the important dishes of the *futari* meal served at night during the fasting month. Noodles, imported from China, are said to have been introduced quite recently ('not long ago', *sio zamani*). Boiled with sugar and cardamom, a packet of foreign noodles becomes *tambi*. Other changes in what people eat are also noted in rural Zanzibar. As I show below, edibles that provide strength to human bodies are used to a lesser extent than before. Some consider this change to jeopardise the health of the current generation. Therefore we may also adopt the perspective that '[f]oodways influence the *shaping* of community, personality and family' (Counihan 1999: 6, my emphasis). My point of departure is, therefore, that food habits are thoroughly incorporated in human beings but are also potentially a response to – or driving forces for – change.

The very availability of electric cookers and freezers provides a potential for transformation in food habits. Goody contributes great significance to the moment when an effective device for producing artificial ice was introduced in England, enabling a catering industry to take off (1982: 162–3). In turn, British culinary practices were transformed. The present chapter dwells on the historical instance when food-related artefacts (electric cookers and freezers) became available to a group of people for the first time. By 2001 these appliances had made their way into people's lives through TV commercials. In addition, demonstrations of electric water kettles were promoted for educational purposes on the same governmental channel. In Swahili dramas, men and women often gather around a restaurant table to consume bottled, sweet drinks, as shown in chapter 5. I never saw electric cookers in use in Swahili dramas, though, which indicates that the government considers their use irrelevant in present Zanzibar.

However, the electric cooker manifests itself on a practical level too, despite its modest distribution in the village. In addition to Asha and Muhamadi, one family in Uroa keep such a device. People are also aware of the cookers used in the surrounding hotels and guesthouses and of my own household's use of electricity for cooking. However, most notably, many Uroans have had personal encounters with electric cookers. In the survey 76 per cent of women and 81 per cent of men said they had tasted food cooked with electricity; 67 per cent of women knew or knew of people who had electric cookers; and 35 per cent said they had tried to cook this way. Uroans are becoming increasingly acquainted with the new technology. This seems to feed a growing discourse of technologies and their links with tasty or proper food. Furthermore, freezers kept in Uroa were not used for storing cooked food. The question of taste again appears in people's explanations.

In the proceeding sections I focus on perceptions of taste in relation to electric stoves and freezers. I start by showing how internal differences are generally played down in questions related to cooked food and their taste. However, on a higher level, food is a significant marker of a shared Zanzibari identity. Then I explore various cooking technologies and their links with taste as Uroans perceive it. I discuss the emerging and partly contradictory discourses on taste from a gender perspective and suggest that this can be regarded as a field of negotiation.

Consumption of cold drinks takes on a more stratified pattern than culinary practices. Here, differences are acknowledged. Partly by focusing on perceptions of the body, I aim to account for why tastes in drinks appear to be in flux while tastes in food remain relatively stable. However, as already indicated, taste is also a multifaceted notion.

Food as a social marker

I draw on selected parts of Pierre Bourdieu's (1984 [1979]) treatment of taste in analysing Uroans' preferences for food. Isabel González Turmo (1997) makes use of Bourdieu's work without relying on predefined categories (see also Lamont 2000: 271 n. 14; Turner and Edmunds 2002: 221–2). She explores how perceptions of tastes in food in rural Spain come about, that is, how they become markers of identification. In Andalucia such processes involve elements of competition. Bourdieu also emphasises the dynamics of how symbolic boundaries are produced and maintained, an approach which is valuable for our purposes. He demonstrates the importance of taste as a discursive and experiential force. Our Uroan case will in certain respects demonstrate the opposite. In this way, it becomes just as important to account for why differences in taste are muted, as it is to show when taste is a prime focus for boundary creation. The notion of taste contains a multitude of interests, perceptions and values. Exploring the notion and how people in Zanzibar variously make reference to taste is therefore an approach with a potential for grasping some of the complexity of life in current Zanzibar.

'Taste' in Swahili, to my knowledge, does not contain a dual meaning as it does in English. For the evaluation of food and its flavours, people in Uroa use the term *ladha*. In comparison, the expression 'a person of taste' is translated into Swahili as *mtu wa akili* (person of intellect or intelligence), *mchaguzi, mteuzi* (meaning both a discriminating and demanding person), or *msaanifu* (someone skilled in art, writing and speaking).[3] The singular meaning of taste related to food in Swahili may appear to clarify the object of study. However, Bourdieu emphasises that tastes in food are inseparable from more general evaluations of lifestyles (1984: 99). In our case, it is not always the creation of difference that matters, but we may still speak of taste as a subtly signifying practice (Ferguson 1999: 93–102).

For the embodied experiences involved, taste in food is at the same time a combination of physical sensations (flavour, texture, consistency, smell) and a conceptual activity (González Turmo 1997: 125, following Toussaint-Samat 1991: 150). González Turmo points to the way such physical sensations are 'received, interpreted and analysed within, and in relation to, the position that each person has in the world, and their perception of this position' (1997: 125). A person's positioning is important as to how 'flavour' is perceived. I start the discussion of taste by looking at how rural Zanzibaris perceive of the food which is processed and cooked within their own community.

Internal differences played down

People in Uroa speak of their cuisine as 'Zanzibari food' (*vyakula vya Zanzibar*). Town is in many respects an important 'other'. However, in terms of cooked food, the Swahilis (*Waswahili*) in Zanzibar at large are considered to have the same knowledge and preferences.[4] Only one couple I talked to could name a typical Uroan dish. This is called *mseto*, and consists of a mixture of beans and rice. Most people, however, would speak of this dish as typically Zanzibari. Many mentioned that fish is characteristic for Uroa, located on the beach as it is. The availability of food products varies across the island. However, more than half of the women in Uroa were not born in the village. Of the men, 85 per cent were. Inter-village family networks linked the population to other villages in crucial ways. Foods were repeatedly transported from place to place.

Nobody expressed the view that meals cooked in Uroa were different from – or better than – dishes prepared in other parts of Zanzibar. González Turmo found the opposite case for Andalucia, Spain. Here, distinct village identities were distinctively played-out in claims as to who possessed the best recipes, flavours and dishes (1997: 120). Such discourses of tastes in food were non-existent in rural Zanzibar and also within the village. In Uroa, we have seen how the (increasing) internal stratification is articulated in areas of consumption such as electric lighting (outdoors, chapter 7) and light, along with TV-watching (indoors, chapter 9). In the present discussion, we shall see that such distinctions appear relevant in the case of cold drinks.

Food habits, in contrast, are not social markers of distinction. Differences are deliberately played down. There are certainly variations in the types of meals people actually prepare and eat. Due to lack of resources, many are forced to make compromises. However, deviations from the ideal of how to prepare a dish pass without comment and do not serve to mark distinctions in a systematic way. The *pilau* Tatu cooked one day serves as an example. Ideally, *pilau* is made of rice, spices (cumin, chilli, cinnamon and cardamom) potatoes, onion, garlic, tomatoes, oil, salt, water and meat (preferably beef, but often made with chicken or fish in Uroa). Just before *pilau* is ready to be served, a mix of fresh tomatoes, onions and lime juice is added on top of the rice. The dish is considered to be the Zanzibari national dish and is primarily reserved for festive occasions. I was repeatedly told of the necessity of adding each particular ingredient.

Tatu had no fish that day. She decided to prepare *pilau*. Plain rice (or rice cooked in coconut milk) does not make a complete meal but needs fish, beans or meat (and preferably vegetables) as an accompaniment. Tatu instead set out to make *pilau*. However, she did not have the required tomatoes, chilli, meat/fish or even cardamom, which is said to be the most important ingredient (in addition to the rice). Still, according to Tatu, the result was *pilau*. Her neighbours (some of them quite affluent and usually able to make *pilau* in the prescribed way) agreed that it is possible to make *pilau* without the 'necessary' (*lazima*) ingredients. Compared to the general descriptions I had received, I was therefore surprised to find that *pilau* can be made in this reduced form and still be called *pilau*. Even though a national symbol, the dish does not require all the ingredients in practice. In comparison, a traditional stew in Andalucia would need the 'correct ingredients' (meat, bones and dried pork/beef) also in practice (Gonzáles Turmo 1997: 123). I think the flexibility found in rural Zanzibar indicates that people do not wish to differentiate between various social units based on what they eat.

The lack of strict rules as to what a dish consists of has a parallel in people's avoidance of commenting on a cook's skills. In general terms, such evaluations pose no problem: 'If she knows how to add a little something it will become better than what other people make' (*Akijua kutia juici-juici fulani itakuwa nzuri zaidi kuliko wengine.*) However, people avoid naming somebody who knows this art better or worse than others. For instance, I asked Silima if his wife's cooking was better than the average. He laughed and hesitated. As I continued to show that I was curious about the matter, he finally agreed that it was. Women also refrain from openly judging their own or others' knowledge of cooking, for better or worse. When a meal is eaten, its particular flavours are never commented on. This attracted my attention, given my background in a cultural setting where the topic of taste automatically accompanies most meals, if only as a gesture of politeness. If I expressed satisfaction during the meals I had in Uroan homes, my words were often returned, friendlily, but as if in surprise. 'Very tasty food!' (*Tam sana!* i.e., *Vyakula vitamu sana*), I would say and the host would reply, smiling: 'Tasty?' (*Tam?*). I never heard anybody else comment on the food as we ate (or afterwards).

Now if the stress on equal skills and a homogeneous cuisine can partly be understood through women's frequent movements across the islands, the virtual taboo against commenting on particular foods needs some elaboration. First of all, there is the question of female identity. A critique of a woman's cooking (which commenting on taste implies) may threaten her purity and reputation. However, in other contexts, such as the evaluation of clothing, judgements that may jeopardise a woman's image of purity are quite common. I therefore turn to another aspect of significance, that of intimacy and fertility.

Cooking's and eating's associations with intimacy has been noted in many cultural contexts (Counihan 1999: 9–10). In rural Zanzibar, the link between sexuality and food is perhaps most clearly demonstrated in the way a husband married to several wives eats and sleeps with each of them in two-day cycles. Evaluating particular foods would, on a social level, imply commenting on how a wife performs within her marital relationship, and in a quite intimate sense. Furthermore, cooking as an image of motherhood and femininity has been linked with procreative powers in general. Recent studies of myth and ritual in Africa support the relevance of treating gender as something more than the relationship between men and women (Blystad 1999: 211–3). From this perspective, which resonates with the treatment of women's wealth in chapter 8, the taste of food concerns the family, and, in turn, the whole descent line's (or even society's) capacity for reproduction in a wider sense, irrespective of which person actually produced the food. A sense of fragility or danger connected to criticising – or appraising – food appears in this light since much more than the cook's reputation would be at stake. These muted food aesthetics somehow resemble the carefully controlled 'aesthetics of darkness' treated in chapter 7. The general fear of evil magic may be a relevant factor in the realm of food too. Harmful medicine is always thought to be prepared in people's kitchens. In this way, critiques of food could in theory involve the risk of insinuating that the cook or related people harbour bad intentions. To take this idea to its most devastating conclusion, criticism could increase the risk of being poisoned on a later occasion.[5] In Carrithers's terms (1992), the aesthetic standards of darkness and the taboo against marking differences in culinary practices, tastes and cooks' skills, allow for less flexibility than may often be the case in other domains. Breaking with what is perceived 'appealing' may here have particularly unfortunate consequences. Differences in taste appear to be a sensitive topic.

Zanzibari food as a point of identification vis-à-vis others

The lack of commenting on the tastes of food cooked in Uroa radically contrasts with the spectacular stories of Zanzibari food that are otherwise told. The expressed distinction between Zanzibari food and non-Zanzibari food is a legitimate way of constructing difference. Celebrating collective identities poses no risks. Obviously, people's relationships with the lump category 'external world' are not unequivocal. I here focus on Uroans' relationship to the Norwegian-headed electricity project that was the subject of chapter 4.

In this process, Uroans depended on the goodwill of the project management. Clearly, they were in a subordinate position vis-à-vis those who had the power to decide where the poles were to be set up. However, Uroans were confident that the foreigners would appreciate their meal. In the aftermath, they also explained the fortunate outcome (electrification) by referring to the superior quality of Zanzibari food. I referred to the way this meal could be said to have seductive overtones. Uroans showed the foreigners who they were. In this way, they seduced the project management into betting on them. They also imposed obligations on the guests (Mauss 1990 [1950]: 39). Through this act, their subordinated position was temporarily set aside and Zanzibari identity and superiority was celebrated. The significant other is, here, non-Zanzibari and linked to the West. Zanzibari food is what made the difference.

'The art of eating and drinking', Bourdieu says, 'remains one of the few domains in which the working classes explicitly challenge the legitimate art of living' (1984: 179). Even though Bourdieu might have underestimated other possible means that dominated classes have for defying power relations, I think the perspective has relevance in the present context. When applied to the meeting between Uroans and the project management, what other means or resources apart from food did the villagers possess that could make an impact? Sharing food of course serves the task of creating social bonds so well. However, the significance of Zanzibari cooking is not limited to such a situation of negotiation. Rather, the event highlights food as an icon around which Uroans construct their shared identity. It is in this context I suggest we consider how various technologies affect foods' taste.

Taste and technologies

Men in Uroa enthusiastically explained how the fire gives food a particular and superior taste. On the fire food is cooked gently (*pole pole*) and slowly made tender (*laini*). In contrast, the heat of electric cookers, they said, is hard to regulate. This has an unfortunate impact on taste. What is more, the smoke from the fire is also cherished. It is seen to leave behind small, significant particles inside (*ndani ndani*) which contribute to the food's delicious taste. In addition, smoke produced from particular trees may have fortunate effects on the body. A teacher explained this by referring to research done by traditional experts on medical diagnosis (*uaguzi*). He concluded that 'for taste, firewood is better, also because of its medical effects'.

The above indicates that men perceive the electric cooker to be detrimental to the taste of food. In in-depth interviews with men I knew relatively well, they all preferred the 'taste of firewood'. They claimed that the quality cannot remain the same without the fire. By using various adjectives, gestures, mimics, and other kinds of body language, they left me in no doubt that they preferred food cooked with firewood. Descriptions of the meal in Uroa at the time of electrification revealed a similar passion for traditionally cooked food. During the census interviews, however, only half of the men said they preferred the taste of food cooked with firewood. The discrepancy between what was said during these formal interviews with eighty men, and the informal conversations with ten to fifteen of them, is interesting. I will return to the same tendency shown also by women presently. For now I hold that due to my association with electricity, men I did not know well might have tended to provide census answers according to what they thought I would agree to and thus emphasised electric cooking. The informal data, including the observation of everyday life, support the claim that men in Zanzibar prefer the taste of food cooked with firewood. This preference partly explains why electric stoves are not in use in Uroa. In addition, of course, electric cooking is far more costly in terms of fuel use than the current 'free' supply of firewood though women's labour.

This articulated preference for traditional taste can also be seen as an extension of people's celebration of Zanzibari cuisine in general. Men's preferences for the fire and its smoke contribute to validating Zanzibari values and styles of living as opposed to foreign ones. Whether this is a question of 'necessity' or not is less relevant (cf. Bourdieu's concept 'taste for necessity' (1984: 374–96)). The boundary between firewood (us) and electricity (them) is created in these replies. This type of electric appliance is conceptually linked with Western ways of living.

Women's views on taste and its relationship to cooking technologies are more varied. In general, during the census interviews, they often seemed less prepared than men to answer questions concerning taste.[6] Compared to men they also appeared less preoccupied with the question of taste as such. This tendency was more marked in in-depth talks and during participant observation, as I show below. By now extending the analysis to the act of cooking, we obtain a broader basis for discussing taste. In Bourdieu's phrase: 'Tastes of particular dishes are associated, through preparation and cooking, with the whole conception of the domestic economy and the division of labour between the sexes' (1984: 185). Now, in chapter 8, we saw how wedding gifts articulated central ideas about a woman's role as a wife and mother. On the other hand, in the previous chapter I pointed to signs of modifications of established gender roles during cross-sex gatherings in front of the TV. These were notably found in a realm where the modern style is particularly strongly emphasised. A study of cooks and their concerns will help us to see links between tastes in food, the various technologies used for preparing them and the degree to which these are influenced by the modern discourse.

A cook's technologies and concerns

Goody has pointed out that in Europe the 'kitchen was the birthplace of many technical operations and apparatus' concerning the preparation and cooking of food. However, 'when these processes left the kitchen for specialist control they generally shifted from the hands of women to those of men' (Goody 1982: 193). Emma Crewe argues that this shift is also true for stove development in the South (1997: 67, primarily referring to the burning of organic fuels). Crewe explains the detachment between developers and the group intended as users of the new technology as an important reason why the massive attempt to introduce efficient stoves in developing countries failed in the 1980s. In short, the new stoves, intended to reduce energy consumption, were not designed to meet the various needs of cooks. The new technologies were not put into use.

Certainly, the few electric cookers found in Uroa have been designed and developed by people socially and culturally detached from rural Zanzibar. From the glimpse provided at the beginning of this chapter, one may ask to what extent these appliances satisfy cooks' needs and concerns. Asha has a deep fear of them, and this she shares with the majority of the population.

Also, we have seen that men are owners of such devices in rural Zanzibar. This signals a further separation between cook and technology. In addition, the electricity bill paid for by men has been highlighted as a barrier for women in the adoption and owning of electrical appliances.

Different types of dishes and impossible ways of making them

Many respondents related to the electric coil element when asked what may be cooked with electricity. The coil element cooker is the cheapest of electric cookers available in Zanzibar and does not provide any possibility for regulating the temperature. Big ovens with plates on the top and one-plate and two-plate smaller stoves have devices for temperature control, but were not kept in the village until 2004. The degrees to which people were aware of alternative types varied as did the relevant taxonomy.[7]

Of the women, 25 per cent stated that one cannot cook all kinds of food with electricity (38 per cent of the men said the same). Among these

Plate 10.1 Ms Mwatima Nassor with electric cooker (coil element type), Uroa, 2001.

respondents, the lack of physical stability and temperature regulation were often seen as limiting the usefulness of such cookers. Bahati associated electric cooking with the coil element and was not particularly impressed with the food she had tasted: 'There was so much heat/power (*moto sana*) that the beans turned strong/bitter/burned (*kali*)'. In contrast, she said that beans cooked on firewood got tender little by little (*yanawiva kidogo kidogo*), resembling men's descriptions referred to earlier. She had never cooked with electricity and did not want to try in the future.

Ugari (mainland Swahili, *ugali*) is the most frequently cited dish that (some) people would not dream of cooking with electricity. It is a thick, heavy porridge usually made with maize flour and water. It takes a lot of muscle power to beat and blend *ugari* and you need to hold on to the pot while doing it. As a result, 'you don't manage to stir when using an electric coil element' *(kwa ringi, huwezi kusonga)*.

As with the beans Bahati had tasted, *Pilau* is generally considered difficult to make when there is no heat regulation. In addition, *pilau* (and *wali*, which is rice cooked in water or coconut milk) needs to be heated from above. A baking effect is normally achieved by placing remaining embers or burning copra on top of the lid towards the end of the cooking time. For

Plate 10.2 Preparing *pilau* requires heat from below and above, Uroa, 2001.

such purposes, the coil element is regarded as having severe drawbacks. In sum, the coil element is unsuitable due to its lack of heat regulation and baking opportunities. For its drawbacks in regard to dishes that need heavy beating, we should also consider the danger associated with the appliance. Holding on tightly to a vessel means getting closer to electricity itself.

The materiality of cooking vessels influences perceptions as to what can be cooked on electric stoves and, in turn, taste. The *dishi* (deep aluminium pot) and *chungu* (clay pot) are in daily use. Women normally also keep an iron frying pan. This is the only type of vessel with a handle in Uroa.[8] The clay pot is the traditional vessel and definitely the one preferred for preparing traditional medicine. Exceptions to the rule are when large quantities must be made, such as when the whole of Uroa had to be ritually protected before electricity's arrival. Clay pots are also generally preferred for soups, for reasons of taste (this stated by men and women).[9] The problem with clay pots is that they crack after a while. If put on a hot coil element it would break into pieces ('stones', *mawe*). However, primarily due to its slightly rounded base, the clay pot is unsuitable for electric cookers which have a flat surface anyway.

In comparison, aluminium pots are said to have been introduced more recently. These are considered suitable for boiling water, rice and vegetables as well as for various porridges (Plate 10.2). They are not galvanized and may corrode but seem to have a longer durability than clay pots. With a flat underside, this is the vessel that goes with electric cookers. It should be mentioned, though, that their surface tends to become uneven

Plate 10.3 Fish and *pilau* ready to be served on the floor, Uroa, 2004.

after use due to their thin construction. Therefore, the technical efficiency would soon become reduced when put on a stove.

There is a sort of hierarchy of taste related to cooking vessels, at least as expressed by the men I met. To quote Rashid: 'The clay pot has [gives] a better taste than the aluminium pot. With the clay pot ... Zanzibari food is better. Tastier. Aluminium is not tasty.' (*Chungu ina ladha yake zaidi kuliko dishi. Kwa chungu ... chakula cha Zanzibar ni bora. Kitamu zaidi. Dishi sio kitamu.*) Still, aluminium pots are widely in use, not least due to their large size. Furthermore, in contrast to Rashid's and other men's similar statements, I never heard a woman complain about the taste of food cooked in aluminium pots, even though they also prefer the clay pot for soups.

We may draw some conclusions from this. First of all, what constitutes an 'electric stove' (*koka ya umeme*) is variously perceived. The particular stove each person has in mind influences his or her perception of the kind of dishes that are possible to cook with electricity. Furthermore, the materiality of clay pots makes these vessels unsuited for electricity. In addition, distinct types of dishes require distinct methods of preparation. Food boiled in water is considered more easily handled with electricity than those which require baking, slow simmering or heavy stirring and beating. However, what is practically possible may be limited due to the interests of preferences in taste. For soups, this dilemma seems to be particularly relevant. From a technical point of view soups may be cooked in aluminium pots on electric coil elements (as Asha's sister did). However, for taste, the clay pot is the preferred vessel. In men's stated dislike for aluminium pots we find a similar tension between what is practical (large amounts and, hypothetically, the use of electricity) and what gives the best taste.

The sketched links between particular stoves, kitchen utensils, various dishes and taste makes up a field of knowledge that is largely undetermined. Each person has his or her view of what is possible and tasty. The complexity involved, including the variation in preferences, seems to undermine a shift towards electric cookers. Similarly, the discourse of the danger inherent in electric cookers prevents them from being put to use. Finally, and linked to this fear, I think it is significant that cooks do not feel they possess the right type of knowledge. In sum, these interconnected elements create barriers towards using such technology. Asha simply refuses to use the coil element cooker. Still, women often showed a positive attitude towards electric cookers and 70 per cent of them, irrespective of their expressed feeling of fear towards electric cookers, said in the census that they want to try to cook with electricity. I will argue that women's rather positive evaluations of electric stoves are linked with their concern for their management of time. We saw in chapter 7 how the pace of life is speeding up at present. I contributed part of this trend to electric light's tendency to blur distinctions between night and day. We will be further prepared to understand cooks' concerns once we have heard them speak about their use of time.

Not losing time: meals down from three to two per day

Most women in Uroa work for money outside the household. They are more preoccupied with minimising time spent on cooking than co-villagers who only work at home. Bi Asiya is an example of the latter group. She looks after the extended family's children during the daytime. When she was asked why she did not keep two fires going at the same time, as other women sometimes do, she replied that she does not need to: 'I just stay here' (*Nakaa tu; nipo*). Her co-wife, Kazija, was listening and commented that Bi Asiya is not preoccupied with doing things quickly (*haraka*) because she stays at home.

However, the large majority of women in Uroa are very focused on their use of time. I argue below that women's concerns for doing things quickly have contributed to reducing the number of meals cooked daily. The arrival of electricity is one of the explanatory factors.

When I initiated talks with women about electric cookers, often explicitly inviting a discussion about taste in food, they tended to lead the topic towards the use of time: 'It is quick'; 'it's done at once' (*mara mmoja, tu*); 'it is express cooking' (*ni kupika ekspress*); 'it makes it easier' (*unarahisisha*). They also compared the 'clean' (*safi*) electric cooking with the inconvenience and health problems connected to the fire: 'no crying due to smoke' (*hamna kulia kwa sababu moshi*); and 'no more coughing and puffing' [demonstrated]. One woman mentioned that the quality of food is improved with electricity: 'you can control the heat better'. She was obviously not thinking of the coil element type. Men also often acknowledged that electric cooking may reduce women's workload. 'It is better with electricity and tasty with firewood' (*Ni bora kwa umeme na tam kwa kuni*), Ibrahim said. The way he contrasted the benefits of each technology indicates that electricity is easy and quick, but leaves no doubt as to his culinary preferences.

Women's emphasis on saving time should be considered in relation to the amount of time traditional cooking demands. On average, women in Uroa today spend twelve hours a week on collecting firewood (distributed between three trips per week). A meal takes on average one hour and twenty minutes to prepare, and in some cases up to four hours. Those families in the survey who used charcoal (nine homes), kerosene (seven) and electricity (one) reported to be using these only occasionally. Therefore the figures primarily represent cooking with firewood. However, behind these figures are also the results of two important changes that have taken place during the last decade. First of all, the number of meals cooked per day has been reduced from three to two. Secondly, breakfast now often consists of purchased bread (produced in factories in Zanzibar) or doughnuts and tea instead of home made bread (chapatti) or staples. Leftovers are served for the third and fourth meal of the day (if a fourth meal is served at all).

It is not the fact that women's new occupations alone have led to these shifts that make them particularly interesting in the present context. In neighbouring villages where seaweed farming is common too, women continue to cook three times a day. In Uroa, it is rather the new habit of earning money combined with electricity's arrival that has produced this effect on women's use of time. Women's re-management of time has generally been noted in chapter 7. Of particular importance in the present context is their wish to watch TV. Meja always speeded up her domestic chores to be ready for the Saturday eleven o'clock Swahili drama. Women who regularly watched TV confirmed that this habit and the fewer meals cooked per day are interlinked. Following the argument in chapters 8 and 9, women in Uroa seem to trade off their increasing share in providing for the household by creating more leisure time. Finding time to relax in new ways contributes to women's rescheduling of time. As a result, women are conscious about how to achieve everything and not 'lose time' (*potea time*).

This shift in cooking practices is an ironic consequence of the arrival of electricity. In chapter 3 we saw that the government regarded electric cooking as a future means for both reducing the work load for women and ensuring a more sustainable environment. However, instead of triggering a supplanting of traditional cooking technologies with new ones, electricity, through TV, seems indirectly to have contributed to the achieving of the above mentioned goals. Women cook less and use less wood for preparing meals today than before electricity's arrival. Many Uroan women would agree that the change has been for the better.

However, the economic situation of electrified households should also be considered. We have seen how the relationship with the utility company binds up people's resources. Therefore, the difference between Uroa and non-electrified villages could also be identified as the Uroans' lack of money to buy, or otherwise provide, enough food. In other words, the reduction from three to two cooked meals per day could mean that the quantity of food has also been reduced. I think it is significant that people in Uroa account for this phenomenon in very distinct ways. Some would ascribe the reduction of meals to a lack of resources. Others would disagree and uniquely point to their concern for saving time. This points to greater differences and to some households' struggle to keep up with changing circumstances. However, I do not have data to clarify whether people in Uroa eat less or more than before, thus the question of nutrition remains open.

Taste and conflicting discourses

When cooking, women do not solely make investments in time, energy, and skills that serve material, social and moral/aesthetical ends, but also invest in their identities as women. Moore's model of embodied experience is fruitful (1994). As touched upon in chapter 9, this author pays attention to the way individuals holding multiple identities invest in some of these identities more than others. This process, she says, depends on the amount of reward a specific identity is associated with. The dominant discourses on gender and food in rural Zanzibar certainly encourage women to make investments in their identities as cooks, wives and mothers. Providing proper food on the hearth is culturally and socially honourable, both within the household and in relation to the wider social network. In addition, I have pointed to the way the hearth and food is linked with procreative powers. However, the development discourse also makes its way into the realm of cooking. I shall provide an example from the survey, where a wife, Akama, and her husband share a preference for firewood. Their answers, however, point in slightly different directions. During the interviews, they were not present at the same time.

Question	Wife's response	Husband's response
Do you find the taste with electricity or firewood better or is it the same taste?	Firewood is better. of food cooked to it (*tumeshazoea*).	Firewood is better. We have become used
May one cook anything with electricity?	Yes, it is development (*maendeleo*). It has become normal to cook with electricity (*Kawaida siku hizi kupika kwa umeme*).	Yes.
Is it dangerous to cook with electricity?	No.	Yes! They can lose their lives (*Wanaweza kupoteza maisha*).
Do you know (of) people who cook with electricity?	No.	No.
Have you tried to cook or tasted food cooked with electricity?	No.	No.
Do you want to try to cook with electricity?	No.	No. Not even if I got much money!

Neither of the spouses had direct experience of electric cookers or of food produced by such appliances. Significantly, he emphasised the danger of cooking with electricity and was very determined about not wanting to 'try'. His emotionally informed way of answering suggests that he had taken an active standpoint against the idea of obtaining an electric cooker. Akama, also likely to have heard her husband's views before my interview with her, supported his view on how to produce the right food; that is, what technology a cook should use (if she had a choice) to maintain the identity of a good wife. Just like her husband, she preferred firewood.

At the same time, and in contrast to most women respondents in these settings, she showed no sign of fear. I suggest that this was linked with her decision about taste and her unwillingness to try. She did not 'need' the reference to danger to account for their non-use of cookers, in contrast to what sometimes seemed to be the case. She instead expressed the view that electric cookers had become normal. The use of 'development' was quite strong in indicating that Zanzibari cooking practices were making 'progress'. This was a tendency she appeared to acknowledge, even though she observed it at a distance in the case of cooking. Akama's holding up of an alternative set of criteria for evaluating performance indicated that a modern cook was one who used electric cookers. We thus see the distinct types of rewards she associated with each of the two cooking technologies. The modern discourse was one set of criteria for evaluation. The other was a thoroughly incorporated set of ideas as to what food should taste like. Her wish not to cook with electricity expressed which of the two discourses she found most rewarding at the time. Her distancing also indicates that she had made up her mind to continue to cook the way she always had. Furthermore, the reference to habits ('we have become used to it') shows a reflexive element in Akama's account. She was not directly excusing her preferences in taste but she made an attempt to explain her non-modern standpoint.

I find this sketch of a woman's position interesting because of the double set of discourses she lined up, which, I think, have general relevance. Most women claimed to have 'modern' attitudes in these settings. Irrespective of their preferences in taste (whether firewood is better or electricity or whether the same) – and, as we have seen, irrespective of their feeling of fear – a large majority (70%) said they wanted to cook with electricity. It is important that these statements were given to a Western anthropologist (or engineer) associated with electricity. It is likely that many found it immediately rewarding to share their willingness to cook in modern ways faced with my presence. Discussing or stating preferences during interviews has the advantage that everyday considerations may be temporarily disregarded. Correspondingly, the answers may be unrealistic. That, however, is not important for the current attempt to describe people's shifting attitudes.

Just as TV habits have become part of women's ways of constructing their modern identities, a willingness to cook with electricity is a similar expression, if only for a moment during the interview. 'Wanting to cook' can of course also be interpreted in a range of ways, from trying once to boil a pot of water to engaging in a fully electrified kitchen. However, the tendency is still an indication of women's orientation towards a modern discourse that, for food, is in direct opposition to incorporated cooking and eating practices.

Everyday food aesthetics appear as a realm with strong elements of continuity in Uroa. However, what we have also seen is that the male discourse on tastes in food, which celebrates firewood, is not quite commensurable with women's concerns and attitudes. Women are preoccupied with their use of time. They judge the prospect of electric cooking within the range of practical constraints and fears it would produce. Still, in given situations they express (or play with the idea of expressing) a willingness to modify cooking techniques. Through this, they play out their modern identities. To men, cooking processes are unrelated to the development discourse; this is different for women. Because men and women perceive these questions quite distinctly, we may think of the question of tastes in food as a subtle battlefield. Tacit negotiations have already led women to modify their cooking procedures. They have changed the types of vessels they use and reduced the numbers of meals cooked each day. Men do not complain about this, despite their stated preferences for the clay pot.

Let me stress that by this I do not mean to say that men perceive cooking as a 'traditional' realm to be contrasted with 'development'. Rather, they do not (need to) refer to the development discourse to promote their preferences because this involves a defence of status quo. I think this is an important nuance in regard to Goody's analyses of the Ghanian case. This author appears surprised, or at least fascinated, when observing that people change their houses to become 'modern' while keeping their cuisine 'traditional'. He writes: 'Traditional food demands traditional treatment. By preference, porridge is often eaten with the fingers rather than with the mediating instruments common in the West' (1982: 177). To me, to the extent that I may assume similarities between Ghana and Zanzibar, this way of classifying practices seems removed from people's own perceptions and experiences.

By 2004 the negotiations had been taken further. Twelve women in Uroa were now using electricity for cooking. One of them said she was able to regulate the heat more easily with the one-plate stove than what was possible on the fire. To save costs, she starts boiling beans, for instance, in an aluminium pot on the fire. As the staple starts to get tender, she moves it onto the stove and adds spices and coconut milk. She said she was pleased with the taste this technology produced and the time she saved by being able to cook several things at the same time. When invited to recount what her husband thought about the taste of food cooked in this way, she significantly answered: 'I have not asked him'.

The twelve women are also owners of these appliances. I touch on this issue in chapter 11 when concluding on the study's central findings. At this point, we note that the field of food and cooking might not be so resistant to change after all. Before ending this chapter, we shall see how perceptions of the body influence discourses and practices connected to food and drinks.

Food and body

The cold reserved for drinks

In a comparative light, and given women's concern for saving time in Uroa, it is striking how seldom food is stored in freezers and refrigerators. Again, the issue of taste is important but on this topic men and women fully agree. When they spoke about cooked foods' incommensurability with freezers, I sometimes was reminded of the way human bodies suffer when exposed to extreme cold. In particular, it was unthinkable to put rice in a freezer, since 'it will be cold and that is no good' (*itakuwa baridi, sio nzuri*). Other people said more specifically that such rice would obtain a watery quality (*maji-maji*). Soups were considered possible to freeze but would lose their taste (*ladha itapotea*). Finally, some pointed to the difficulty of reheating frozen food on the fire in contrast to the way this can be achieved with electric ovens. I shall not dwell on the variety of accounts, but simply note that the cold storage of food is avoided as it affects taste.

For drinks, however, cooling is highly valued. Here we have a realm in flux since the arrival of electricity and freezers and refrigerators. Goody observed that preferences for drinks in Ghana expressed social distinctions to an extent that was not found for food (1982: 178–9). Similarly in Uroa, at least on a directly observable level, differences in affluence were reflected in what people drank and not by what they ate. During Ramadan, the distribution of cold drinks takes on a particular significance.

More affluent families tend to consume Coca Cola, Sprite, Fanta or Ginger Ale during Ramadan, in accordance with modern styles promoted through various channels. After the half past six evening prayers and a full-day fasting, Hija passes by a shop to drink a cold bottle immediately. Then he brings several sodas home for the family to consume during and/or after the meal. Sodas seem to provide an experiential sensation which is highly cherished. Shops double their sales of mineral water in the fasting month. In 2003, on the celebration of Idd's first day (when Ramadan is over), one of the largest shops in Uroa sold ninety-two crates of sodas, in contrast to the usual one crate on a normal day. In comparison, Meja and Khamis, and most of their closest neighbours and relatives had not had a single soda since 2001 when I met them again in 2004.

Plate 10.4 The use of freezers, Uroa, 2001.

When poorer families have cold lemonade or water during Ramadan, this is perhaps their creation of a dignified alternative to the bottled, cold soda they would have wanted if they had a choice. Differences observed in what people drink seem ultimately more like variations on a theme (contrasting the ordinary with the cold) than expressions of differences in taste. Therefore Goody's observation that distinctions are produced in what people drink appears to be the case on the empirical level. However, people of different economic standing seem to hold similar preferences regarding cold, sweet drinks. These preferences are also influenced by perceptions of what the cold does to the human body. Such theories are found among the poorest and among people of relative affluence.

Playing with the cold

Many people in Uroa, particularly elderly men, expressed a concern for the unfortunate effects cold drinks have on the human body. 'Cold water use/eat up the body.' (*Maji baridi yanapuua mwili.*) 'Normal water is better than cold water (*maji wa kawaida ni fresh kuliko maji baridi*) because your body doesn't become cold.'[10] Cold drinks may give you a cold (*mafua*) or a fever (*homa*, not here taken to mean malaria). Children are particularly vulnerable in this respect. When the weather is cold, that is, the rainy season, one should avoid things that produce cold. This is why freezers and fans are seldom used in the rainy season. Cold drinks represent a threat to the general balancing of hot and cold. Also, some particular foods and drinks are classified in terms of their capacity for heating or cooling a body, although I do not treat these at present (see Middleton 1992: 146; Caplan 1997: 248 n. 6).

Older men sometimes said they preferred to break the fast with the water from young coconuts (*madafu*) but added that nowadays these were difficult to obtain. In the past, Silima said, coconuts were put in the shade to be cooled down. This practice stopped when freezers arrived (when a change to cold drinks, homemade sweet drinks or sodas took place). We here see a continuity in people's preferences for the cold. Furthermore, people also pointed to the importance of the sequence in which you drink: it is better to start with ordinary water, then have the typical, thin porridge (*uji*) served for *futari*, and maybe sodas or cold drinks towards the end of the evening. A young woman said that if she starts with cold soda she feels as if her 'stomach gets a shock' (*tumbo linashtuka*) which makes her unable to eat. This corresponds to other accounts where sweet drinks in particular are said to make one feel full (*shiba*); an unfortunate condition to be in when facing the first meal of the day.

The unhealthy effects of cold drinks seem to be widely acknowledged, but people relate to this threat in different ways. Women were often quite relaxed with regard to themselves: 'I just like cold water' (*Napenda maji baridi tu*). However, in order for their children to obtain a balanced state, they would be at least as attentive as men to the potential danger of drinking cold liquids. Wealthier men also often showed a relaxed attitude: 'It is here. … Cold things are dangerous for the health but, still, we do smoke [cigarettes].' (*Tayari. … Baridi ni hatari kwa afya, lakini, still, tunavuta.*) The cold is not ideal but, rather, irresistible.

A generational difference sometimes appeared when people contrasted themselves with other groups, as summed up in two quotes from men, the first young and the second old. 'The old is porridge, the young is soda.' (*Wazee ni uji, vijana ni soda.*) The old man was worried about young people's consumption of cold drinks: 'They don't know what may cause them danger/pain. The body becomes weak, soft/tender. A little problem; they are not used to it.' (*Hawajui madhara yake. Mwili unaregea, unakuwa laini. Tabu kidogo; hawajazoea.*) Thus the generational opposition treated in chapter 5 between occult knowledge and the development discourse has a parallel in drinking habits. The young oppose traditional knowledge while elders pity the young who do not know what is best for them. We return to some sort of distinction here. However, the variety in preferences across gender categories and generations, and differences between theories and practice, do not allow for strict classification in terms of preferences for cold drinks.

Building up and jeopardising bodily strength

The need to balance hot and cold is related to the importance of possessing strength (*kuwa na nguvu*). However, although too much cold liquid may be temporarily unfortunate, the substance itself that the body consumes has a more enduring effect. Certain foods are considered crucial in this respect. In short, heavy (*zito*) foods such as cassava, sweet potatoes, green bananas and beans provide a strong body. Persons who feel particularly vulnerable are inclined to make sure they eat enough heavy foods. For example, one woman in Uroa, Zainabu, had had stomach-aches for a long time. She was in the middle of a conflict with her in-laws and ascribed the aches to an evil spirit they had sent her. She cooked heavy meals every morning and avoided light (*epesi*) foods such as bakery bread. Implicitly, and essential to the discussion, the process of cooking 'strong' foods involves cooking them on fire. Significantly, the cooking must be done by a woman. In the quite unusual case to follow, the central role played by the female cook in this process will be illustrated.

Normally, men who live on their own go to relatives' houses to eat. However, one man I met used to cook his daily food using an electric coil element. He said he prefered the taste of food cooked on the fire. It would, however, have been unthinkable for him to sit by the fire himself. Uroan aesthetics, otherwise quite flexible, do not allow for a man to do so. In his bachelor days, the alternative technology offered a way for him to cook whilst keeping his masculinity intact. However, and not surprisingly, when he married his wife took over the cooking. Consequently, there was no longer a need for the coil element and it was stored away. This story tells us how fundamental a woman and her hearth are for the purpose of producing proper food. A household in Uroa is incomplete without a wife. Hearth, woman and tasty foods that provide strength are inseparable units.

Heavy foods make up the main portion of the Ramadan evening meal. People spoke of these dishes and their tastes with enthusiasm. Bourdieu points out that ideas about food and how it affects the body are related to perceptions of taste, and this has relevance in Uroa (1984: 190). The taste of heavy food is linked with building up a strong body. Today, however, the most commonly eaten and cherished staples are the less heavy ones, particularly imported rice. Again, taste is important but this is less connected to health-bringing effects here. 'If the children could decide, we would have rice every day of the week', one man sighed when telling me that he preferred his wives to cook meals of all sorts to obtain enough variation and thus strength. Uroan cuisine is perceived to have changed in this respect and this is sometimes looked upon with regret, as in this man's account.

People in the past were stronger, of better quality (*madhubuti*). They became old of age. It is very hard these days to see people who live to eighty or ninety.

Before they did. They also had a strong health. You would like to know why? Because people in the past ate food with strength (*chakula cha nguvu*). They ate vegetables which they boiled for a little while only. They ate fish, also boiled for a little while, not fried in oil for a long period of time as we do today. They ate maize, as we do now, but maybe the whole piece boiled in water, or grained. They did not eat much flour, rice and sugar. In this way they got more vitamins and better health than we do today. You see now: cancer, pressure, I don't now what. And people die before they turn fifty, or maybe forty. In the past, if they got a problem, they used herbs and roots. They did not have a hospital, no medicine. ... The medicines of today work, yes, but their effects cannot compensate for the types of food we eat. Food is the most important thing.

We see how much attention is given to the cooking process in this account of a better past. Ingredients have changed in a historic light. However, the transformation from boiling techniques to frying is likewise important. Taken together with men's cherishing of the smoke and the tastes it produces, its health bringing effects, and the symbolic importance of the hearth, this expressed worry for how changed eating patterns affect the body results in resistance towards transforming cooking processes any further. There are many reasons why electric cookers were, until very recently, not in use in Uroa.

Tastes at rest, tastes in flux

The discussion presented on food and taste is largely based on Uroans' answers to hypothetical questions. There were few possibilities to observe practices connected to electric cooking and preferences for food as they materialised when people actually ate. Central parts of the findings must therefore be taken for what they are: a discussion of people's conceptualisations of food, taste and technologies. Furthermore, I have pointed to the way my position and presence contributed to the production of what was said. This, however, does not make the data 'biased' in the sense that they are less 'scientific'. By rendering visible the discursive field in which people's accounts were produced (cf. Hastrup 1995, see chapter 1), I have tried to show that the intersubjectivity at work provides us with particular insights.

Nevertheless, as accounted for in the introductory chapter, there is a problem of representation in that men, to a large extent, were the ones to provide me with more in-depth theories of the phenomena in question and how life has changed over the years. The silencing of women's voices on such topics could of course be related to my own methodical shortcomings. However, I would like to stress that I always tried to search for women's ways of looking at things too. So instead of regarding the gender differences as a weakness in textual representation we could treat it as reflecting a real discrepancy in women's and men's concerns.

The question of tastes in food as a signifier of identity has been treated on two levels. First of all, rural Zanzibaris celebrate their uniqueness in relation to the outside world. Here, food is an important marker of distinction. It may be suggested that Uroans' reluctance to modify their cooking practices serves to protect the boundary vis-à-vis the outside world.

Secondly, the motivation for maintaining the status quo in the realm of food preparation also appears rooted in internal village life in important ways. We saw that differences in dishes and their tastes are muted in everyday life. This silence is partly linked with the egalitarian ideology and women's frequent movement around the isles, but cannot only be explained by this. Here, I pointed to the close links between food and procreative powers. Culinary practices are connected to the question of fertility in its widest sense. More specifically, perceptions of the human body were found to be central. Uroans are concerned with obtaining enough strength to meet with uncertainties and dangers in life. The penetrable nature of human bodies has been noted in the way spirits and evil magic may enter human beings. This permeable aspect is also related to the food people ingest. Eating heavy foods which have been cooked on the fire is a way to obtain strength. Moreover, inherent in the rural Zanzibari food aesthetics is the woman who attends to her fire. The prospect of using electric cookers breaks with these prescriptions as to how proper food should be produced. Proper food, in turn, is the food of one's liking; that which entails a preferred taste.

Similarly, food that has been frozen loses some of its important qualities. When Uroans say the taste becomes reduced in such cases, this should also be considered in relation to the importance of obtaining strength. The state of cold food is described as unfortunate in the same way it is thought that people should not become too cold. Foods, in a way, also possess a 'health' that must be guarded so as not to disturb the balance strived for in human bodies. In consequence, Uroans do not keep food in their freezers.

Nevertheless, the analysis has also shown that the village is not represented by one single voice. Uroans continue to play down differences in the taste of food which is actually produced. However, in village discourse there is a growing disagreement between spokespeople who defend the traditional hearth, on the one hand, and those more open to change, on the other. The former group highlights the supreme taste of food cooked on firewood. I have indicated that this articulated preference for smoke goes hand in hand with a discourse concerning the danger associated with electric cooking. Dangers may indeed be real, but we also noted the 'suitability' of this discourse when people say they prefer the status quo. Although there are exceptions on both sides of the disagreement, and the aspect of perceived danger is found to be general, I showed the significance of a gender difference. This is what I have labelled a tacit field of negotiation.

I think there are two interrelated reasons why women appear more attuned to changing cooking technology than men. First of all, positioned as cooks, they are particularly concerned with the practical implications of such a shift. There is no question about female earners' concern for saving time on cooking. For them, the electric stove represents a way to provide more time for other chores. With this appliance they can spend less time fetching firewood. They also perceive cooking time to be reduced with this technology. Secondly, and also related to cooking as an important women's task in Uroa, women cooks appear to find resonance in the development discourse when (potentially) cooking in new ways. Therefore, in contrast to men's emphasis on the superior taste of food cooked on firewood, women bring up development when discussing cooking techniques. In addition, they say they want to try electric cookers. By 2004, we actually see a manifestation of this trend in practice. In this way, two distinct sets exist in parallel for constructing female identities and evaluating a woman's performance as a cook. Put simply, a cook is torn between providing Zanzibari food in a safe and aesthetically prescribed manner, on the one hand, and risking her health but saving time by cooking in a modern way, on the other. The internal negotiations within a single cook are of course related to the amount of reward and punishment she expects from her social surroundings from each alternative (cf. Moore 1994). If she brings up this topic for verbal negotiations with her husband, a proposal for change is likely to be met with resistance. However, there are clear signs that negotiations are going on in reality. We see this in the reduced number of meals, in women's use of aluminium pots and, not least, in the very new tendency to acquire and use electrical appliances. As a result we can see that Uroan culinary practices do change. As Carrithers (1992) tells us, aesthetic standards allow room for flexibility and change. For rural Zanzibari culinary practices there is evidently a dynamic of 'repetition with constant variation' at work, as long as the changes in question take place in silence.

For drinks, there are more internal distinctions in people's consumption patterns. There might always have been differences in what people have drunk in Uroa. However, the arrival of cold drinks is generally cherished and the ideal appears more or less the same among Uroan households, albeit modified here and there in view of the unfortunate effects cold drinks may have on the body. This is why I called differences in what people consume 'variations on a theme' rather than expressions of distinctions in taste.

The way Uroans have grasped the possibility of consuming cold drinks can be contrasted to the relatively strong reluctance to change cooking practices. I suggest that the flexible pattern in people's drinking habits, and their stronger articulation as markers of distinction, appear for several reasons. First of all, drinks are less connected to building strength and providing fertility, compared to food. Too much cold, though, is not good. However, cold drinks seem to have a more temporal effect than that which solid food has on the body. Secondly, drinks are not as interwoven with gender relations as is food preparation. Thirdly, cold drinks are continuously presented as part of a modern life in the national discourses. When men in Uroa say they cannot resist cold, sweet drinks, I think they sum up the phenomenon quite effectively. Cold drinks are objects of desire and they are possible for a man to provide in aesthetically acceptable ways. In accordance with the way modern men provide their families with TV shows, they also signify their ability as modern providers when they purchase, store and produce cold drinks.

The issue of tastes in food is fascinating in the way it encapsulates a range of conceptualisations, positions and preferences. Due to its manifestation in immediate judgements, 'taste' provides the ethnographic task with a possibility for richness. If women, with their fears and aspirations, seem less interested in taste than men, it is in fact through their perceptions of taste that the notion's complexity and elasticity is revealed.

Notes

1. Asha's emphasis on religious reading marks the couple's orientation towards Islam as a contrast to those who openly confirm their regular dealings with spirits or magic protection. What remains uncertain is to what degree she associated my question of spiritual and magic protection with the previous topic of discussion (the danger of electric cookers). I found it a bit crude to ask if she prays more than usual when planning to use the cooker. However, this issue turned out to be irrelevant.
2. Normally the kitchen forms a corner of the yard (*uani*) and has a palm roof (see figures in chapter 9). In this house all roofs are made of iron sheets. Most families do not keep tables, except for those with a TV set. In wealthier families tables are also found in the bedrooms. However, in kitchens tables are extremely rare.
3. A standard English–Swahili dictionary. 1999 [1939]. Nairobi: Oxford University Press.
4. The exceptions are Indian, Arab and other Asian families who are considered different in terms of their distinct ways of dressing, cooking and eating, etc. Furthermore, Uroan's view that Zanzibari food is the same all over the island could very well be perceived differently in town.
5. I did not come across instances which explicitly confirmed people's fear of what they were being served by others. Unni Wikan holds that in Bali, coffee is considered much more dangerous than tea because the liquid conceals traces of poison (1990: 49). During fieldwork, the only instance when poisoning became a verbally articulated threat was during election times. People feared that members of the political opposition would poison the water in Uroa. Guards watched the wells at night-time for several weeks.
6. In the census, 36 per cent of women said they preferred the taste of food cooked with firewood and 38 per cent thought the two distinct means of cooking gave similar tastes to the food. In addition, as for the men, 13 per cent said 'electricity tastes better'. 13 per cent of women had no opinion.
7. The coil element may be labeled '*ringi*', '*sahara*' (lit. 'cloth used for turban' (Issak 1999)), '*springi*' (lit. 'spring'), '*jiko*' (stove), but also '*koka*'. The oven/stove may be labeled '*jiko kubwa*' (big stove), and, again, '*jiko*' and '*koka*'. One-plate and two-plate stoves are called '*plati moja*' and '*plati mbili*' though I did not hear people speak explicitly about such devices until 2004.

8. Nowadays these utensils may be bought in some of the shops in the village or from salesmen who occasionally visit the village by moped to offer various goods. In town, casseroles and saucepans made of stainless steel are available, but Uroans do not buy and use these. The cost of a stainless steel casserole is at least ten times higher than a *dishi* or *chungu*.

9. Juma Ali Juma, a Zanzibari scholar working for the Forestry Department informed me that the aluminium pot is not suited for making soups. In Zanzibar (including Uroa) soups always contain acid ingredients such as tomato and lime juice. The surface may oxidize because of these and liberate unhealthy substances into the food.

10. Interestingly, the man in his thirties who said this also saw excessive heat from the sun (*joto*) as being able to make a body 'cold'. Cold is in both cases used as an antonym for 'fresh', a word he uses to describe a balanced condition.

Chapter 11

ELECTRICITY MAKES A DIFFERENCE

In the preceding chapters we have followed electricity's historical and spatial trajectories in Zanzibar. What we have encountered is the technology's multiple interconnections with the dense fabric of social life. Its introduction has been advocated, contested, ignored and approved by distinctly positioned protagonists. Its uses are negotiated and selected. Some of the services electricity provides are objects of desire (illuminated space and TV programmes) while others are less relevant (electric cookers). These choices are socio-culturally and economically conditioned and are the result of negotiations. They have not only reinforced some power relations (villager–state, have's–have-not's) but have also produced changes in the dynamics of various sorts of relationships (gender relationships, generational relations, human–spirit relations). To Zanzibaris, electricity is perceived to be linked with 'development', but not in static ways. Its organisation also has some difficult aspects. Even so, electricity's impact implies increased human well-being in many respects. This chapter provides conclusions as to the book's central findings.

What does electricity promise?

From the Soviet rural electrification program, to the United States' model Tennessee Valley Authority project, to the new South Africa's township electricity programs, electrification has provided the twentieth century with perhaps its most vivid symbol of modernization and development. Fusing a powerful image of universal connection in a national grid with the classical Enlightenment motif of illumination of the darkness, electrification has been an irresistible piece of symbolism for the modernist state. ... It was no different in Zambia, where the electrification of the townships was a compelling symbol of inclusion, a sign that Africans, too, were to be hooked up with the 'new world society'. In the new Zambia, electricity (like those other primary goods of modern life, education and health care) would link all of the country's citizens in a universal, national grid of modernity.

James Ferguson, *Expectations of Modernity*

In this quote, Ferguson refers to the electricity grid in Zambia and elsewhere as a prime example of an icon of development (1999: 242–3). In Zanzibar too, various governments (past and present) have regarded electrification as a means for achieving progress and development. Their ideologies and goals for development have been quite distinct, but electricity remained central in each era. There was a strong aesthetic dimension involved, which has generally been linked to projects taken on by modernising states (see Scott 1998: 224–5). With the technology in question, the 'geographical imagination' was, in each period, brightly reflected in the contrast between darkness and illuminated space. However, although electricity is generally a compelling symbol of development for authorities who provide the technology, it is wise not to presuppose that such links exist in people's own conceptualisations. Ferguson provides a highly context-sensitive and rich account of Zambians' encounter with development in the 1990s. However, it is somewhat surprising when the author categorically declares that electricity had a strong symbolic significance in Zambia. He does not go into detail as to how the Zambian grid evolved and we are left with little understanding of how Ferguson reaches this conclusion.[1] It appears to me that simply stating the symbolic importance of electricity has the effect of masking some of the variation that might have existed. Such variation in present-day Zambia is otherwise impressively captured by the author. This reduction becomes especially striking when he compares the 'promises' of modernity as they were articulated in the electricity grid during its formative period with today's unreliable network and customers' problems paying their bills (ibid.: 243).[2] In this way, he partly uses the history of electricity as a case for disclosing modernisation as a myth and a lie (ibid.: 253). In order to reach this conclusion, I think we need to have known more about how electricity was perceived in the first place and not just by the modernising state.[3]

This book has provided an account of how lasting symbols (of development or other significant values) may come into being. For electricity grids in Zanzibar such representations appear more unequivocal in the aftermath of a certain degree of stabilisation having been reached, than at their time of creation. This 'mainstreaming' in attribution of meaning is partly linked to the materiality of a heavy infrastructure such as electricity. Poles, lines and transformers are simply difficult to remove from the landscape, once installed. Moreover, linked to their staying capacity, dominating discourses continue to impose their interpretations on symbols after their manifestation as enduring objects. This is in line with Moore's (1996) valuable perspective on the constitution of the spatial order. The configuration of a 'tracee' of power lines or a living room is not random. In addition, they reflect, Moore says, not real social relations, but representations of such. In the Zanzibari case, electricity's association with development appears unquestioned in its aftermath.

Electric networks in their creation

In its moment of creation and implementation, electrification is a very unsettled matter, politically as well as symbolically. Despite my choice of a 'success' story, such as Uroa's, which involved a high level of participation, we came across the contested nature of electrification processes which not only applies to rural Zanzibar. Furthermore, it is significant that the various Zanzibari villages approached the arrival of electricity in quite distinct ways. The process in Uroa differed from that of the majority of the villages that became electrified in more passive and conventional ways. Uroa's success in terms of village satisfaction, street lighting and a high degree of household connections was explained exactly in relation to their need to mobilise for electricity. I stress, however, that there is always a certain degree of local agency at work. The central question is to what extent the framework for a given intervention takes the aspect of community involvement into account. I contend (see chapter 4), that 'community development' continues to bear relevance as a promising approach to increased well-being in rural areas.

Local agency can of course also act counter to the goal of intended interventions initiated from the outside. In Binguni, another village on Unguja, the effort to electrify resulted in disaster (elaborated in Winther 2005: 302–6). Binguni village here represents a radical contrast to Uroa. In short, there had been no protagonist or locally-based legitimacy in Binguni for welcoming the electricity grid. The village leadership had received a written letter two weeks before the project was due to start. The 'tree owners' who control the land of the spirits had not been involved in the process and they became upset when project staff started clearing the bush close to sacred spots in the forest. Correspondingly, they called for the spirits to intervene. In short, local resistance put a stop to electricity. By pushing too hard for development, non-development may ultimately result. This is what happened in Binguni. I can draw this conclusion because people in Binguni today sincerely regret the outcome. I contribute a large part of the explanations for the non-electrification of Binguni to asymmetric relationships embedded in projects initiated from outside (ibid.). Also relevant was the need for project management to reach predetermined goals within financial and time constraints. Maia Green's notion of development as 'manageable realities' captures this limitation (2003a). This is also her way of explaining why projects in many places tend to turn out so similarly. It reflects the fact that local participation in practice is often limited in its effects.

A hierarchical order existed in Uroa due to the project management's continuous mandate to decide on various matters. This is related to the nature of intended change in general (cf. chapter 4). There were also asymmetric relations at play within the village. The village leadership, with its considerable influence, represented one particular faction within the local political context. The street lighting outside the Chairman's house reflected his position and his potential to influence the project in a direction that served his own group. Furthermore, women were not active during the planning and implementation of electricity. I have accounted for this by pointing to women's general position in Islamic Zanzibar (reduced possibilities for ownership of houses, moving at the time of marriage, high risk of divorce) and their role in the village (attending meetings only to a limited extent, not holding many formal positions and not being as active as men in communal work). A central question is whether women's participation would have changed the way electricity ended up in the village and the grid's spatial distribution. In relation to this, would their participation at an early stage have provided them with a larger share of electricity's benefits in the long term? This is probable. The village mill and the kindergarten constitute two institutions in Uroa which women consider important. The fact that none of these have been included in the network so far is a sign of men's greater say in these matters.

In the overall picture, however, these hierarchical problems have had limited significance in Uroa. This is so, first of all, because the Chairman and his group appear to have been determined to work in the interests of the community at large. It was also project policy to support public services and the water supply. As a result, electricity has radically improved public services of which women are the most significant beneficiaries. Running water and the services provided at the electrified health centre are free and available for all (see below). Secondly, the quality of the process vis-à-vis the project management overcame many of the problems often associated with top-down structures. Due to their significance, I now reiterate the main characteristics of the relationship between village and project. I hold that the case of Uroa reveals important aspects of participatory development related to technological change and how this can be achieved in practice.

The success of Uroa was heavily determined by the particular relationship that evolved between the village leader and the project management. Now, if this relationship and the project outcome had only been the result of the two protagonists' particular personalities, the case would not have had much general relevance. I have argued, however, that some of the characteristics of the process were also crucial to the result.

The two groups belonged to, and drew on, quite distinct knowledge systems which constituted a discontinuity. They represented distinct world views (Long 1989). They communicated, but more through bits and pieces than by agreeing on the meaning contained in each message. This did not threaten the parties' shared sense of equivalence (Hobart 1993). On the contrary, it was the partial character of their understanding, and the protagonists' acknowledgement of such partiality, that contributed to the positive outcome. It is important, in this respect, to point to the Chairman's position in the village and his great skill in making things turn out as he wanted. Significantly, for his co-villagers to reflect and decide on whether electricity was a good idea, time was the most important thing needed. The high level of conflict, the protection rituals, the many meetings, in sum, the discourses of development and ignorance required effort and time. In contrast, in Binguni, the lack of time for such moral discourse led to the refusal of electricity.

It goes without saying that such reflexive processes can only be handled internally. Furthermore, it is not a coincidence that occult practices became relevant during the days of electrification, both in Uroa and Binguni (and in most villages I have visited in rural Zanzibar). Occult practices in Africa are 'a set of discourses on morality, sociality and humanity; on human frailty' (Moore and Sanders 2001: 20). Times of rapid change trigger a need for such discourses. My material strongly supports Moore and Sanders's (and their co-authors, such as Fisiy and Geschiere 2001) demonstrations of the close interconnections that exist between occult practices and modern realities. In both villages, there was a prospect for a given change (electricity). Here, the realm of the occult provided a means for each of the groups (and, in Uroa, the sub-groups) to reflect upon and articulate their concerns, intentions and worries. In brief, they used occult knowledge and practices to work on, negotiate and express their modern experience related to the (potential) arrival of a given change. I dwell on the relationship between the occult and the modern experience for two reasons.

First of all, the experiences from Uroa and Binguni and their opposed results with regard to electrification effectively demonstrate one of the common erroneous presumptions inherited from modernisation theories, which I also encounter from time to time. This relates to the contention that 'tradition' or 'culture' constitutes a barrier to development. However, as has been widely demonstrated in the literature, the involvement of the occult does not mean that we are dealing with a 'traditional' phenomenon directed against change. Quite the contrary, the use of occult knowledge is as much made use of in the service of change (Uroa) as in resistance to change (Binguni).

Secondly, and linked to this, attempts to achieve intended social change in Africa should be attuned to acknowledging the importance of occult knowledge. Moore and Sanders's thesis and the Zanzibari material here find resonance in another study with a slightly different focus. Erica Bornstein has studied Protestant NGOs in Zimbabwe and argues that religious groups' explicit focus on questions of morality is what constitutes their main advantage in the development setting (2005: 170). She writes: 'Christian development provided a discursive space for negotiation with jealousy and evil spirits, with the material success of some and the impoverishment of others, with moral struggles that could not always be resolved. That the discourse of Christian development was inclusive of unseen spiritual forces … made it more powerful in the Zimbabwean context' (ibid.). I would claim that this is also the characteristic and strength of the (various) local knowledge systems captured as 'the occult' at large. The discourses at work may be subtler and less approachable to outsiders, but they are of vital importance. Project schemes that do not allow for local, moral discourse to influence the process (including turning it down) are likely to produce unfortunate results.

This is partly in line with Arce and Long's (2000) argument that people always actively and critically respond to the ideologies that discourses of development entail. The authors employ the notion of 'counter-development' to account for such local response. However, Arce and Long appear to assume that the Western origin of such ideologies is a central point. Based on the Zanzibari case, and the body of literature on modern experiences in the Swahili area, I find this assumption to be a little exaggerated. True, Minou Fuglesang's findings in Lamu to some extent show an articulated anti-Western attitude in the way people relate to objects perceived to have their origin in the West (1994), which fits with Arce and Long's perspective. But although the body of recent works on Swahili modernities (see chapter 2) point to people's disappointment with the prevailing living conditions, they do not emphasise that a Western origin of things is perceived to be significant.

If we return to the contrast between Uroa and Binguni, was Binguni more anti-Western than Uroa? I think not. The tree owners fought a concrete battle against those who demolished sacred spots in the forest, not an abstract concept of Western modernisation. In addition, what took place in Uroa was both a protest against electricity and a movement to make electrification a reality. Which of these groups of actors acted most 'anti'? And what were they hostile to? In my view there is a problem with the manner in which this model highlights the Western point of reference to which local agency acts counter. It also somehow assumes that responses for or against changes in the past were of a qualitatively different order than what we see today. Neither of these assumptions appear to apply to rural Zanzibar. The friction that occurs in times of change appears most closely linked to the existing tensions in the local political context. Today, the most important influence which in Uroa is explicitly referred to as Western (and also negative) is the unfortunate effect of tourists' improper behaviour, drinking habits and dress codes. Similar negative influences perceived as Western reach people in Zanzibar through the medium of TV.

However, ideas of progress and development, and the negotiations of what changes are appropriate for which reasons, have a distinctive local reference. That said, there is one important realm in which traces of opposition to Western ways and ideas can be interpreted. I return to the realm of food and cooking towards the end.

Electrification and human well-being

Throughout this book on electricity in rural Zanzibar, I have followed the anthropological tradition of trying to ground the analysis in people's own practices and perceptions. This also applies for the way I have treated the notion of development and the impact of electricity on social life in a time period characterised by a wide range of socio-material change (see in particular chapter 5). Similarly, by way of making conclusions about the effect of electricity on human well-being in rural Zanzibar, the experiences and evaluations of women, men and children will be my main focus. Here, Douglas's notion of poverty as a relational and social phenomenon is worth recapitulating (1982, see chapter 1). Viewing consumption and poverty as two sides of the same coin, she argues that the drives for increasing consumption are rooted in our wish to include other people in our lives. For doing so, as the previous chapters have shown, we need material objects, for example an illuminated, extended living room (chapter 9) or a novel appliance (chapters 8 and 9) or ingredients for cooking a proper, traditional meal (chapter 10). Consumption is thus intrinsically a social phenomenon, and so is its counterpart, poverty, which Douglas takes to mean a state where a person experiences a lack of material resources and thus a lack of ability to include other people in their lives. A feeling of lack of dignity results. This relative perspective on poverty can both be used internal to the village and vis-à-vis other locations and the outside world.

The emphasis on experience and social exclusion has certain resemblances with recent trends in development thinking which emphasise so-called 'participatory' approaches to understanding poverty. As I return to shortly, this implies paying attention to the ways people themselves define and experience the condition of poverty. The shift does not, in my view, mean that conventional ways of measuring and comparing poverty (e.g., the UN's Human Development Index) in terms of general indicators such as health, education and economic growth are not important for monitoring the situation and informing policies intended to improve the well-being of the poor. This book has demonstrated the relevance of several of these factors to people's well-being in rural Zanzibar – and electricity's significance within this picture. Today covering areas in which 80 per cent of the rural population lives, electricity has provided people with easy access to clean water, improved health facilities (chapter 3), and an empowering environment for learning (chapter 5). The technology's positive effects on services in the public sector and women's and young girls' time-use are a considerable contribution to the current political ambitions of the Tanzanian and Zanzibari governments to reduce absolute poverty in rural Zanzibar (chapter 3). Access to clean water is also a human right. Due to the way in which electricity conditions water supply, one might even go as far as to consider access to electricity as a human right in itself. This has been suggested (Dugard in press). Electricity alone does not provide improved water supply, but in Zanzibar the technology constitutes an important condition for achieving such a goal. I believe, therefore, that the positive impact that access to electricity has on water supply and people's health alone provides a justification for further investing in this infrastructure elsewhere.

To the women and men I came to know in Zanzibar, this thesis on electricity's significance in relation to health, water and women's time-use was obvious. Their perceptions and experiences here fit some of the conventional criteria for measuring, and means for combating, poverty. However, they would also have other concerns as to what constitutes a good life – including what role electricity plays, or could play, in making the quality of life improve. During census interviews, men and women were asked what they considered to be the most important factor for living the good life. Many people tended to mention various objects and issues that are common in the village, but which they do not possess or control themselves.[4] This indicates that people, when asked about the good life, are focused on the things they feel they lack in relation to what other people possess. It both shows people's fear of social exclusion and the notion's significance in grounded poverty research. Due to the sensitive nature and socially stigmatising term of 'poverty' (*umaskini*) in Zanzibar (and elsewhere) and the study's specific focus on consumption, I have found this field ethically challenging to approach (see chapter 1).

That being said, and keeping in mind the (increasing) social stratification that will be summarised below, electricity has enhanced life in rural Zanzibar in many more ways than simply through its impact on public services. Let us review some glimpses from the proceeding chapters. Some 20 per cent of rural households have obtained electricity connection in Unguja, despite the incredibly high cost this represents to them (chapters 1 and 6). By this, they demonstrate their desire for the new technology. More than 80 per cent of the people in Uroa watch TV regularly and perceive this to be an important step towards development (chapter 5). New ideas and images from elsewhere, are considered to be vital to the ongoing process of changing one's life for the better. The entertainment aspect is also important and people now relax in new ways. TV might also have an impact on people's awareness of human rights. In an evaluation report of the Bangladesh rural electrification project, such effects (through TV programmes) have been emphasised (NRECA 2002). It is likely that in

Zanzibar too, increased access to information, through various channels, on health, education, gender equality and other human rights may have a long-term and positive effect. A multitude of discourses and aesthetic expressions reach the village after electrification and there is little doubt that the new access to global information provided through TV programmes, computers and the Internet have far-reaching consequences. Electricity also quickly becomes adopted for religious aims (chapter 5). Parents strongly support all these developments and they are passionate about providing a proper education for their children. We have seen their stress on this in practice also, when sending children to night classes (chapter 7). A relevant question is how these changes may be interpreted in terms of one of the current approaches to poverty and well-being.

Amaryta Sen has emphasised the role of state and non-state actors in protecting the rights and entitlements of poor and vulnerable groups. As Sen points out, people are *entitled* to the services they themselves find necessary and important in order to live a good life (Sen 1983, see also Banik 2005: 16). Through the study of people's acquisition and use of electricity in rural Zanzibar, and its rapid normalisation, it is clear that people consider the new practices as a central aspect of modern, good living. Following Sen and others who argue for a human rights-based approach to development, we could suggest that since people consider electricity to be a significant element in their understanding of a good life, someone actually has the obligation to provide them with this technology at an affordable price.

I started this book by maintaining that electricity matters in rural Zanzibar. Subsequently, I have shown why and how it matters. This being said, the relational approach to poverty and well-being adopted in the present work has also revealed that certain fundamental challenges persist. These might even have become graver with the introduction of electricity: Social differences are on the rise; gender inequalities continue to bear relevance; and the control of the state over citizens has taken on new weight. As the title of this chapter indicates, electricity makes a difference in positive terms, but it also reinforces and produces social boundaries. I sum up these points after having discussed electricity's effect on people's access to income and resources, and some of the environmental aspects related to electricity's arrival and use.

Electricity's effect on people's financial vulnerability

So far, electricity has had a limited effect on people's level of income in rural Zanzibar. Electricity is not used for fishing and seaweed farming, which, together, constitute the two most important realms of production in rural, coastal areas. Tourism, in contrast, depends on electricity and is becoming Zanzibar's most important financial sector. I have shown, however, that most ordinary Zanzibaris are excluded from this realm. This is what produces some of the main obstacles to combating poverty in economic terms at present.

Nevertheless, a range of entrepreneurial initiatives are being made at the local level. In chapter 3, I mentioned some of the (modest) ways in which people at present are trying to make use of electricity with the aim of enhancing their financial power. Also, a host of women's corporations have been established in recent years.[5] In general, most of the groups are engaged in micro-credit projects concerned with the small trade of various items. As long as they focus on trade, the effects of electricity on people's economical performance are likely to be more indirect (access to water, more time for income-generating activities, etc.) than direct. Finally, there are all the little shifts in people's everyday rhythm caused by the arrival of water pumps and electric light which, in sum, affect their level of production. The day has, after electrification, become twenty-four hours instead of twelve. This implies a new full range of choices as to what to do when, which observably makes people more efficient. At the same time, these new choices make them feel more short of time than before. With electricity, the pace of life is speeding up.

After a certain time with electricity, my data has shown that the number of cooked meals per day in rural Zanzibar goes down from three to two. This is a result of women's new opportunities to earn money, the time saved by an improved water supply and also their desire to watch TV in the evenings (chapter 10). The implications of this in terms of nutrition have not been investigated. Therefore it is not possible to conclude whether this shift implies that people in electrified villages over time eat less than before or less in comparison to non-electrified villages. Given the significant investment electricity represents and the normalisation of costly appliances such as TVs and freezers, the question deserves further attention. The observation that households who make between one and two dollars per day are tying up large amounts of their resources, with fluctuating and marginal incomes and rapidly increasing transport prices, is somewhat worrying.

On the other hand, access to electricity makes people less dependent on oil and kerosene, the price of which has dramatically increased in recent years. In 2005, the calculated pay-back time for investment in electricity was nine years for an ordinary household (SUM 2005). This is the point in time at which the use of electricity in an ordinary household becomes cheaper than the alternative of kerosene for light and batteries for radio. In 2006, the pay-back time was reduced to three to five years due to the high kerosene prices. In sum, to people in rural Zanzibar there is a high financial risk involved in whatever technology they choose. Electricity appears to be the better solution given that people have the available means to investment in it, although electricity prices are also subject to increases (SUM 2006). What I wish to emphasise is the extreme financial vulnerability of the people in question. Energy policies in Zanzibar, as elsewhere, should, accordingly, be very carefully developed. In sum, electricity has provided a range of changes people perceive of as improvements. To a considerable extent, these shifts match governmental objectives. However, apart from the tourist industry, electricity is not often used for generating income. To obtain development in its macroeconomic sense, the exploitation of the potential inherent in electricity appears to remain a challenge. Nevertheless, it appears highly unjustified to thereby conclude that electricity has failed to contribute to bringing 'development' to this area. This is clear from the presented material. If poverty is taken to mean the absence of what people feel they need to live a good life, electricity qualifies as a remedy in many respects. Still, in rural Zanzibar, the most trusted effect of electricity's arrival, as seen by the people in question, has not yet been realised, but is retained as a hope for the future: Through good health, education, and the virtue of 'getting new ideas', electricity is regarded as an investment in the generations to come and their ability to make a better life.

Environmentally sustainable development

Electricity's social aspects have been my main focus in the preceding chapters, but from time to time the analysis has also touched on issues related to the environment. In terms of people's physical surroundings, electrification caused a loss of trees and fields in inland areas (e.g., Binguni), for which the owners were compensated economically by the project. We have noted that people–spirit relations also influenced the way people perceived the cutting of bush in the forest to prepare for the coming of the grid. In a development context, this approach constitutes what Croll and Parkin (1992a; 1992b) would label a holistic perspective on the people–environment relationship. I have treated such aspects because they form part of the story of how electricity was introduced and the consequences of its use. In a wider sense, I would argue (with Croll and Parkin) that insights into how such people–environment relations are constituted (verbally and as practised) form an important point of departure for interventions that in intention or effect are linked to the natural environment. In Zanzibar, where deforestation is considered a challenge by the authorities, the means for addressing such problems should take people–environment relations into account, in line with other important factors such as gender, ownership of land and other socio-economic aspects.[6]

As for the global environmental challenge and climate change in particular, the shift from fossil fuels to hydroelectric production evidently constitutes a positive step. To central and local protagonists, however, electricity's economic advantages (also in terms of not having to provide spare parts for diesel generators) appear to be more relevant arguments for the centralised electricity system rather than a response to the threat of global climate change (chapter 3). Be that as it may, it has been my concern to demonstrate some of the subtler dynamics related to the global environment which on an aggregate, global level, are likely to have severe effects. Through the study of housing construction in chapter 7, I showed the way in which various technologies are linked. Changes in one technology, such as obtaining an electricity connection to one's house, lead to other kinds of changes, such as new types of waterproof roofs which do not allow for natural ventilation. This leads to more sealed constructions, which, together with the heat produced by incandescent light and other appliances, contribute to people's increased sense of discomfort during the hot season. In turn, the drive for fans (and probably soon also air conditioning) is rapidly increasing.

My point is that this could lead to a spiralling consumption pattern which could have been avoided. With the present low coverage of electricity in most African rural areas and the pressing need to invest in this infrastructure to combat poverty, it is crucial that such possible links are examined and a sustainable solution achieved before widespread deployment occurs. Electricity systems in many Southern contexts are facing a formative period at present. To meet the threat of global climate change, development agencies tend to highlight the need to produce electricity from renewable energy sources. Less is said and done on the consumption side, including what measures that could provide sustainable electricity use also in the future. In several European countries the so-called 'White Certificates' have recently been introduced which have considerable energy saving targets and results (ADEME – WEC 2007). These pose obligations on the energy company to include energy-efficiency measures in their customers' households or premises (for example by offering customers a certain number of compact fluorescent light sources for free or at a cheap price, or providing solar cells, solar water heaters, etc.). Similar measures have been suggested for Southern contexts by Eoin Lees (ibid.) and appear to warrant urgent consideration. The energy choices people are provided with at an early stage of electrification will profoundly influence their behaviour, and thereby also the environment, for many years to come.

Are kinship relations losing significance?

The analysis of the changes in the production sector and the increasing focus on money in Uroa indicate that family enterprises are in decline. After electrification and other coinciding socio-economic changes, people spend more time working independent of family networks. As individuals, they have a moral right to spend their money as they want. Does this mean that the individual's realm is expanding at the cost of the significance of the extended family?

No, this is not the case. When we studied how people used these devices, the importance of the extended family reappeared. TV programmes were shared and living rooms extended to accommodate the family and the neighbour network in the evenings. The same pattern is found when owners of freezers let relatives cool their drinks during Ramadan. Consequently, the reproduction of relationships which confirm the values of solidarity and equality is increasingly sustained through acts of consumption. Family relations appear no less important today than in the past, but the means for reproducing them have taken on new forms. This observation of continuity would be missed had we focused on the production sector alone. Similarly, had we considered consumption as uniquely related to markets and prices, we would not have understood why people buy the objects in question and how they handle this in the social context. The mother-in-law who is invited in to watch Swahili dramas in the evening, and who is entitled to stay as long as she wants, also constitutes an important object of study for understanding the dynamics of electricity consumption in Uroa. We need to see the whole chain to grasp the significance of its various parts. On another level, this book cals methodological attention to the vallue of focusing on family relations, kinship and gender (see below) in studies and policies that address development interventions.

Family cooperation formed an important part of men's strategies to obtain electrical appliances. Without brotherly cooperation, there would have been far fewer electrified houses in Uroa than is actually the case. Men who have immigrated to the village have fewer opportunities to engage in financial enterprises with other people. Those with an identified origin in Pemba are more or less excluded from such possibilities. Furthermore, and given that coins always have two sides, we also saw the relevance of one's family network at times of making dangerous acquisitions. Here, the balance between showing modesty and submitting to a desire for a new object is threatened. I argued that sanctions are more likely to come from one's equals, from those left behind, and that the offering of TV programmes should be considered in the light of a person's concern for demonstrating a willingness to share. It should also be noted that Zanzibaris highly value being together in groups, which applies for men as much as for women.

There is thus considerable continuity in the significance of family networks. Two changes are important, though, and the first relates to the growing differences within the village community. I have shown that increasing economic stratification is a fact and is likely to modify former relationships. New types of goods and ways of displaying modern styles enter Uroan households daily, but, within a given family network, such aspects and knowledge are unequally distributed. Uroa is becoming a less egalitarian place, also on the intra-family level. I do not emphasis this because I want to romanticise a 'better' past where people in fact had less recourses and fewer opportunities to get new ideas from the world at large.[7] I think the shift may be significant for Uroans' balancing of concerns and the values that ultimately inform their ways of relating to each other.

The other change that has been indicated is that the number of children per man, and also per woman, appears to go down with the arrival of electricity. I have shown how the arrival and rapid normalisation of electricity appears to delay men's entry into marriage. People acknowledge that it has become more expensive to provide a proper house for a wife. Utility regulations that prohibit men from connecting several houses (that is, several wives) to one meter enforce this process (cf. chapter 6). In addition, we have seen a change of moralities in this respect in that younger people speak mockingly of elderly men who have several wives but no electricity installed. Fifteen years after electricity's arrival, the current continues to some extent to be a marker of generational belonging.

Other mechanisms also appear to reduce the future reproduction rate in Uroa. Parents' emphasis on education makes many of them focus on supporting those children they have with more resources than before. Furthermore, due to people's watching TV at night, husbands and wives spend less time alone than before. If people's complaints about this tendency reflect their changed behaviour, a general tendency supported by Garnert, the arrival of electricity has had an impact on Uroan sexuality (Garnert 1993, see chapter 9). Again, the result will be that fewer babies may be born.

Negotiating gender relationships

Women's new sources of income have provided them with increased autonomy. Having your own income means more control and moral legitimacy to decide. However, women increasingly spend their money to support the household, thus, indirectly, they contribute to the financing of electricity and appliances, while still being referred to as those 'provided for'. Due to Islamic rules of inheritance, women seldom own houses. This is the single most important reason why I have argued that Islamic informed rules limit women's access to electricity and control thereof. In the case of divorce, there is also an ambiguity inherent in what a woman may take with her. Perhaps partly because of this, but most notably related to the 'maleness' associated with electricity and its organisation, a woman does not invest in electrical appliances. She does not buy, or receive at her wedding, appliances which have the peculiar characteristic of constituting a financial burden once in use. Instead, women appear to devote themselves to securing their children's development. Compared to the adult generation, in which women were illiterate to a greater extent than men, in girls' and boys' equal access to school we see that parents also have expectations for their daughters' future beyond becoming wives and mothers.

Gender relations, and how they may be changing at present, have also been explored by focusing on the spatial reorganisation of the living room (chapter 9). The husband has 'come home' since the arrival of electricity and TV, which constitutes a significant change in social relations between husbands and wives, and the couple as against the extended family. For 2001, I showed how the reorganisation of the room allowed for a mix of genders without jeopardising the ideal of sexual segregation. I also pointed to the way husband and wife were sitting together and the way they met the guests from a privileged position. Here, I suggested that Moore's (1996) model of continued power relations could be nuanced. True, the idea of male superiority continues to be a dominant representation in rural Zanzibar too. This is reflected when the husband fetches and turns the appliance on. By doing this, he symbolically provides for his wife. However, due to the spouses' position in the room, her right to comment and, notably, their way of performing in this modern style with great confidence in front of a wider audience, I suggested that something new might be being reflected. The strong impact of the development discourse at least invites us to question how this fits in with the idea of male superiority. I drew on Moore's later work (1994) to account for how distinct discourses may have enduring effects on people's embodied experiences and, in turn, their identities. I suggested that the hostess appeared less subordinate to men when performing in a modern style in this particular setting than in other contexts. Here, Miller's (1994) perspective was illuminating. People's uses of material objects not only reflect but also *produce* values, identities and power relations, i.e., 'structures'. As of 2001, living rooms in Uroa can thus be seen to objectify a modified, or alternative, set of values and moralities, which find legitimacy in the development discourse. Extended family relations remain important, but the value of being able to relax in this particular way temporarily overshadows the importance of male dominance.

With yet another reorganisation of this space between 2001 and 2004 (same-sex gatherings in front of the TV and fewer evening guests in TV-equipped homes) I indicated that these developments could affect the hostess's (and host's) previously levelled status. Without an audience to watch them perform, this could to some extent become the case. However, couples having the ability to withdraw to their own living room in this way maintain their modern status vis-à-vis others. The criteria for judgement embedded in the development discourse allows for an alternative interpretation, or creation, of space, values and identities to those inherent in the male-female hierarchicy.

From the study of food we also came to see some of the dynamics of how practices are reshaped. Women have modified their cooking utensils despite men's preferences for the taste of food produced in clay pots; and the reduction in the number of meals cooked per day due to the coming of seaweed, electricity and TV has been noted. I pointed to the silence in which such negotiations and shifts appear to have taken place, which is in accordance with Zanzibari aesthetics. It is significant that a woman may modify her way of performing as a wife if she has legitimate reasons for doing so. To note, here, is the fact that what constitutes 'legitimate reasons' is quite unclear, which is in line with the undetermined nature of life in rural Zanzibar. What is more, when we explored perceptions of how electric cookers affect tastes in food, I showed that the gender difference that appeared was related to men and women's distinct positions. Women and men are not unequivocally influenced by external discourses and this reinforces the ongoing gender negotiations.

When such processes materialise into changes in practice, we get the possibility of exploring them further. It is interesting to see how the introduction of electric cookers in 2004 appeared to be managed. First of all, the women had taken out loans from the new school project fund (see chapter 7) for buying these appliances. Secondly, and also a fundamentally new practice, the spouses in these particular families now shared the cost of electricity consumption. Often, the husband would pay 60 per cent of the bill and the wife would pay the rest. One woman actually paid the whole bill herself. Significantly, the husband would receive the money from his wife at home before going to pay at the CCM office. The ideology of male providers continues to be relevant, and it seems vital to keep up this image vis-à-vis other people. I have repeatedly emphasised the 'male' electricity bill as being a barrier for women owning appliances. Now, it seems, such dilemmas have been solved through negotiation. The effects in the long run are yet to be seen.

Women and men in Uroa have grasped the possibilities offered by new economic realities, new objects and ideas from elsewhere in their attempts to reshape their lives for the better. They employ various strategies for coping with economic fluctuations and other risks. As is noted elsewhere for the East African region, people in rural Zanzibar always seem to be acting in the 'subjunctive mode' (Whyte 1996: 4).[8] This implies the perception that few things are certain, risks are many and strategies for handling risks may always fail.

What I have also stressed is the need to possess knowledge and resources in order to perform in any particular way. Women 'immigrants' from within the island do not know how to catch octopus. Men from town do not necessarily know how to operate a canoe. These are small examples of how important it is to be at ease with a style in order to master it. The risk of failure is ever present. I now conclude by talking about Uroan men's position as utility customers in relation to uncertainty, knowledge and their strategies for coping with risk.

Electrified worries and the need to get in control

People and households registered as customers with the state company become locked into specific ways of acting (chapter 6). Customers must make their homes accessible and they must show up in time with sufficient money. In addition, they must certainly not interfere with the scripts of objects such as the meter. In short, they are to behave as obedient and competent customers. Scott maintains that authoritarian modernist projects seek to simplify existing structures so that the state may deliver development services (1998: 224–5). I would say the script of any monopolised infrastructure, such as electricity in Zanzibar, has this trait attached to it. The distribution of electricity must be effective and simple. The script of the system, as described in chapter 6, is intended for such purposes. Each element is delegated a specific purpose for the smooth delivery of current in exchange of payment. The electricity bill is the utility company's regular feedback to customers on how they are performing.

However, there is also a motive of political control among authoritarian regimes, according to Scott (ibid: 224). He argues that the state seeks to make people better objects for political control through development projects. In Zanzibar, the (re-) introduction of the multiparty system has actualised the regime's authoritarian traits. The government strives for control. I often observed such strategies in everyday life and, notably, the surveying of the electrical system is also used for the political control of Zanzibaris. The entering of private space to read meters implies an intrusion in two respects. First of all, it means that the social relationship between the employee and the customer is tested and sometimes challenged. This is reciprocal. Secondly, the government's access allows it to monitor what posters a person may have on the walls inside their house (an important marker of political affiliation) or if there are party flags up, or critical conversations going on. Informants for the government are everywhere in Unguja. The utility company's right to enter houses has created new boundaries between safe and unsafe space.

Another important trait of the electricity system is that customer relationships are based on contracts with named people. In this way, in contrast to the rather diffuse ways in which other kinds of objects are purchased and become shared in everyday use, the electricity bill rests with a single person. This fits with the Zanzibari morality of individual financial responsibility. However, the consequences of this contract are quite distinctive from other kinds of practices. The tendency that people are approximately five months behind with their payments speaks of the extent to which customers remain isolated with their commitment. This new dependent relationship with the state constitutes an important effect of electrification. It increases people's fear of the consequences of failing as customers. In addition, I showed that men's worries here are not only linked with payment. The configuration of the system, along with the accounting system and bills issued in English, prevents people who are already in a vulnerable position from performing as informed, modern customers within this bureaucracy. This radically contrasts with the way we saw powerful customer groups in the past negotiating their interests vis-à-vis the electricity company. The position of today's rural customers has striking parallels to that of the people living on the Other Side in the colonial period (see chapter 2).

I think the risk rural customers experience today is particularly painful because there are few authorities to turn to. Or rather, the main authority is the state corporation itself, but due to the antagonistic relationship between customer and company, people do not seek advice from the very party they trust the least and fear the most in this context. In addition, no matter how much electricity's secondary objects are shared within the extended family, the bill is addressed in the singular. Perhaps the new trend of some women helping finance the electricity bill speaks of couples becoming a stronger unit than before. The evidence that couples are increasingly together at home in the evenings also points to a stronger emphasis on the nuclear unit. However, it remains the registered person's responsibility to settle his bills with the utility company. Vis-à-vis the corporation, one's liability remains in the singular.

With the increased governmental control, the post-payment system and the incomprehensible electricity bills, one could consider electricity to be one of the pitfalls of development. In this light, it is appropriate to ask Ferguson's question as to whether development has fulfilled what it promised. In a parallel process, volatile world markets affect life to an extent that has never been experienced before. Consequently, Uroans' current economic position is strikingly vulnerable, and in 2004 this seemed increasingly to be the case. Despite the many changes that had occurred in the name of 'development', people were striving just to make ends meet to an apparently increasing extent. Meja and Khamis, for instance, said they do not get enough to eat (*hatushibi*) three to four times a week. In 2001, I had not heard such complaints. Therefore, for the household finances, we may say that people's tying up resources in lasting equipment and appliances lock up the family's resources in ways that are detrimental to subsistence. This constitutes a severe and paradoxical situation but, as noted, the alternative (to rely on kerosene for lighting) is not a financially sustainable solution in the long run.

Electricity customers' new exposure to risk requires new strategies for dealing with uncertainty. Here, risk management as a joint family enterprise is not currently relevant. We may ask how customers adjust to the new reality. The practice of saving money in the bank coincided with electricity's arrival. 'To put aside money' (*kuweka pesa*) is a strategy to allow planning for the future. The phenomenon of 'singular' debt could very well contribute to this focus. However, few men brought up the issue of savings when telling me about their lives and how they handle financial challenges.

In contrast, I have mentioned Abdalla who is a member of one of the new fishing corporations in Uroa (chapter 5). He had been to a government-organised course where participants were informed about the possibility of getting loans. Abdalla said it was here that he learned how to write a budget (*budjeti*). He repeatedly emphasised the importance of 'getting in control' (*kupata kontroli*) by making 'plans' (*mapango*). A written budget had been required when he obtained a loan for investing in modern fishing gear and his fishing corporation keeps a detailed accounting system. Abdalla is an innovative person and constantly has new projects on the go. Like everyone else in the village, though, he struggles to make ends meet. However, he voices a commitment to planning systematically for the future more than others. Does this emphasis on control indicate a shift in how he handles risk?[9]

In certain ways it appears that he seeks to eliminate risk rather than striving to be prepared for various scenarios. However, it is not a clear-cut task to interpret such signs of changing risk-management in the Uroan context. The fisherman's emphasis on control could have been adopted from the particular discourse in town without having too much conceptual or practical significance. We have seen people's general concern for reducing uncertainty and managing risk. Abdalla does not use occult knowledge to any lesser extent than anyone else in his striving for prosperity. Labelling his strategies 'control' does not fundamentally change their content or orientation. Writing a budget instead of thinking one out does not eliminate the risks involved.

Abdalla would agree on the latter point but stress that control puts you in a better position to judge how to spend your money. As a relatively wealthy person, he has increased the scale and range of his investments. This appears to trigger a more acute need for planning in a systematic way. The consequences for failing become more fatal when the stakes are high. When, as an individual, he seeks prosperity in ways that transgress normal limits, he simultaneously appears more isolated in handling the consequences. This is partly so because he cannot expect his relatives to be able to help him if projects fail. However, morally too, he has taken on risks in more personal terms than what is normally seen to be the case. The personal history of another man from Uroa is revealing of such moralities. Today, this man is admired but notably also criticised for having been strong (*wa nguvu*) in the past. He extended his business too much, it was said, and therefore ended up ruined. His many children are evidence of the man's former power. However, without the financial ability to keep up with 'development', by providing his house with electricity, for example, his glory is gone.

We here return to the heart of the dilemma in Uroan economic and moral life, which is the tension between the articulated individual responsibility and the need to demonstrate group solidarity. Hence the question related to risk-evaluation, control, and change must be to ask the following: is the tension between responsibility in the singular (as articulated) and handling of risk in the plural (as practised) being provided with new content at present? Despite the strong elements of continuity I hold that a shift is taking place. 'Getting in control' does not necessarily mean to (try to) eliminate risk. However, the expression points to an individual's duty to handle ups and downs also in practice. 'Control' is not accomplished as a shared project (the exceptions are the corporations mentioned). The notion characterises the solitary situation only some Uroans, such as Abdalla, appear to face actively. However, significantly, every Uroan is equally isolated in their position as long as they remain electricity customers. For the majority, I thus find a discontinuity in how the bureaucratic system defines them (as individual customers) and how they manage to relate to this in practice. Most Uroan customers confront the new situation defensively. They are exposed to a type of risk they probably did not expect when signing up as customers. Together with the incomprehensibility of the system and the mutual antagonism between utility company and customer, I concluded that the electricity system in rural Zanzibar is far from stabilised. It is unsettled and highly disputed.

'You don't tell someone with a bike to buy himself a car!'

The idea that life can and should be changed for the better with the help of education and new objects and ideas can be traced back long in time in Uroa. However, electrification and a range of other recent changes have intensified the local development discourse. I argue that the massive impact of these transformations, combined with the presence of government institutions, has transformed 'development' from being an idea of progress to becoming an increasingly permanent set of criteria for judgements and behaviour. Here, the value of change is celebrated, sometimes at the cost of other, culturally informed virtues, which ultimately leads to legitimising difference. This trend gains further moral momentum from the visible patterns of stratification that emerge at present. Electric light has a force in making enduring differences observable. At the same time the egalitarian ideology remains powerful.

Uroan aesthetics are informed by a range of contradictory moralities, and social life is characterised by a lack of fixity.

People in Uroa relate to their new, impersonalised counterparts in town or elsewhere in ambivalent ways. They lack control over world markets and utility tariffs. However, the new medium of TV and, for example, the increased use of tape recorders for religious education, involves Uroans in external networks in a way that they greatly appreciate. This reinforces the national and global discourses' power to affect the way people live and evaluate their lives. For this reason, it is highly relevant to speak of people's increasing experience of globalisation phenomena in rural Zanzibar. How have these processes modified Uroa as a meaningful place?

I touched on Edwin Ardener's (1987) perspective of 'remote areas' when accounting for how Uroa has become more 'like a town' with the arrival of electric light (chapter 7). Such descriptions indicate that Uroans today consider their place to be less remote in relation to town and more levelled in status compared with other villages. In other words, Uroa is not so much placed 'on the other side' as it was before. People's perceptions of their being included in a national grid of modernity contribute to rendering Uroa meaningful as a place.

The village–town relationship could be taken a bit further. Historically, as seen from Uroa, life in town was of relatively little relevance. Today, the daily transport of people, goods and TV broadcasts bring the 'two worlds' closer together. These new connections produce a particular paradox. We see that the premises for Uroans' comparisons with life in town at present lie precisely in the new means of communication and the extended contact. I hold that the daily images of a modern life in town also contribute to constructing Uroa as a remoter place than before. This is so because differences between town and village persist and have become so readily observable. Within the development discourse, life in town is the ideal.

Uroans have an ambivalent relationship to life in town. Material objects from the centre are admired. In encounters with institutions such as the utility company or with individuals from town, Uroans modify their behaviour and appear vulnerable. The town aesthetic seems to dominate rural styles when the two actually meet. However, Uroans also contrast the hard work they put in with what they perceive as an easier life in town. Furthermore, they stress solidarity as a typical feature of life in rural areas. There is a sense of moral superiority and dignity to life in the village as Uroans see it.

Throughout this account of people and electricity in rural Zanzibar, we have encountered how carefully men and women introduce new objects into their lives. External discourses have an impact and the materialisation of electricity in the village constitutes a drive of its own. However, Uroans also select which elements and advice to reject. When I asked a man in Uroa why people do not cook with electricity, he said: 'You don't tell someone with a bike to buy himself a car!' By this, he implied that he is content with cooking practices as they are. However, unlike most men, he did not refer to the superior taste of Zanzibari food (or the danger involved in electric cooking, see chapter 10). Rather, he made a reference to modesty. Furthermore, with the words 'you don't tell' he appeared to blame the questioner for insinuating that Zanzibaris should change their way of treating their food.

The man's statement may further enlighten us as to why men in particular find electricity unappealing in the context of food. Electric cooking and the cold storage of food are foreign ideas that break with the Zanzibari aesthetic for treating foodstuffs. We remember food's significance as a marker of people's shared, Zanzibari identity. Perhaps in this respect Uroans' perception of electricity as something Western make this marking of a boundary particularly important (cf. Arce and Long 2000). The man can be read as saying: 'we accept these parts of your development but not the rest'. Due to my associations with the electrification project and my expressed interest in cookers, I was struck by his bicycle/car metaphor. In any case, we may have come closer to understanding how Zanzibaris select some elements from various surrounding discourses and disregard others. People in Uroa claim the right to construct their own identities and the styles through which these are performed. This resonates with historical accounts of how adaptive the Swahilis have been to external influences and how, despite various transformations, they have maintained a sense of common identity. It is also a strong case for arguing that people living in various parts of the world today shape their own, particular modernities (Moore and Sanders 2001; Knauft 2002; Sahlins 1999; Caplan 2004; Comaroff and Comaroff 1993).

The present is far from 'the end of development' for people in Uroa. To them, the coming of electricity, new objects and jobs, and also people and ideas, constitutes development as long as it implies changes for the better. They continue to express hopes for future progress. On a collective level today, electricity is a sign of Uroa's common achievement. At the time of its introduction, the picture was more varied and disputed. Furthermore, enacting modern styles is legitimate for normalised practices, such as sending children to school or watching TV, but acting in this modality requires new types of knowledge, careful performance and may still be risky. This is particularly so in relation to the utility itself.

Long-term values, such as equality, solidarity, modesty and respectability, continue to be relevant after electricity's arrival. However, I have shown that people reproduce and articulate these values in slightly shifting ways at present. I have pointed to the appearance of a more stratified Uroa and to how new objects become part of some people's projects for self-definition.

The transformations taking place at present give increasing impetus to moral and existential issues that were 'always' relevant in Uroa. However, the pace of change is increased and new solutions must continuously be invented and justified. The particular, modern expression we find in Uroa is far from the result of a 'homogenisation process', leading everywhere to similar cultural forms. True, the impact of transnational and national connections on life has been demonstrated, some of which have also made Uroans more vulnerable at present. At the same time, though, I have emphasised the selective ways in which new influences are included in men's and women's lives. More specifically, I hold that Uroans' meaningful uses of electricity and electrical appliances are not arbitrary. People's 'current styles' are, in a literal sense, the results of a technological system's scripts and the shifting social, cultural and material context in which electricity was introduced. As was the case following electricity's arrival, its uses are also continuously subject to men's and women's various and shifting interests and choices. Electricity's impact in rural Zanzibar could not have been predetermined, but clearly, the new technology has made a difference.

Notes

1. Ferguson gives one reference to Coopersmith 1992 (Fergusson 1999: 243) who has treated the history of Russian electrification.
2. It is unclear which era Ferguson refers to when describing the network as unifying the Zambian state. According to the home pages of Zambia Electricity Supply Corporation, the largest supplier of electricity in Zambia today, it was not until the 1950s that at least four of the various power stations were connected in a grid (http://www.zesco.co.zm/).
3. I do not wish to imply that I question Ferguson's general argument about how deceived Zambians feel about the misleading promises of the modernising project. Life in the 'Copperbelt' certainly involved dramatic socio-economic changes first, at the time of the rise of the modern 'illusion', and then with its breakdown some decades later. In comparison, the historical and present rural Zanzibari experience of development seems more sober. Economic fluctuations on world markets and the government's shortcomings in supplying public goods have not erased people's belief in such projects. And in Ferguson's defense, it is of course impossible to investigate every kind of variation in one single study.
4. For example, nine people without electricity connection mentioned the importance of electricity (only one person with such a connection gave the same priority); six women living further away from the village taps than the average highlighted the need for easy access to water; a childless woman pointed to the importance of having children; and two men from Pemba focused on the need to be on good terms with one's neighbours. Other issues, such as access to money, business, a nice house and good health were also often mentioned.
5. In Uroa alone, eight new groups were registered between 2001 and 2006.
6. In earlier chapters I have pointed to the unfortunate effects of two other changes. The FINNIDA tree planting project has, in practice, resulted in the privatisation of the land around Uroa (chapter 5). As a result, most women must walk farther than before to fetch firewood than they used to. Secondly there is the unfortunate environmental effect of seaweed production in that women prefer to cut down living trees to obtain poles for their fields. I have not treated the possible environmental effects of seaweed farming on the shore or in the sea.
7. Todd Sanders speaks of the 'aesthetics of anthropological explanation' and how certain ideas about the relationship between the past (better) and the present (worse) are embedded in much work (communicated at a seminar at the University of Oslo, 29 March

2005). This is illustrated when occult phenomena are treated as resistance to socio-economic changes, such as the spread of capitalism. He also relates this aesthetic to anthropologists' concern with providing political and moral sensibilities to social analysis. De-exoticising 'the other' by rationalising behaviour and beliefs forms part of the picture.

8. Whyte (1996: 24) adopts this notion from Byron Good (1994: 153) who cites Jerome Bruner: 'To be in the subjunctive mode is ... to be trafficking in human possibilities rather than in settled certainties'.

9. Marianne Lien makes use of Charles Taylor's (1992) cultural approach to modernity in her analysis of a Norwegian marketing enterprise (Lien 1997: 280–7). Lien holds that the difference between non-modern and modern contexts is not the extent to which doubt and ambivalence occur. Rather, there is a distinction in how people relate to such uncertainties. People in traditional communities, the anthropologist argues, seek to avoid risk only to integrate it at another level (referring to Douglas 1966). In contrast, people living in modern contexts attempt to eliminate doubt. Here, Lien holds, people act 'as if' control of future events were possible. Combined with a Western focus on authenticity and inwardness, i.e., the existence of a 'real', inner quality of things and people which can be revealed, the notion of control is interesting. The paradox in the Norwegian context is that people act as if control and rational planning were possible and simultaneously acknowledge the unpredictable ways in which things actually happen. However, Taylor's notion of inwardness is specifically Western and I find universal models for modern traits of this sort quite problematic.

GLOSSARY OF SWAHILI TERMS

baraza – bench outdoors, often placed outside private dwellings.
bui-bui – black, long veil used by women in the countryside when going to Zanzibar Town.
chungu – clay pot used for for cooking.
dala dala – small buses used for collective transport.
dishi – aluminium pot used for cooking.
elimu – education; knowledge.
futari – evening meal served during the month of Ramadan.
hadharani – in public.
halhabari – witch-hunting ritual.
haraka – hurry.
haya – modesty; shyness.
hodi – hello (uttered before entering someone's premises).
kanga – two-piece wraps or cloths worn by women.
kanzu – long, white robe worn by men on Fridays and during weddings and funerals.
kazi – work.
ladha – flavour or taste (in food).
lazima – important/necessary.
maendeleo (also *maendesha*) – development; moving forward.
malai (lit. 'angel') – frozen, sweet ice.
maulidi – eulogy on the Prophet's life.
mchawi (pl. *wachawi*) – witch or sorcerer.
mganga (pl. *waganga*) – healer.
mila – tradition.
mita – electricity meter.
msaada – help.
mtu mbaya (pl. *watu wabaya*) – bad person with evil intentions.
muhimu – important.
mzimu (pl. *mizimu*) – sacred spots where spirits reside.
nguvu – strength.
pendeza – be appealing.

pilau – pilaff.

pumzika – relax.

ringi – electric cooker of the coil element type.

sawa – equal; ok.

shetani – spirit.

siri – secret; secretly; hidden.

taarab – popular music genre in East Africa.

ukumbi – living room.

umeme – electricity.

umeme direct (also *komba*) – unauthorised connection to the electricity grid whereby a non-registered consumer is linked up via a neighbouring electricity customer.

yuniti – electric units (kilowatt-hours).

zamani – a long time ago.

BIBLIOGRAPHY

References

Akrich, M. 1994 [1992]. 'The De-scription of Technical Objects', in W.E. Bijker and J. Law (eds), *Shaping Technology/Building Society*. *Studies in Sociotechnical Change*. Cambridge, MA: Massachusetts Institute of Technology Press.

Andersson, J. and Z. Ngazi. 1998. 'Coastal Communities' Production Choices, Risk Diversification, and Subsistence Behaviour: Responses in Periods of Transition. A Case Study from Tanzania', *Ambio* 27(8): 686–93.

Appadurai, A. 1986. 'Introduction: Commodities and the Politics of Value', in A. Appadurai (ed.), *The Social Life of Things. Commodities in Cultural Perspective*. Cambridge: Cambridge University Press.

Arce, A. and N. Long. 2000. 'Reconfiguring Modernity and Development from an Anthropological Perspective', in A. Arce and N. Long (eds), *Anthropology, Development and Modernities. Exploring Discourses, Counter-tendencies and Violence*. London and New York: Routledge.

Ardener, E. 1987. '"Remote Areas": Some Theoretical Considerations', in A. Jackson (ed.), *Anthropology at home*. London and New York: Tavistock Publications.

Askew, K.M. 1999. 'Female Circles and Male Lines: Gender Dynamics Along the Swahili Coast', *Africa Today* 3(3–4).

Bader, Z. 1991. 'The Contradictions of Merchant Capital, 1840–1939', in A. Sheriff and E. Ferguson (eds), *Zanzibar Under Colonial Rule*. Dar es Salaam: Historical Association of Tanzania and London: James Currey.

Banik, D. 2005. 'Introduction', in D. Banik (ed.), *Poverty, Politics and Development. Interdisciplinary Perspectives*. Bergen: Fagbokforlaget.

Barth, F. 1993. *Balinese Worlds*. Chicago and London: University of Chicago Press.

Bender, B. 2002. 'Time and Landscape', *Current Anthropology* 43: 103–12.

Bijker, W.E. and J. Law. 1994. 'General Introduction', in W. Bijker and J. Law (eds), *Shaping Technology/Building Society: Studies in Sociotechnical Change*. Cambridge, MA: Massachusetts Institute of Technology Press.

Blystad, A. 1999. '"Dealing with Men's Spears". Datooga Pastoralists Combating Male Intrusion on Female Fertility', in H.L. Moore, T. Sanders and B. Kaare (eds), *Those Who Play with Fire. Gender, Fertility and Transformation in East and Southern Africa*. London: Athlone Press.

Bornstein, E. 2005. *The Spirit of Development. Protestant NGOs, Morality and Economics in Zimbabwe*. Stanford, California: Stanford University Press.

Bourdieu, P. 1977. *Outline of a Theory of Practice*. Cambridge: Cambridge University Press.

———. 1984. *Distinction. A Social Critique of the Judgement of Taste*. Cambridge, MA: Harvard University Press. (Originally published in 1979 as *La Distinction: Critique Sociale du Jugement*. Paris: Les Editions de Minuit).

Caplan, P. 1984. 'Cognatic Descent, Islamic Law and Women's Property on the East African Coast', in R. Hirschon (ed.), *Women and Property – Women as Property*. London: St Martin's Press.

———. 1997. *African Voices, African Lives. Personal Narratives from a Swahili Village*. London and New York: Routledge.

———. 2004. 'Introduction', in P. Caplan and F. Topan (eds), *Swahili Modernities. Culture, Politics and Identity on the East Coast of Africa*. Asmara: Africa World Press.

Carrithers, M. 1992. *Why Humans Have Cultures. Explaining Anthropology and Social Diversity*. Oxford: Oxford University Press.

Carsten, J. and S. Hugh-Jones. 1995. 'Introduction', in J. Carsten and S. Hugh-Jones (eds), *About the House: Lévi-Strauss and Beyond*. Cambridge: Cambridge University Press.

Chambers, R. 1995. 'Paradigm Shifts and the Practice of Participatory Research and Development', in N. Nelson and S. Wright (eds), *Power and Participatory Development. Theory and Practice*. London: Intermediate Technology Publications.

Comaroff, J. and J. Comaroff. 1993. 'Introduction', in J. Comaroff and J. Comaroff (eds), *Modernity and Its Malcontents. Ritual and Power in Postcolonial Africa*. Chicago and London: University of Chicago Press.

Cornwall, A. and R. Jewkes. 1995. 'What is Participatory Research?', *Social Science and Medicine* 41(12): 1667–76.

Counihan, C.M. 1999. *The Anthropology of Food and Body. Gender, Meaning, and Power*. New York: Routledge.

Cowan, R.S. 1983. *More Work for Mother. The Ironies of Household Technology from the Open Hearth to the Microwave*. New York: Basic Books.

Crewe, E. 1997. 'The Silent Traditions of Developing Cooks', in R. D. Grillo and R. L. Stirrat (eds), *Discourses of Development. Anthropological Perspectives*. Oxford and New York: Berg.

Croll, E. and D. Parkin. 1992a. 'Anthropology, the Environment and Development', in E. Croll and D. Parkin (eds), *Bush Base: Forest Farm. Culture, Environment and Development*. London: Routledge.

———. 1992b. 'Cultural Understandings of the Environment', in E. Croll and D. Parkin (eds), *Bush Base: Forest Farm. Culture, Environment and Development*. London: Routledge.

Curtis, D. 1995. 'Power to the People: Rethinking Community Development', in N. Nelson and S. Wright (eds), *Power and Participatory Development. Theory and Practice*. London: Intermediate Technology Publications.

Depelchin, J. 1991. 'The Transition from Slavery, 1873–1914', in A. Sheriff and E. Ferguson (eds), *Zanzibar Under Colonial Rule*. Dar es Salaam: Historical Association of Tanzania; and London: James Currey.

Douglas, M. 1966. *Purity and Danger*. London: Routledge & Kegan Paul.

———. 1982. *In the Active Voice*. London, Boston and Henley: Routledge & Kegan Paul.

———. 1996 [1970]. *Natural Symbols*. New York: Routledge.

————. 1999 [1972]. 'Deciphering a Meal', in M. Douglas, *Implicit Meanings. Selected Essays in Anthropology*. London: Routledge.

Douglas, M. and B. Isherwood. 1996 [1979]. *The World of Goods: Towards an Anthropology of Consumption*. London: Routledge.

Dugard, J. In press. 'Power to the People?: A Rights-based Analysis of South Africa's Electricity Services', in D. McDonald (ed.), *Electric Capitalism: Recolonising Africa on the Power Grid*. Cape Town: HSRC Press (Human Sciences Research Council of South Africa).

Ellen, R.F. (ed.). 1984. *Ethnographic Research. A Guide to General Conduct*. London: Academic Press.

Fair, L. 1994. 'Pastimes and Politics: a Social History of Zanzibar's Ng'ambo Community, 1890–1950', Ph.D. dissertation. USA: University of Minnesota.

Feld, S. and K.H. Basso. 1996. 'Introduction', in S. Feld and K.H. Basso (eds), *Senses of Place*. Santa Fe, NM: School of American Research Press.

Ferguson, J. 1999. *Expectations of Modernity. Myths and Meanings of Urban Life on the Zambian Copperbelt*. Berkeley, Los Angeles and London: University of California Press.

Fisiy, C.F. and P. Geschiere. 2001. 'Witchcraft, Development and Paranoia in Cameroon: Interactions Between Popular, Academic and State Discourse', in H.L. Moore and T. Sanders (eds), *Magical Interpretations, Material Realities. Modernity, Witchcraft and the Occult in Postcolonial Africa*. London and New York: Routledge.

Foley, G. and P. Moss. 1983. *Improving Cooking Stoves in Developing Countries*. London: Earthscan.

Fuglesang, M. 1994. 'Veils and Videos. Female Youth Culture on the Kenyan coast', Ph.D. dissertation. Sweden: Stockholm Studies in Social Anthropology (32).

Gardner, K. and D. Lewis. 1996. *Anthropology, Development and the Post-modern Challenge*. London and Sterling, Virginia: Pluto Press.

Garnert, J. 1993. *Anden i Lampan. Etnologiska Perspektiv på Ljus och Mörker*. Stockholm: Carlssons Bokförlag.

Goffman, E. 1959. *The Presentation of Self in Everyday Life*. Middlesex: Penguin Books.

González Turmo, I. 1997. 'The Pathways of Taste. The West Andalucian Case', in H. Macbeth (ed.), *Food Preferences and Taste*. Oxford: Berghahn Books.

Goody, J. 1982. *Cooking, Cuisine and Class. A Study in Comparative Sociology*. Cambridge: Cambridge University press.

Green, M. 2003a. 'Globalizing Development in Tanzania. Policy Franchising Through Participatory Project Management', *Critique of Anthropology* 23(2): 123–143.

————. 2003b. *Priests, Witches and Power. Popular Christianity After Mission in Southern Tanzania*. Cambridge: Cambridge University Press.

Grillo, R.D. 1997. 'Discourses of Development: the View from Anthropology', in R.D. Grillo and R.L. Stirrat (eds), *Discourses of Development. Anthropological Perspectives*. Oxford and New York: Berg.

Hastrup, K. 1992. *Det Antropologiske Prosjekt – om Forbløffelse*. Copenhagen: Nordisk Forlag AS.

————. 1995. *A Passage to Anthropology. Between Experience and Theory*. London and New York: Routledge.

————. 1998. *A Place Apart. An Anthropological Study of the Icelandic World*. Oxford: Clarendon Press.

Hobart, M. 1993. 'Introduction: the Growth of Ignorance?', in M. Hobart (ed.), *An Anthropological Critique of Development. The Growth of Ignorance*. London: Routledge.

Hughes, T.P. 1983. *Networks of Power. Electrification in Western Society, 1980–1930*. Baltimore and London: Johns Hopkins University Press.

Hutchinson, S.E. 1996. *Nuer Dilemmas: Coping with Money, War and the State*. London: University of California Press.

Issak, I.E. 1999. *Swahili–Norsk Ordbok*. Oslo: Spartacus Forlag AS.

Johnson, M. 1998. 'At Home and Abroad: Inalienable Wealth, Personal Consumption and the Formulations of Femininity in the Southern Philippines', in D. Miller (ed.), *Material Cultures. Why Some Things Matter*. Chicago: University of Chicago Press.

Kempton, W. and L. Montgomery. 1982. 'Folk Quantification of Energy', *Energy* 7(10): 817–27.

Knauft, B.M. 2002. *Critically Modern: Alternatives, Alterities, Anthropologies*. Bloomington: Indiana University Press.

Lamont, M. 2000. *The Dignity of Working Men. Morality and the Boundaries of Race, Class, and Immigration*. London and Cambridge, MA: Harvard University Press.

Lane, J. 1995. 'Non-governmental Organizations and Participatory Development: the Concept in Theory Versus the Concept in Practice', in N. Nelson and S. Wright (eds), *Power and Participatory Development. Theory and Practice*. London: Intermediate Technology Publications.

Larsen, K. 1995. 'Where Humans and Spirits Meet: Incorporating Difference and Experiencing Otherness in Zanzibar Town', Ph.D. dissertation. Norway: University of Oslo.

———. 2004. 'Change, Continuity and Contestation: the Politics of Modern Identities in Zanzibar', in P. Caplan and F. Topan (eds), *Swahili Modernities. Culture, Politics and Identity on the East Coast of Africa*. Asmara: Africa World Press.

Latour, B. 1987. *Science in Action*. Cambridge, MA: Harvard University Press.

———. 1994. 'Where Are the Missing Masses? The Sociology of a Few Mundane Artefacts', in W.E. Bijker and J. Law (eds), *Shaping Technology/Building Society. Studies in Sociotechnical Change*. Cambridge, MA: Massachusetts Institute of Technology Press.

Leach, M. et al. 1999. 'Experiencing Poverty in Africa. Perspectives from Anthropology', *World Bank Poverty Status Report*, Background paper 1(b).

Le Guennec-Coppens, F. 2004. 'The Monetization of Matrimonial Prestations in the Comorian Great Marriage', in P. Caplan and F. Topan (eds), *Swahili Modernities. Culture, Politics and Identity on the East Coast of Africa*. Asmara: Africa World Press.

Lien, M.E. 1987. 'Fra Boknafesk til Pizza. Sosiokulturelle Perspektiver på Mat og Endring av Spisevaner i Båtsfjord, Finnmark'. Occasional papers (18), Department of Social Anthropology, University of Oslo, Norway.

———. 1997. *Marketing and Modernity*. Oxford and New York: Berg.

———. 2003. 'Shifting Boundaries of a Coastal Community: Tracing Changes on the Margin', in T.H. Eriksen (ed.), *Globalisation: Studies in Anthropology. Anthropology, Culture, and Society*. London: Pluto Press.

Londos, E. 1993. *Uppåt Väggarna i Svenska Hem. En Etnologisk Studie av Bildbruk*. Stockholm: Carlsson Bokförlag.

Long, N. 1989. 'Introduction: the Raison d' tre for Studying Rural Development Interface', in N. Long (ed.), *Encounters at the Interface: a Perspective on Social*

Discontinuities in Rural Development. Wageningen Studies in Sociology 27. Wageningen, the Netherlands: Wageningen University Publications.

McGruder, J.H. 1999. 'Madness in Zanzibar: "Schizophrenia" in Three Families in the "Developing" World (Tanzania)', Ph.D. dissertation. USA: University of Michigan.

Maliyamkono, T.L. 2000. 'Zanzibar's Economy. Part II: Zanzibar's Financial Benefits from the Union', in T.L. Maliyamkono (ed.), *The Political Plight of Zanzibar*. Dar es Salaam: TEMA Publishers Company Ltd.

Marvin, C. 1988. *When Old Technologies Were New. Thinking About Electric Communication in the Late Nineteenth Century*. Oxford: Oxford University Press.

Mauss, M. 1990. *The Gift. The Form and Reason for Exchange in Archaic Societies*. London: Routledge. (First published in 1950 as *Essai sur le Don* by Presses Universitaires de France).

Mazrui, A. and I.N. Shariff. 1994. *The Swahili: Idiom and Identity of an African People*. Trenton, NJ: Africa World Press.

Mbwiliza, J. 2000. 'The Birth of a Political Dilemma and the Challenges of the Quest for New Politics in Zanzibar', in T.L. Maliyamkono (ed.), *The Political Plight of Zanzibar*. Dar es Salaam: TEMA Publishers Company Ltd.

Meyer, B. 1998. 'Commodities and the Power of Prayer: Pentecostalist Attitudes Towards Consumption in Contemporary Ghana', *Development and Change* 29(4): 751–76.

Middleton, J. 1992. *The World of the Swahili. An African Mercantile Civilization*. New Haven and London: Yale University Press.

Middleton, J. and J. Campbell. 1965. *Zanzibar: its Society and its Politics*. London: Oxford University Press.

Middleton, J. and M. Horton. 2000. *The Swahili: the Social Landscape of a Mercantile Society*. Oxford: Blackwell.

Miller, D. 1994. *Modernity. An Ethnographic Approach. Dualism and Mass Consumption in Trinidad*. Oxford and New York: Berg.

———. 1998. 'Why some things matter', in D. Miller (ed.), *Material Cultures. Why Some Things Matter*. Chicago: University of Chicago Press.

Mintz, S.W. and C.M. Du Bois. 2002. 'The anthropology of food and eating', *Annual Review Anthropology* 31: 99–119.

Moore, H.L. 1994. *A Passion for Difference. Essays in Anthropology and Gender*. Cambridge: Polity Press.

———. 1996 [1986]. *Space, Text and Gender. An Anthropological Study of the Marakwet of Kenya*. New York and London: Guilford Press.

Moore, H.L. and T. Sanders. 2001. 'Magical Interpretations and Material Realities. An Introduction', in H.L. Moore and T. Sanders (eds), *Magical Interpretations, Material Realities. Modernity, Witchcraft and the Occult in Postcolonial Africa*. London and New York: Routledge.

Mosse, D. 2004. 'Is Good Policy Unimplementable? Reflections on the Ethnography of Aid Policy and Practice', *Development and Change* 35(4): 639–71.

Myers, G.A. 1993. 'Reconstructing Ng'ambo: Town Planning and Development on the Other Side of Zanzibar', Ph.D. dissertation. Los Angeles, USA: University of California.

Nelson, N. and S. Wright. 1995. 'Participation and Power', in N. Nelson and S. Wright (eds), *Power and Participatory Development. Theory and Practice*. London: Intermediate Technology Publications.

Nisula, T. 1999. *Everyday Spirits and Medical Interventions. Ethnographic and Historical Notes on Therapeutic Conventions in Zanzibar Town.* Saarijärvi: Gummerus Kirjapaino OY.

Nurse, D. and T. Spear. 1985. *The Swahili. Reconstructing the History and Language of an African Society, 800–1500.* Philadelphia: University of Pennsylvania Press.

Nustad, K. 2001. 'Development: the Devil We Know?', *Third World Quarterly* 22(4):479–89.

Nyamwaya, D.O. 1997. 'Three Critical Issues in Community Health Development Projects in Kenya', in R.D. Grillo and R.L. Stirrat (eds), *Discourses of Development. Anthropological Perspectives.* Oxford and New York: Berg.

Nye, D.E. 1990. *Electrifying America. Social meanings of a new technology, 1880–1940.* London and Cambridge, MA: Massachusetts Institute of Technology Press.

Olsen, E.F. 1999. 'Dealing with Conflicts. An Anthropological Study of Joking Relationships Among Women in a Zanzibari village', dissertation submitted as partial fulfilment of requirements for Cand. Polit. degree, Department of Anthropology, University of Oslo, Norway.

Pantzar, M. 1997. 'Domestication of Everyday Life Technology: Dynamic Views on the Social Histories of Artifacts', *Design Issues* 13(3): 52–65.

Parkin, D. (ed.). 1994. *Continuity and Autonomy in Swahili Communitites: Inland Influences and Strategies of Self-determination.* London: School of Oriental and African Studies.

———. 1995. 'Blank Banners and Islamic Consciousness in Zanzibar', in A.P. Cohen and N. Rapport (eds), *Questions of Consciousness.* London: Routledge.

Parry, J. and M. Bloch. 1989. 'Introduction: Money and the Morality of Exchange', in J. Parry and M. Bloch (eds), *Money and the Morality of Exchange.* Cambridge and New York: Cambridge University Press.

Pottier, J. 1997. 'Towards an Ethnography of Participatory Appraisal and Research', in R.D. Grillo and R.L. Stirrat (eds), *Discourses of Development. Anthropological Perspectives.* Oxford and New York: Berg.

Rogers, B. 1981. *The Domestication of Women. Discrimination in Developing Societies.* London and New York: Tavistock Publications.

Sahlins, M. 1999. 'Two or Three Things that I Know About Culture', *Journal of the Royal Anthropological Institute* 5: 399–421.

Saleh, M.A. 2004. '"Going with the times": Conflicting Swahili Norms and Values Today', in P. Caplan and F. Topan (eds), *Swahili Modernities. Culture, Politics and Identity on the East Coast of Africa.* Asmara: Africa World Press.

Sanders, T. 2001. 'Save Your Skins: Structural Adjustment, Morality and the Occult in Tanzania', in H.L. Moore and T. Sanders (eds), *Magical Interpretations, Material Realities. Modernity, Witchcraft and the Occult in Postcolonial Africa.* London: Routledge.

Schivelbusch, W. 1988. *Disenchanted Night. The Industrialisation of Light in the Nineteenth Century.* Oxford, New York and Hamburg: Berg. (First published in German in 1983 as *Lichtblicke. Zur Geshichte der Künstlichen Helligkeit im 19 Jahrhundert.* München: Carl Hanser Verlag).

Scott, J.C. 1998. *Seeing Like a State. How Certain Schemes to Improve the Human Condition Have Failed.* New Haven and London: Yale University Press.

Sen, A. 1983. 'Development: Which Way Now?', *The Economic Journal* 93(372): 745–62.

Sheriff, A. 1991a. 'Introduction. A Materialist Approach to Zanzibar's History', in A. Sheriff and E. Ferguson (eds), *Zanzibar Under Colonial Rule*. Dar es Salaam: Historical Association of Tanzania and London: James Currey.

———. 1991b. 'The Peasantry Under Imperialism, 1873–1963', in A. Sheriff and E. Ferguson (eds), *Zanzibar Under Colonial Rule*. Dar es Salaam: Historical Association of Tanzania and London: James Currey.

———. 1991c. 'Conclusion', in A. Sheriff and E. Ferguson (eds), *Zanzibar Under Colonial Rule*. Dar es Salaam: Historical Association of Tanzania and London: James Currey.

Shove, E. 2003. *Comfort, Cleanliness and Convenience: the Social Organization of Normality*. Oxford: Berg.

Shweder, R. 1997. 'The Surprise of Ethnography', *Ethnos* 25(2): 152–63.

Sillitoe, P. et al. 2005. *Indigenous Knowledge Inquiries. A Methodologies Manual for Development*. Rugby: Intermediate Technology Publications Ltd.

Southerton, D., B. Van Vliet and H. Chappells. 2004. 'Introduction: Consumption, Infrastructures and Environmental Sustainability', in D. Southerton, B. Van Vliet and H. Chappells (eds), *Sustainable Consumption: the Implications of Changing Infrastructures of Provision*. Cheltenham: Edward Elgar Publishing.

Spear, T. 2000. 'Early Swahili History Reconsidered', *The International Journal of African Historical Studies* 33(2): 257–90.

Talle, A. 2002. 'Kvinner og Utvikling – Tjue år Seinere', *Norsk Antropologisk Tidsskrift* 13(1–2): 47–61.

Tambila, K. I. 2000. 'Aspects of the Political Economy of Unguja and Pemba', in T.L. Maliyamkono (ed.), *The Political Plight of Zanzibar*. Dar es Salaam: TEMA Publishers Company Ltd.

Taylor, C. 1992. 'Inwardness and the Culture of Modernity', in A. Honneth et al. (eds), *Philosophical Interventions in the Unfinished Project of Enlightenment*. London and Cambridge, MA: Massachusetts Institute of Technology Press.

Turner, B.S. and J. Edmunds. 2002. 'The Distaste of Taste. Bourdieu, Cultural Capital and the Australian Post-war Elite', *Journal of Consumer Culture* 2(2): 219–40.

Walley, C.J. 2004. 'Modernity and the Meaning of Development within the Mafia Island Marine Park, Tanzania', in P. Caplan and F. Topan (eds), *Swahili Modernities. Culture, Politics and Identity on the East Coast of Africa*. Asmara: Africa World Press.

Weiner, A.B. 1976. *Women of Value, Men of Renown. New Perspectives in Trobriand Exchange*. Austin: University of Texas Press.

White, L.A. 1943. 'Energy and the Evolution of Culture', *American Anthropologist* 45(3): 335–56.

Whyte, S.R. 1996. *Questioning Misfortune. The Pragmatics of Uncertainty in Eastern Uganda*. Cambridge: Cambridge University Press.

Wikan, U. 1990. *Managing Turbulent Hearts. A Balinese Formula for Living*. Chicago and London: University of Chicago Press.

———. 1992. 'Beyond the Words: the Power of Resonance', *American Ethnologist* 19(3): 460–82.

———. 1996. *Tomorrow, God Willing. Self-made Destinies in Cairo*. Chicago and London: University of Chicago Press.

Wilhite, H. 2005. 'Why Energy Needs Anthropology', *Anthropology Today* 21(3): 1–3.

———. 2006. 'Why is Consumption Changing in Kerala? An Ethnographic Approach', Ph.D. dissertation. Norway: University of Oslo.

————. In press. *Consumption and the Transformation of Everyday Life: a View from South India*. New York, London and Delhi: Palmgrave Macmillan.

Winther, T. 1991. 'Social and Economical Aspects of Rural Electrification, Zanzibar, Tanzania', thesis submitted as partial fulfilment of requirements for the Master of Science degree, Department of Electrical Power Engineering, University of Trondheim, Norway.

————. 2005. 'Current Styles: Introducing Electricity in a Zanzibari Village', Ph.D. dissertation. Norway: University of Oslo.

Reports

ADEME (French Environment and Energy Management Agency) – WEC (World Energy Council). 2007. 'European Experience of White Certificates' (Lees, E.), in 'Energy Efficiency Policies Evaluation: a Worldwide Review'. London.

Centre for Development and Technology, University of Trondheim (O'Keefe, P. et al.). 1990. 'Project Profile 3: Zanzibar Rural Electrification Project (RUREL)', in 'Evaluation of Norwegian Assistance to the Energy Sector of SADCC Countries'. Trondheim, Norway.

IEA (International Energy Agency). 2002. 'World Energy Outlook 2006.' Paris

————. 2006. 'World Energy Outlook 2006.' Paris.

NORAD, (Aasen, B.). 2006. 'Lessons from Evaluations of Women and Gender Equality in Development Cooperation. Synthesis Report 2006/1'. Norway.

Norconsult (consulting engineering company). 1994. 'Rural Electrification Projects, Zanzibar. Project Review Report, February 1994'. Norway.

NRECA (National Rural Electric Cooperative Association) International Ltd, (Barkat, A. et al.). 2002. 'Economic and Social Impact Evaluation Study of the Rural Electrification Program in Bangladesh'. Dhaka.

NVE (Norwegian Water Resources and Energy Administration)/ECON (Nordic consulting company)/E-CO Partner (Norwegian-Danish energy engineering company). 2003. 'Appraisal of Zanzibar Rural Electrification Project. Phase IV. June 2003'. Norway.

SFPC (State Fuel and Power Corporation). 1995. 'Zanzibar and Pemba Islands Rural Electrification Project, Phase IV. Project Document'. Zanzibar.

————. 1998. 'Electrical Masterplan Report (1)'. Zanzibar.

————. 2001. 'Zanzibar and Pemba Islands Rural Electrification Project, Phase IV.' Zanzibar.

SUM (Centre for Development and the Environment, University of Oslo), (Winther, T. et al.). 2005. 'Project Report, Information Project Zanzibar Rural Electrification Project, Phase IV'. Norway.

————. (Winther, T.). 2006. 'Social Impact Evaluation Study of the Rural Electrification Project in Zanzibar, Phase IV (2003–6)'. Norway.

Tanzanian Ministry of Planning, Economy and Empowerment. 2005. 'Poverty and Human Development Report 2005.' (Prepared by the Research and Analysis Working Group of the Government of Tanzania's Poverty Monitoring System). Dar es Salaam: Mkuki na Nyota Publishers.

―――. 2006. 'MKUKUTA: National Strategy for Growth and Reduction of Poverty. Status Report 2006.' (Prepared by the Research and Analysis Working Group, MKUKUTA Monitoring System.) Dar es Salaam: Creative Eye Ltd.

UNDP (United Nations Development Programme). 2001. 'The Human Development Report 2001. Making New Technologies Work for Human Development.' New York.

―――. 2006. 'The Human Development Report 2006. Cultural Liberty in Today's Diverse World.' New York.

Zanzibar Forestry Development Project. 1993a. 'Fuelwood in Zanzibar Town. Zanzibar Forestry Development Project Technical Paper No. 3'. Printed in Vantaa, Finland.

―――. 1993b. 'Report on the Assessment of the Stove Activities of the ZFDP. Zanzibar Forestry Development Project Technical Paper No. 4.' Printed in Vantaa, Finland.

Archival sources (Zanzibar National Archives)

ZA-SB1-8: 428. (1909). Description of commercial activities within the British Protectorate.

ZA-AB6-14/1. (1910). Warning to customers for failing to fulfil the contract.

ZA-AB6-14/3. (1912). Change to 24 hour tariff due to customers' behaviour.

ZA-AB6-14/15, 20. (1912). Complaint and reply regarding increased tariffs; Mosques' free current during Ramadan.

ZA-AB6-14/21–8. (1916). Coal crisis, electricity rationing, increasing rates.

ZA-AB6-14/36. (1916). Complaint about dark streets.

ZA-AB6-14/44–8. (1918). Refusal of request from Ismails Council for lower charges.

ZA-AB6-14/53–7, 74–86. (1918–19). Internal discussions regarding request from factory for lower charges leading to general reduction of power rates but not for light customers.

ZA-AB6-14/117, 123. (1923). Letters from Indian National Association: requests for lower tariffs.

ZA-AB6-14/128–131. (1924). Internal minutes discussing reduction of tariffs.

ZA-AB6-15/36. (1928). Evaluating households with regard to electric cooking.

ZA-AB6-56/97. (1938). Letter from the Commissioner of Police to Financial Secretary regarding Saateni residents' application for electric street lighting.

ZA-AB6-56/118. (1951). Letter from Zanzibar Township Council regarding insufficient street lighting in Ng'ambo area.

ZA-AB6-56/128. (1952). Correspondence between Township Council and utility office regarding improvements in Ng'ambo

ZA-AB6-5/3A. (1954). Opening of Saateni power station

ZA-AB6-20/1,10–11. (1957). Complaint and reply about change from direct to alternating current.

ZA- AB6-30/1–4. (1957). Complaint from disconnected customer, discussions and reply.

ZA-AY1-30/6C,7. (1964). The Board summing up of events after the revolution.

ZA-BA88-23. (1964). Techno-economic considerations and recommendations related to the development of electric power supply in Zanzibar and Pemba areas for the period 1965–1976.

ZA-DB1-33. (1980). Letter from Zanzibar Minister to TANESCO regarding tariffs.

INDEX

men's ownership to 160
modified construction techniques 139, 143
and settlement patterns 78, 139
see also environment, spiralling electricity consumption
Hutchinson, Sharon 12–13, 15

Identity
African 25
meter-reader's dual 110–111
modern 135, 166, 207, 231
multiple 183, 204
Muslim 95
processes of objectification 20n6, 184
Swahili 22–25, 238
Tanzanian 25
women's 155, 195, 204–7, 214
Zanzibari 25, 68, 192, 196–97, 213, 238
see also men, as family providers
independence 41
inheritance 154, 160, 230
Internet 99, 133, 225
irons 82n8, 106, 167n7
Islam 14, 22, 25, 95–96, 98, 131–32, 144–45, 179, 215n1
and global networks 145
and women's limited control of electricity 160, 220, 230
see also tourism, critique of tourist styles

Kanga 15, 86, 114, 135, 143, 155–56, 159
kinship 17–18, 149–50, 157–58, 229–30
see also extended family
kitchens 13, 17, 48n36, 65, 109, 150, 155, 171, 173, 189, 196, 198, 207, 215n2
knowledge
and agency 3, 72, 75, 81
anthropological 11–12
occult 25, 66, 102–3, 161, 163, 210, 221–22, 235
systems of 74–75, 81, 220, 222
scientific 75
see also electricity bills, customers' knowledge of
Koranic schools 95

Larsen, Kjersti 24, 42, 93, 171
Latour, Bruno 19n2, 72, 111–12
Le Guennec-Coppens, Françoise 158, 167n5
Lien, Marianne E. 111, 166n2, 184, 191, 240n3
light, electric
and the pace of life 18, 146, 202, 226
quality of 108, 176
security 136, 138
and spirits 15, 18, 130, 137–38
street lighting 30, 33, 41, 60, 73–74, 80, 82n10, 129, 219–20
as a symbol of power 18, 28, 30, 42, 105, 129–30, 135, 146, 236
living rooms 18, 171–72, 186n2, 219, 231
meter-reader entering 109, 111, 170
physical transformation of 172–74, 223, 231
as a place to relax 174, 186
load-factor 34, 46n19
Long, Norman 3–4, 10, 74–76, 81, 238

Marriage
cross-cousin 27
electricity's effect on patterns of 4, 123, 142–43, 230
see also divorce
Maulidi reading 86–88, 183
Mazrui, Alamin M. 23–24
men
as family providers 88, 150, 159, 182–83, 215, 232
see also electrical appliances, ownership to; houses, men's ownership to
Middleton, John 22–24, 26–27, 80, 163, 210
Miller, Daniel 7–9, 20n4, 20n6, 184, 213
modesty
economical 18, 27, 88, 95, 102, 134, 158, 164, 166, 229, 238
respectable conduct 88, 146, 181
money
and electricity 51, 71, 80, 82n10, 107, 114, 120, 123, 155, 161, 183, 232–33, 235
increasing importance of 17, 74, 86, 88–90, 100, 102, 148, 203–5, 226, 229
monthly generation of income in Uroa 89
and the school 132–33
and secrecy 164
and the sharing of expenditures between husband and wife 159, 230
and tourism 85, 90, 134, 145
uneven distribution of 15–16, 99
and weddings 155, 157–58, 167n6
see also good life, the; seaweed production
Moore, Henrietta L. 80, 134, 170, 182–84, 204, 214, 218–19, 221, 231, 238
Myers, Garth Andrew 31, 37, 41–43, 45n5, 47n23, 47n25, 48n37, 53

Neo-liberal influences 52–53
Nisula, Tapio 24, 26, 36, 41, 45n5, 53, 80
normalisation of objects 2, 5, 9, 18, 105, 142, 158, 165–66, 175, 181, 205–6, 225–26, 230, 238
Nurse, Derek 22–24
nursery school, see education, nursery school
Nustad, Knut 3, 72–73, 82n11
nutrition 204, 226
Nyamwaya, David O. 72, 82n11
Nye, David E. 17, 19n2, 42, 45n2, 46n15, 135

Occult, the 25, 66, 76–77, 79–81, 98, 102–3, 112, 135, 161, 163–64, 210, 221–22, 235, 240n7
Olsen, Elisabeth F. 84, 171–72

Parkin, David 24, 96, 227
Parry, Jonathan 157, 167n6
Pemba 20n3, 22–23, 25–26, 48n39, 49, 51, 54, 58, 78, 133, 154, 229
political antagonism/impasse 26, 41, 54
and the ban on aid 54–55
effects in the village of 25, 54, 78, 110, 215n5, 233, 229
effect on research of 21n10, 103n4
see also Pemba
privatisation of land
see firewood, effect of tree-planting project on people's access to